7.95
B ✓T

A Q
Baghdad

Tehran

Esfahan

I R A N

KUWAIT

Persian
Gulf

BAHRAIN

QATAR

D I

Riyadh

B I A

TRUCIAL OMAN

Gulf of Oman
Muscat

and OMAN

MU

SOUTH YEMEN
(Once Aden)

Mukalla

E.G.M

HUSSEIN

To J.F.S.

PETER SNOW

HUSSEIN

A Biography

ROBERT B. LUCE, INC
WASHINGTON · NEW YORK

Hashemite Branch of the Prophet's Family

Hussein
Proclaimed King of Hejaz 1916
Abdicated 1924 Died 1931

li
g of Hejaz
24–5

Abdullah
Born 1882
Founded Transjordan 1920
Assassinated 1951

Feisal I
King of Iraq
Died 1933

dul Illah
ent of Iraq

Naif

Talal
Born 1909
King 1951
Abdicated 1952

Ghazi
Died 1939

ina=HUSSEIN=2*Muna*

Mohamed
Born 1940

Hassan
Born 1948
Crown Prince 1965

Basma
Born 1951

Feisal II
Assassinated
July 1958

56084

Aliya
orn 1956

Abdullah
Born 1962

Feisal
Born 1963

Zein
Born 1968

Aisha
Born 1968

ILLUSTRATIONS

ACKNOWLEDGEMENTS

I would like to thank the scores of people who have revealed their often very personal memories of Hussein and their assessments of his character and policies. The extremes of bitterness and devotion evoked by Hussein's rule and personality and the highly subjective nature of most Arab testimony have enormously complicated the task of writing a balanced account. But the challenge has been irresistible. It is one of the limitations of writing about a living person that many of those who deserve most to be thanked cannot be named, but among those I can identify I mention—in particular :

Sir Alec Kirkbride, Lt-Gen Sir John Glubb, Zeid Al-Rifai, Kamal Rifaat, Sherif Nasser bin Jamil, Salah Goher, Suleiman Naboulsi, Wing Commander Dalgleish, Mrs Golda Meir, Abdul Moneim Rifai, Bahjat Talhouni, Ali Abu Nuwar, Field Marshal Sir Gerald Templer, Sir Philip Adams, Sir Charles Duke, Sir Geoffrey Furlonge, Sir John Henniker-Major, Mrs Yael Vered, Major-General Zeid bin Shaker, Munif Razzaz, Nabeel Sha'ath, Ali Hiyyari, Major General Strickland, Princess Dina, Major Robert Young, Major General Ma'an Abu Nuwar, Sir Charles Johnstone, Rahat Chattari, Moraiwid Tell, Dr Abdul Salaam Majali, and for his own account of many of the key events in his life King Hussein himself.

Thanks are also due to Major Robert Young for his pictures and to Hagop Toranian of Amman for his cover picture and other photographs.

Peter Snow,
Summer, 1972

ACKNOWLEDGEMENTS

CONTENTS

11

FOREWORD

AGAINST ALL THE ODDS

Few men have lived as dangerously as Hussein, King of Jordan. So precarious is his existence that he would recognise, as I do, that his life could end in the few weeks between the writing of this book and its publication. He has been shot at more times than he can remember and has nearly killed himself in a number of motor accidents. His enemies have tried every stratagem to prise him from his throne. In a world where kings are out of fashion, he has outruled all other Arab leaders and outfaced the current enthusiasm for régimes closer to the people. His life has run against all the odds.

But if Hussein's courage is universally admired, his politics are not. He has survived only by the constant reassertion of his authority through the military, and his government is still an autocratic *élite* in which every decision of importance is referred to him alone. He has allowed his people to participate in the process of making decisions only in so far as they have agreed with him, and since his thinking on key political problems has been out of step with the mainstream of Arab thinking, his policies have rarely received widespread popular acclaim.

However, in the Arab world, embittered and emotionally disturbed by its struggle with Israel, popular policies are seldom wise, and while there are many who abuse Hussein, there are many others who respect what they regard as his realism and admire his resistance to the prevailing clamour from the Left. Hussein's career has a good claim to be considered as substantially more than a mere exercise in personal survival.

So this book is the story of his ceaseless exposure to danger, his escapes and his adventures, but it is also an examination of how the explosive combination of emotion and reason in his character has affected the confrontation between Hussein and his opposition inside and outside Jordan. This is primarily the story of a man, intensely human and sensitive but capable of ruthless determination; it is also the story of a land and a people whose

13

fate has depended for twenty years on the lonely and largely instinctive judgement of one man. And when the story is told, we must look at the record of Hussein's rule, and establish what more he has achieved than his own survival and the preservation of the Hashemite dynasty in Jordan.

Hussein could well claim his family have a right to be preserved. They were descended from the Prophet Mahomed, the original liberator of the Arabs in the seventh century, and at the beginning of this century they raised the first successful Arab revolt against the Turks. Less than twenty years before Hussein was born, his family seemed to be riding high on a wave of popular enthusiasm to rule a free Arab world.

But by the time Hussein became king, at the age of sixteen, the family that had been the champion of the Arab cause was beginning to look as if it had more enemies than friends. And the boy who had been born to be king was born to a life of unending danger as well.

Hussein's story really begins with the fortunes of his family in 1914. . . .

PART ONE

THE BOY KING 1935–1954

I

BORN OF THE DESERT

One afternoon in Cairo, shortly before the outbreak of the first world war, Lord Kitchener, Britain's overlord in the Middle East, had a visitor. It was a young Arab prince—Hussein's grandfather, Abdullah. He came from Mecca, the holiest city of the Arabs, which was then one of the subject cities of the Turkish Empire. It was a tired empire, and although most of the Arab world was still within its grip, its days were numbered. Abdullah's father, Sherif Hussein, was the leading member of the Hashemite family, who were the traditional guardians of the holy cities of Mecca and Medina.

Neither Abdullah nor his father had any connection at that time with the land that later became Jordan. It was an undefined wilderness of desert, mountain, and valley hundreds of miles away to the north of Mecca—another slice of the Turkish empire; neither its townspeople nor its Bedouin owed any allegiance to the distant Hashemite family in Mecca. But, like the Hashemites, they were Arabs, and their rulers were Turks.

Abdullah was ambitious. He was also gifted with an enthusiastic taste for intrigue, and a sparkling sense of humour. He lived with gusto; he enjoyed the company of women and the other pleasures of life; he was not a remarkable soldier, if we are to believe Lawrence of Arabia, who says he was 'not serious enough for leadership', but preferred to win his battles by the force of his remarkable personality. He was, above all, a realist, and his courage and authority were forceful and full-blooded: few people argued with him. He was later to be the most lasting of the many influences on his grandson, Hussein.

Abdullah's talk with Lord Kitchener had a decisive influence on the history of the Middle East. Abdullah said that he and his father feared the Turks were out to reduce even further the power of local rulers like the Hashemites. He said his family were not going to stand for it, and that the Turks could not rely on the continuing loyalty of the Hashemites if war broke out in the

Middle East. It was a conversation that Kitchener and the British government did not forget. When war did break out that same year, and when Turkey sided with Germany, Britain knew she had an ally in Abdullah's family. It was the beginning of an alliance that both sides observed faithfully through half a century, and if many people since then have judged that Britain was backing the wrong horse, nobody doubted the wisdom of the alliance when it was first made.

In 1916 Abdullah's father, Sherif Hussein, proclaimed his revolt against the Turks. Britain promised him political support in establishing an independent Arab state in a series of letters from the British High Commissioner in Cairo, Sir Henry MacMahon, and gave him military assistance as well as the brilliant, eccentric military advice of Colonel Lawrence. In a year, Abdullah's younger brother Feisal had thrown the Turks out of Aqaba and was advancing on Syria, and by October 1918, Feisal, Lawrence and the British army were marching into Damascus. Abdullah missed the triumph: he spent the war reducing the Turkish garrisons at Taif and Medina nearer home. But victory was complete and the Hashemites now expected their reward.

It did not come as cleanly as they had been led to expect. Britain and France had done a quiet deal behind Sherif Hussein's back at the time he was launching his revolt. They had agreed to split the Arab world, once they had won it, into British and French spheres of influence. Although this secret 'Sykes-Picot' agreement talked vaguely of 'Arab suzerainty', it was clearly intended to fall far short of granting full independence. So when Feisal's new Arab government in Damascus was overthrown by the French two years later, the British did not lift a finger to help him: Britain had quietly agreed to leave France alone in Syria and Lebanon, if France would leave Britain alone in Palestine and Iraq. But Britain gently told Feisal—and Abdullah who had an eye on the throne of Iraq—to bide their time, and promised them both that their interests would be reconsidered.

If Arab feelings were hurt by British and French double-crossing over Syria, their passions were permanently aroused by the Balfour Declaration of 1917 and the dynamic Jewish settler invasion that followed it. Britain intended them to be reassured by that part of the British Foreign Secretary's Declaration which went on to say—after proposing the establishment of a Jewish National Home in Palestine—that it was clearly 'understood that nothing shall be done which may prejudice the civil and religious rights of existing non-Jewish communities in Palestine. . . .'

But over the years it became clear that the rights of the Arabs in Palestine were not compatible with such a determined influx of Jews, and extremists on either side were so set on destroying any chances of integration that the British were powerless to maintain any kind of social or political order. However impartially the British mandatory authorities struggled to keep a balance between the Arabs and the Jews, Britain was permanently damned in Arab eyes for having opened the door to the Jews to enter Palestine in the first place. And if Britain was damned, so were those Arabs like the Hashemites who attached themselves to her or depended on her. The Americans and their Arab friends were caught in the same position, which became even worse than Britain's twenty years later when America became the principal patron of the State of Israel. The aftermath of the first world war set off the emotional unheaval that disrupted politics in the Middle East from then on. And just next to the point where the upheaval was to be most violent, the small kingdom of Jordan was founded by Hussein's grandfather—Abdullah—in 1920. . . .

It was first called Transjordan: the land beyond the Jordan. In the time of the Romans it had been part of the rich granary of the empire, and towns like Jerash and Amman were fashionable and prosperous; they were the frontier towns where the Roman Empire did business with the East.

But by the time the British took over from the Turks, Transjordan was the most primitive land in the Middle East. It contained few natural resources. Only 350,000 people lived there. Most of them worked the land in the Jordan valley and around the hilltowns of Irbid, Ajlun, Salt, Jerash and Amman. They were a mixture of peoples: Circassians from the north, Christian and Moslem villagers, and from the desert a large Bedouin element that had settled in and around the towns and villages over the years. Further south and to the east were the nomadic Bedouin.

There were no firm boundaries between these different peoples, nor was there a clearly defined focus for them, socially or commercially. There was little trade anyway and what there was—mainly farm produce—moved north and south along the line of the Hejaz railway into Syria and Arabia, and west into Palestine.

It was a primitive land politically too. The pattern of tribal diversity discouraged the British from governing it attentively. The dominant tradition was the patriarchal Conservatism of the Bedouin, but neither the Bedouin nor the townspeople saw the need for any loyalty outside their own families, towns, or tribes. The two main Bedouin tribes, the Beni Sakhr in the north, and the Howeitat in the south had no common bond and regarded each other with bitter hostility. The families in the towns were always intriguing against each other, and were regarded with some contempt by the Bedouin. The land needed a leader, but Britain simply left the tribes to manage their own affairs under the eyes of a number of British political officers.

Into this vacuum—on a November day in 1920—stepped Hussein's grandfather, Abdullah. It was four months since his brother, Feisal, had been expelled from Syria. Abdullah, with his father's permission, had decided to try to retrieve the family's position in the north, which the British had promised them, and which they felt they had earned by their revolt against the Turks. Abdullah travelled up from Medina on the old Turkish railway, and as the train pulled into the station at Ma'an in southern Transjordan, he and a band of armed followers stepped out and surprised the world by announcing their intention to occupy Syria. At first Abdullah was greeted with some laughter, but the prestige of his name and his uncompromising demeanor soon had their effect: when he arrived at Kerak in the heart of Transjordan, the British representative, Mr Alec Kirkbride, felt there was no alternative but to go and greet him.

'Welcome, sir', said Kirkbride, who had no instructions from the British government to say anything at all. Abdullah enquired politely about the form of government in Transjordan and its international status, and Kirkbride replied that he was not quite sure, and that it was academic anyway in view of Abdullah's arrival on the scene.

'Ah,' said Abdullah, leaning forward with a twinkle in his eye, 'I was sure we would understand each other.'*

* Kirkbride tells of his experiences with Abdullah in his book *A Crackle of Thorns.*

Abdullah arrived in Amman, summoned all the tribal leaders, and told them he was assuming power in Transjordan. If his panache impressed them, it certainly was not his money or his army : he had neither. But popular enthusiasm was with him, and the British had shown that they were not against him. That was enough.

The new 'Emirate' of Transjordan was born. The British quickly accepted Abdullah : Winston Churchill, then Colonial Secretary, met him in Jerusalem and offered him a budget of £5000 a month, and Abdullah recognised Britain's mandate over Transjordan. He was promised independence at a later date, and Churchill gave him enough military and political support to establish and maintain his position in Transjordan. He was told that the Jews would settle in Palestine but was assured that they would not move into Transjordan. Meanwhile Abdullah's brother, Feisal, was given the kingdom of Iraq, to make up for his loss of Syria.

Abdullah ruled Transjordan in the best Arab tradition. He was kind and generous to those who were loyal to him, and ruthless with those who opposed him. He spent what money he had almost exclusively on buying the allegiance of sheikhs, and if he could not buy them, he fought them. He put down a number of rebellions in his first year, and in 1923 he had to ask the Royal Air Force to help him subdue a revolt by the Adwan tribe. A year later the RAF came to his rescue again. The Wahabis from Saudi Arabia invaded Transjordan, and were soundly defeated by Abdullah's tribesmen with British air support. A year later the Wahabis had their revenge : they expelled Abdullah's family from Mecca and Medina for good.

By the late 1920s the pattern of Abdullah's rule was established. It was a benevolent tribal autocracy dependent on Britain for its money and protection. The enthusiasm of Syrian and Palestinian nationalists for the new Arab régime soon evaporated : Abdullah had quickly made it clear that although he had personal ambitions in Palestine and Syria, he would lend no help to those who wanted to make them republics independent of France and Britain, and would give no support to the campaign of violence against the Jews led by the Muslim leader in Palestine Haj Amin Al Husseini, whom Abdullah personally detested.

Abdullah had no time for democracy : the elected council had no effective power. Although the British were continually pressing Abdullah in public to modernise his government, they recognised in private that it was the only way Transjordan could be run. Britain and Abdullah worked hand in hand : British officials, businessmen and soldiers became a part of the system and Abdullah sent his son Talal to Harrow, a British public school.

But Abdullah's power was not dependent only on the British. His family tree gave him a religious and tribal legitimacy in the eyes of the deeply traditional Bedouin, who were the dominant political force in the chaos of Transjordan when Abdullah arrived. He was a Bedouin himself, and he knew how their loyalties worked. He was always accessible to them, always generous to them. When he came to form an army, it was from the Bedouin that he took most of the recruits : the Arab Legion was a largely Bedouin force fiercely devoted to the ruler, who was one of their own stock and descended from the Prophet himself. Their loyalty was to be the key to Abdullah's power within Transjordan, and Hussein, his grandson, would never have survived without it.

In 1930 a young British officer called John Bagot Glubb was called in from Iraq to put this Bedouin force together. He was a small man with a kindly face and a chin that did not work properly because of an injury. He was almost a Bedouin himself —reserved, intensely self-sufficient, but emotional and sensitive. He immediately formed a close friendship with Abdullah, together with the tall, good-humoured Kirkbride, who later became British Resident in Transjordan, and then Ambassador in Jordan. Soon after Glubb arrived, Britain signed a treaty with Abdullah which promised him help if attacked, and allowed Britain to station forces in his country and look after his defence and foreign policy. Transjordan was one of the stablest countries in the Middle East, and the main source of its stability was its close link with Britain.

Into this colourful desert kingdom, on November 14th, 1935, Hussein was born. His parents were first cousins, both Hashemites. His father was Abdullah's son, Talal, a man as gentle as Abdullah was forceful, as retiring as his father was assertive. To those who knew him, Talal was a warm, kindly friend, highly intelligent and cultivated : to his father, he was a failure, totally unfit to assume the tough job of ruling a kingdom; to Hussein he was a devoted parent—and above all a family man with no ambition to rule. Talal was a thoughtful introvert. He had hated Harrow, where he had started his career by being dumped unroyally into a pool. Many thought that his time at Harrow and his own Arab intellectual leanings inclined him against the British but people like Kirkbride, who knew him well, felt that this was not enough to make him an unreliable ally if he came to succeed his father.

Hussein's mother was a different character altogether: Zein was a woman of power, the central figure in the family. She had a strong personality and a keen political instinct that later, after Abdullah's death, made her a powerful backstage influence on the affairs of the country. Hussein was the eldest of their four children; the others were Mohamed, Hassan, and Basma, a girl.

Amman, in the thirties, was a small town whose focal point was still the old Roman theatre. To the north, on a hill, was the Raghadan Palace built by Abdullah when he first arrived and beside it stood the small house where Hussein was born. When he was two, his father moved to a house which had belonged to Kirkbride on another of the hills surrounding the centre of the town. It was built of grey stone and was uglier than most of the houses in Amman, but it had a number of spacious rooms, and a large garden with a stable block where Talal could keep his horses. He enjoyed riding, and would sometimes take young Hussein perched on the saddle in front of him. In those days the house overlooked open country on three sides; later it was surrounded by other buildings, and the empty brown hillside opposite was covered by the hastily erected dwellings of the thousands of Palestinian refugees who poured into Amman after the wars with Israel in 1948 and 1967.

Most of Hussein's early days were spent on that corner of Jebel Amman. He went to school there: first to a nursery school 200 yards away, then to the Christian Missionary School just round the corner from the house. It is still there—the walls of Hussein's own classroom now pock-marked with shrapnel craters after the hammering his tanks and artillery gave it in September 1970, when it was occupied by Palestinian commandos. His teacher there, Miss Frayeh, remembers a very quiet, contemplative little boy, who used to sit at a desk by the window. He was not one of the brains of the school. His report for 1942-3, when he was seven, says that he got an A for English, but a D for

English dictation—the worst in the class—and his arithmetic was below average too. His favourite subject was Arabic poetry. One of his best friends at school was Zeid Rifai, the son of one of the country's regular Prime Ministers, Samir Rifai. Zeid was no better than Hussein at work, and much naughtier in class. The two boys struck up a friendship that lasted.

Not far away from Talal's house on Jebel Amman was the British Residence and the Headquarters of the Arab Legion. Both Glubb, who took over command of the legion in 1939, and Kirkbride, at the British residency, became firm family friends and were frequent visitors. They preferred to keep their visits hidden from Abdullah, who they feared would be jealous and resentful. Both of them recall the small dark-haired, rather shy little boy who was always a model of politeness and respect. Sometimes Hussein would go on shooting expeditions with his father and Kirkbride. Kirkbride would drive them all out to the oasis of Azraq, deep in the desert east of Amman, where the duck migrated through Transjordan in the winter. Hussein's small figure would be almost lost in a pair of plus-fours. On one shooting trip the car got stuck in the mud, and Hussein's father had to wave down a passing cyclist, commandeer his bicycle, and ride five miles to the nearest police post for help.

Hussein's was a simple, almost suburban household, but the happy family life was not to last. A tragic mental illness hit Talal with growing effect, like a slowly spreading poison, and finally made life with him impossible for his wife and children. At first, the schizophrenia was hardly apparent at all. Then came—at long intervals—strange fits, when he was transformed from a gentle, civilised man into someone dangerously possessed. And finally, when he became murderous during his mental seizures, it was obvious that he would have to live permanently under care. But at this early stage, while Hussein was still a boy, and his grandfather Abdullah ruled, the fits that affected his father were something that everyone learned to live with. People who were talking to Talal would suddenly see his eyes change expression, and would know it was time to leave: his illness was embarrassing but tolerable.

To Hussein, who loved his father dearly, the experience of Talal's illness was doubly tragic. For Hussein was also devoted to his grandfather, Abdullah, who made no secret of his contempt for Talal. Abdullah had the almost animal contempt of the strong for the weak, and was deeply disappointed that his son would never be the proud Bedouin that he was.

Hussein found it painful that Abdullah was blind to the suffering of his own son. He was a deeply sensitive boy, like his father, and because Talal's relationship with his family was unusually close and intimate, Hussein felt as if he shared much of the pain and shame of his father's suffering. But his grandfather was the king, and Hussein also found himself responding to another instinct as strong as his affection for his father. It was, simply, a compelling urge to do his duty for the Hashemites, and like Abdullah, he believed that his family's god-given mission was to care for the people of Transjordan. This conviction, which Hussein has often referred to, is cynically dismissed by many who have watched him at press conferences as a convenient excuse for staying in power. But it is a conviction sincerely held, and it helps to account for much of his later firmness of character, and his determination to preserve his throne against all attacks. He wants to preserve not just himself, but the Hashemite dynasty; to Hussein, the survival of the line is as important as his own survival.

This explains why, in those early days, he found himself emotionally divided between his father and his grandfather and responded to both. To Abdullah, who was a realist, it was one further indication that the man who would one day effectively succeed him would not be Talal, but Hussein.

II

IN THE SHADOW OF GRANDFATHER

1946–JULY 1951

Hussein was a boy of fifteen when his grandfather was shot dead before his eyes. It was an event that revealed to the young prince with terrifying impact the reality and responsibility of power in a turbulent modern state.

In the three or four years that led up to the king's murder, the little country of Hussein's childhood was transformed. The explosion in Palestine wrenched Abdullah's kingdom from its desert seclusion and threw it into turmoil, and the prince, who was to live with the turmoil long after his grandfather's death, watched it develop from his schoolroom. . . .

Hussein's was hardly a king's education; it suffered from the enmity between his father and grandfather. Talal was concerned that Hussein should give priority to his Arabic: Abdullah was keener on religion and English. Hussein's schools and tutors changed too often, particularly at the secondary stage, for him to settle down and make many close friends: something he always found difficult anyway. He went to three secondary schools before he was sixteen, when his education was cut short by events.

The two best years were the ones he spent at that most British of public schools—Victoria College, set, not among the rolling hills of southern England, but in the sultry Egyptian city of Alexandria, where King Farouk had his palace.

There Hussein was given the hearty boarding school education that Britain normally reserves for her own future leaders—and in his own way, Hussein loved it. He liked the football, the cricket, the sense of comradeship and community, and the spartan life of the long bleak dormitory that he shared with thirty other boys. He remembers the cold showers they had to take every morning, and the way he had to watch every penny of his pocket money. In a book—largely his own work—that he

helped write in 1962, he recalls that his family was not rich, and
that he had to repair his own school blazer because he knew
his parents 'could not possibly afford to buy me another one'.*
In the 1940s, although Abdullah's expenditure as ruler was
limited only by his credit, his son's family had to manage on a
very modest annual allowance.

At school, Hussein did not excel at games, though he won a
medal for fencing in his last term at Victoria College. But he
took a keen interest in everything with a grave determination
to do his best and to be seen trying even if he did not win. People
began to notice that courage was his most evident quality. The
rest of his character lay hidden, for the moment, beneath his
polite reserve.

Although Hussein enjoyed his two years at Alexandria, he
never took to the Egyptians. Despite the scolding of the British
teachers at Victoria College, the Egyptian children there used to
bully him. In a way he was a natural for it : he was smaller than
average, with a head and shoulders that seemed somehow too
big and wide for his body, and he was too quiet and well-behaved
to be popular. Besides, although Hussein was to a great extent
insulated from politics during his schooldays, everyone knew that
his grandfather was King Abdullah and Hussein was made increasingly aware that Abdullah's attitude to the new state of
Israel contrasted dangerously with that of most other Arabs. . . .

The story of Abdullah and Israel takes a few pages to tell. It
is a story that Hussein took a direct part in only at the end—
at its violent climax—but what he saw of it during Abdullah's
last years was a vital part of his political education.

When Hussein was eleven, Abdullah became King of the independent state of Transjordan which he renamed 'the Hashemite
kingdom of Transjordan'. But no one really believed that Transjordan was properly independent : British forces had an almost
free run of the country and without British money, Abdullah's
economy would have collapsed within weeks; Transjordanians
were importing four times as much in value as they were export-
ing. In Syria and Egypt, where republican feeling was running
high, and King Farouk was fast becoming an absurdity,

* King Hussein, *Uneasy lies the Head*, p. 12

Abdullah's revised treaty with Britain was attacked on the grounds that it simply recognised the British 'occupation' of his country.

None of this particularly worried Abdullah. He, Glubb and Kirkbride now ran the country as a triumvirate, with the aid of a rotating sequence of Prime Ministers. There was a parliament, the Majlis, and there were elections to it, but most people voted for the King's nominees, and the government took its orders from the king anyway.

There was little of importance that the ruling trio disagreed about: Kirkbride and Glubb found that the great secret with Abdullah was never to say 'No' to him—just 'Yes, sir, but . . .' Although Abdullah, after 1946, had the ultimate power of decision, his two main advisers, if united, could usually coax him in the direction they wanted on a matter of detail, on which his own judgement was frequently poor and always obstinate. He was incorrigible over money, which he spent lavishly—although never on himself. The strict financial control that London tried to exert on him in the past was, at Kirkbride's urging, dropped in the 1940s and Abdullah was given a free hand to spend it as he wanted. Kirkbride's reply to his critics was always: 'As long as this little country is a stable, loyal friend of Britain's, what are you worrying about?'.

It was not to stay stable for long. In 1947, fighting broke out in Palestine between the Arabs and the Jews. The United Nations called for the partition of Palestine but the Arabs refused to accept it. They refused to contemplate the partition of a land in which they had until recently been the overwhelming majority of the population. The Jews in Palestine, reinforced by the vast exodus of Jews from Europe during the second world war to a total of some half a million, were now determined to create their own state. The Arabs, under the wild leadership of the Palestinian nationalist Haj Amin Al Husseini, were equally determined to stop it. Abdullah, no friend of Husseini's, remained aloof. But his instinct was to look for an accommodation with the Jews that would allow him, and not the Husseinis, to rule as much of Palestine as possible.

Abdullah had two conversations with the Jews before the war with Israel. The chief Jewish representative on both occasions was Mrs. Golda Meyerson, later the Israeli Prime Minister Golda

Meir. She told the author—in April 1972—that Abdullah's position changed dramatically between the first meeting, in November 1947, and the second, on May the 10th 1948—four days before the declaration of the State of Israel. Both meetings were held in top secret, the first at the Palestine Electricity Plant on the east side of the Jordan at Naharayim, the second in the house of Abdullah's driver in Amman : Mrs. Meyerson disguised herself in the white scarf of a Palestine woman to escape notice. In November Abdullah appeared ready to accept the UN partition of Palestine; he said he would take over the Arab state as part of Transjordan and then come to a peaceful agreement with the Jewish state. But, according to Mrs. Meyerson, his conciliatory attitude had evaporated by April. He said that if it came to war, he would have to take over the whole of Palestine and that there would no longer be any room for a Jewish state, but he was happy to discuss measures to guarantee the Jews full political and religious rights in his Greater Transjordan. Mrs. Meyerson told the King that he must know very well that they could not accept that, and the meeting ended with no agreement.

It was, anyway, too late for talk. The Arabs were experiencing one of those periods of fatal delusion when they thought they could win an all-out war with the Jews. The Arab League was calling for war, and appeals were coming from leading Palestinians across the Jordan. In his own country Abdullah was under growing criticism and even open attack, for not giving material support to the Arabs already fighting in Palestine.

And so it was that Hussein's grandfather found himself, on the 14th of May 1948, being called on by all the Arabs to send his army into Palestine and extinguish the newly-declared State of Israel. Even the British had quietly told him a few weeks earlier, through the Foreign Secretary, Mr Bevin, that they would expect him to occupy the Arab part of Palestine if it came to war with the Jews. Abdullah was not unwilling : his ambitions in Palestine were well-known, and he had long been preparing for this day.

When war began on May the 15th, Glubb's Arab Legion had 4,500 men available to fight in Palestine. The Israelis had about 30,000 on all fronts. Officially, Abdullah, as Commander-in-Chief of all the Arab forces, had been promised help and fully co-ordinated battle plans by Lebanon, Egypt, Syria and Iraq.

The only help he got was from Iraq. The Egyptians—jealous of Abdullah's determination to enlarge his kingdom—even went so far as to confiscate a shipload of British ammunition for the Arab Legion on its way through the Suez canal to Aqaba, and Abdullah could do nothing to get it released.

The war lasted, on and off, for about nine months. The Egyptians were routed; the Syrians and Lebanese hardly moved out of their own territory. The Jordanian Arab Legion successfully held onto most of that part of Palestine they had occupied, but they lost the towns of Lydda and Ramle, which Glubb had told Abdullah they could not defend, and they failed to stop the Israelis capturing the Negev desert and the port of Eilat. It was useful ammunition for those who opposed Abdullah and wanted to find scapegoats for the Arab defeat. Glubb, the British officers, Britain and Abdullah himself were blamed for restraining their men, and for giving up Arab territory by agreement with the Jews.

Abdullah, who felt the Jordanian forces had acquitted themselves well, rejected all this abuse with contempt. One large group of demonstrators besieged his palace shouting for victory over Israel and accusing the Legion of betraying the Arabs. Abdullah, not content to leave his guards to ward off the menacing crowd, walked down the steps and slapped the leader of the demonstration sharply across the face.

'What nonsense is this?' Abdullah roared at his suddenly hushed audience. 'You want to fight the Jews? Very well, there's a recruiting office just over there : those who want to fight, join up at once; those who don't, go home and shut up!'*

The main source of opposition to Abdullah was still the Palestinian group led by Amin al Husseini, who in September 1948 set up their own 'All Palestine Government' in the Gaza strip. But in December, another important group of Palestinians held a special congress at Jericho and asked for union with Transjordan. It was an open invitation which Abdullah had done everything to encourage. Although the authority of the Congress to speak for all Palestine was open to question and its legality very dubious, Abdullah regarded himself from that moment as King of the Arab part of Palestine on the West Bank of the Jordan, and formally annexed it in April 1950 with Britain's

* Kirkbride, *A Crackle of Thorns*, pp. 30–1.

approval. The kingdom of Transjordan became the kingdom of Jordan.

By this one action, Abdullah presented himself and his grandson Hussein, with the most dangerous throne in the world. Palestinians now outnumbered Transjordanians by two to one, and the Palestinians were desperately bitter and dejected people. They owed no particular loyalty to Abdullah, who, they felt, had let them down in the war. They resented his links with the British, who were partly responsible for what had happened in Palestine, and they brought with them a flood of refugees from Israel, who fed eagerly on Egyptian and Syrian anti-Israel propaganda and were to form the nucleus of the Palestinian guerilla movement. Abdullah immediately gave the Palestinians full Jordanian citizenship and half the seats in his parliament. But Abdullah's rule was still virtually oblivious of parliament, and the Palestinians soon made it clear that this was not good enough : they were intelligent, ambitious people and they wanted more than a token participation in the running of the country. The enlargement of the kingdom had more of the making of a clash than a merger.

Events now moved quickly towards the gun battle in Jerusalem that thrust Hussein from his cosy school life into the turmoil of politics.

Abdullah took the risk of reopening the contacts he had had with the Israelis in an effort to salvage something of the Arab territory lost to the Jews in the war. On several occasions he received Israeli emissaries secretly at his palace at Shuna in the Jordan valley. These meetings are attested by Glubb and others who bear no malice towards Abdullah : there is no doubt that they took place. The secret negotiations came to nothing; the Israelis were unwilling to make the territorial concessions that Abdullah needed if he was to take the risk of making peace with them.

But Abdullah made one great mistake. He entrusted a man called Abdullah al Tell with the task of arranging these meetings. Tell was a Colonel in the Arab Legion and a particular favourite of the King. He had been promoted fast to be military commander in Jerusalem, and Abdullah gave him the job of carrying messages to and from the Israelis. But when Glubb and Abdullah refused to promote al Tell to Brigadier, only a year after he had been appointed a Colonel, he resigned in a fit of pique and made off to Egypt with photostats of those secret documents. There he made common cause with another of Abdullah's implacable foes—Amin al Husseini—and the two of them are thought to have activated the conspiracy that ended in the Aqsa Mosque in Jerusalem on the 20th of July 1951.* Abdullah had pressed his luck too far.

During the first three weeks of July, Hussein spent a lot of time with his grandfather. He had the clear impression that the old man had selected him for special attention. Hussein's father was by now a very sick man : in May 1951, he had been sworn in as Abdullah's deputy, but the very next day he had a seizure and his embarrassed family flew him off to Beirut, and announced that he was suffering from a nervous breakdown. Abdullah had another son, Naif, who was popular with the army but whose mother was not, like Talal's, a Hashemite. Naif was a favourite of Abdullah's because he was strong and active, but he was not gifted with the judgement and finesse that would make him a king. Hussein was only sixteen, but seemed the likelier bet.

Hussein would often be up at 6 a.m. He would drive himself in one of the royal cars from his father's house down the hill, through the town and up to the Raghadan Palace. For a long time, Hussein kept his driving secret from Abdullah : he was not sure whether the old man would approve. But one evening, after they had spent a day together, Abdullah surprised Hussein by coming out of the palace after they had said good night and finding him in the driving seat. Hussein was extremely embarrassed, but all Abdullah said was, 'I see you are going home. Well, be careful, won't you?'

When Hussein arrived home five minutes later, his grandfather was on the telephone—just to make sure he was still in one piece.

Those days with Abdullah would start with a lesson in religion, English and Arabic. Sometimes Hussein would translate English into Arabic for Abdullah, whose English was poor. They would

---

* Abdullah Tell told the author in December 1971 that he never plotted the death of Abdullah, only his removal in favour of Talal. Tell denies that he left Jordan in a huff; he was, he says, afraid that his conspiracy was about to be uncovered.

spend long days together at conferences, receptions, and meetings with the Arab Legion. Abdullah was a man of great charm, humour and generosity but with a ruthless impatience for those who displeased him. None of this was lost on Hussein, who began to try to model himself in his grandfather's image.

In Cairo a conspiracy was brewing. Evidence which appeared later at their trial showed that Abdullah Al Tell and Musa, a relation of Amin Al Husseini, were plotting the King's death as early as 1950.* Doctor Musa al Husseini was a respected figure in Jerusalem at this time and although he was a relative of Amin, no one suspected that he shared the same hatred for Abdullah. The King had even asked Musa to stand in the coming elections in Jerusalem. He was 42, and a graduate of London University.

In September 1950 Musa went to Cairo and secretly met Abdullah Tell. He was given £70 towards the fee for an assassin. The following May, Musa met a young Palestinian called Mohamed Ukka just outside Jerusalem. He gave him £200; Mohamed and his brother Zakariya were to find Musa a revolver and act as assistants; they would advise him of the King's movements. Finally, Musa brought in a Jerusalem vegetable merchant called Musa Ahmed al Ayyubi: this was the man who was to find him an assassin.

On the 19th of July 1951, Mohamed Ukka told Musa that the King was coming to Jerusalem to say prayers at the Aqsa Mosque the following day. Musa did not believe him at first, but it was soon officially confirmed. Meanwhile Ayyubi had found an assassin—a young tailor's apprentice called Shukri Ashu. Ayyubi gave him some money and a talisman with a short inscription on it.

There was a strangely unsettling atmosphere in the Middle East in July that year. It was a time when extremist groups like

* Tell strongly denies all implication in the assassination plot of July 1951. He says false evidence was produced at his trial by the Palestinian conspirators in order to demonstrate that their plot had the support of East Jordanians too. Tell came from the East Bank town of Irbid. Hussein later told Tell, during a visit to Cairo in 1955, that he believed he was innocent in spite of Tell's constant public attacks on Abdullah's dealings with the Jews.

B

the Muslim Brotherhood were in the ascendancy—and there
was an undercurrent of violence too. On the 16th of July the
Lebanese Prime Minister was driving out to the airport at Amman
after talks with Abdullah, when his car was peppered with
machine-gun fire from an overtaking car. He died instantly.

Sir Alec Kirkbride left for a holiday in Scotland. He could
smell the violence in the air and before leaving, he had said to
Abdullah:

'Sir, please do not go to the Aqsa mosque in Jerusalem to pray
while I am away; go anywhere else, but not there.'

Jerusalem was in the heart of Palestine, where opposition to
Abdullah was strongest, and the Aqsa was always thronged with
people. Abdullah replied with an old Arab proverb: 'Until my
day comes, no one can harm me; when my day comes, no one
can guard me.'

Hussein was very excited. His grandfather has asked him to go
with him to Jerusalem. They would go to Amman airport first,
to present 'wings' to Jordanian air force pilots. Hussein wore his
army uniform: Abdullah had just appointed him an honorary
captain, as a reward for his success in fencing at Victoria College.

Hussein and his grandfather had lunch in a hangar at the
airport after the presentation and Wing Commander Bill Fisher,
the British officer who commanded the Jordan air force taxied
out the King's aircraft—a Dove. After lunch, the King took off
for Jerusalem; Hussein went by road.

Friday the 20th was a warm day. Hussein and his grandfather
breakfasted early, and Hussein was surprised when Abdullah
asked him why he was not wearing his uniform. Hussein had
sent it back to Amman by car to be pressed, but Abdullah was
so insistent that he wear it, that someone had to be sent after the
car to bring the uniform back. After some delay they set off
to spend the morning in Nablus. After that, Abdullah had decided—against nearly all advice—to go to prayers in the Aqsa
Mosque in Jerusalem. They had coffee with the Mayor of Nablus,
who suggested that Abdullah should pray at the Nablus mosque
this time. But, no, Abdullah was adamant.

At noon, Abdullah and Hussein were back in Jerusalem. Glubb
had ordered Colonel Habes Majali, his commander there, to take

all possible precautions, and Hussein noticed the streets full of troops. When they reached the old city, their car stopped as near the mosque as possible. A man opened the car door and bowed low to Abdullah. It was Doctor Musa al Husseini.

Hussein and Abdullah walked towards the mosque. The military guard was so big that Hussein turned to an officer and asked if it were a funeral procession.

Abdullah found the escort cramping too. He strongly disliked being guarded, and as he entered the large courtyard of the mosque, the soldiers pressed feverishly against the huge crowd of Friday morning worshippers who wanted a glimpse of the King. Abdullah turned to Colonel Majali.

'Don't imprison me, Habes,' he said. Majali relaxed the cordon a little, and Abdullah insisted on stopping now and again, to talk to some of the people pressing in on him. Some of them he knew, others were strangers.

It was dangerous, and Majali knew it. Quietly he signed to some of the soldiers to wrap themselves closer round their King. But Abdullah would not have it. As he reached the steps of the mosque, he spoke again, curtly, to Majali, and the guard stepped back to allow him to walk through the door ahead of the others.

On Jordan Radio, listeners could hear the morning prayers from the Aqsa Mosque, live from Jerusalem. Someone was reading the Koran.

Abdullah moved through the door. Hussein was a pace or two behind him. The old sheikh of the mosque waited inside to greet Abdullah and kiss his hand.

But he never did. A young man stepped out from behind the huge door. It was Shukri Ashu, holding a revolver. He took a couple of paces from the door and pointed the muzzle at Abdullah's right ear. It was only a few inches away, and when Ashu pulled the trigger, the deafening explosion blasted all life from the King: the bullet passed behind his ear and out through his eye.

The body crumpled to the ground at Hussein's feet. His grandfather was dead.

III

THE ARAB PUBLIC SCHOOL BOY

JULY 1951–AUGUST 1952

For an instant everyone stood still. There was a wisp of smoke at the end of the small, black revolver.

Then Hussein lunged at the murderer who turned to escape. Bearded dignitaries and friends of the dead King scrambled to avoid the gun battle they knew must follow.

The bodyguard moved forward behind Hussein, but for a moment nobody dared fire in the confusion. Then suddenly, Hussein found himself face to face with the murderer who was trapped, and had turned to fight it out. This time he pointed the revolver at Hussein.

Hussein turned slightly away from the man. The gun went off and the bullet flashed at Hussein's chest, struck a medal at an oblique angle, and ricocheted off. Hussein reeled backwards, and a number of bullets from the bodyguard put an end to Shukri Ashu. The talisman was still round his neck : the Arabic inscription read, 'Kill, and thou shalt be safe.'

Radio listeners heard the chatter of the guns behind the deep voice of the man chanting the Koran.

Hussein and some of the bodyguard carried Abdullah's body to hospital on an improvised stretcher made out of a carpet, and Hussein was given an injection—for shock. Then he and the other bewildered members of the King's party were driven to Jerusalem airfield. Glubb and the Jordan government wanted him back in Amman safely as soon as possible. Wing Commander Fisher was told to fly the King's body home to Amman, and a second aircraft was ordered to Jerusalem to collect Hussein.

The man who piloted the second Dove was Squadron Leader Jock Dalgleish—a big, friendly Scotsman with a rocky, wind-swept face, who had a healthy disrespect for authority and, like Hussein, a boyish passion for adventure. It was to be the start of a long friendship. Dalgleish saw young Hussein standing alone

on the tarmac at Jerusalem airport, as the large Cadillac arrived
carrying the King's body. Soldiers of the Arab Legion, still mad-
dened with fury at what had happened, leapt out of their escorting vehicles and carried the body—in its bloodstained robes—
into the plane.

The loneliness that Hussein felt at that moment was intense,
His father had left ten days earlier for five weeks of medical
treatment in Geneva, and there seemed no one whom he could
turn to. When Dalgleish came up to him and gently told him,
'I'll look after you', he felt he had a friend.

Hussein and Dalgleish flew back to Amman, as Glubb's troops
moved to secure the country against any follow-through by the
men who had planned the murder. If there was any dissension in
the Arab Legion, it did not dare assert itself. Hussein's uncle,
Naif, who was Talal's half brother, was appointed Regent in
Talal's absence, and Kirkbride cut short his holiday in Scotland.

Who was to succeed Abdullah? The decision was made by
two men, Kirkbride and the Jordanian Prime Minister Taufiq
Abul Huda, a thin, dry, astute little man who, like all Jordanian
leaders recognised that Britain's hold over his country's finances
made her consent an essential part of all important political
decisions.* Glubb was closely consulted, but always scrupulously
avoided taking part in any political decision-making himself.

There were two choices for the succession, Naif, the Regent,
and Talal. Naif was popular and ambitious, but had not Talal's
intelligence : both Kirkbride and Taufiq thought him quite un-
suitable for rule. But Talal, the natural successor to Abdullah
through his Hashemite mother, was hardly more suitable : he
was mentally unstable, and too shy and introverted to give Jordan
strong leadership. Moreover, when overtaken by one of his fits,
he was known to rant and rave about the British in such a way
that many thought he might change Jordan's political alignment.
Glubb and Kirkbride, who knew him well, understood that this
was the fantasy of a schizophrenic, but Arab nationalists in Jordan
and elsewhere who knew him less well, had high hopes of him.

What really decided the British and Taufiq for Talal was the
fact that Hussein was his son. Abdullah had recognised Hussein's

---

* The degree of Jordan's dependence on Britain at this time encouraged
a number of countries, led by the Soviet Union, to refuse to recognise
Jordan as an independent sovereign state.

strength of character early, and its beginnings were clear to the others too. If Hussein was eventually to succeed, a period of rule by his father would give him legitimacy. It would be awkward to expect the succession to pass from Naif to Hussein : Naif might have other ideas. The only problem was Talal's madness, but the chances were that he would soon show himself incapable of ruling anyway, and the throne could pass to his son. So the choice was made. Quickly, secretly, an extra guard was put on Hussein, and Glubb kept an eye on Naif, who was still acting as Regent.

Hussein, suddenly exposed to the intrigues of palace politics as everyone shuffled for position, found himself being groomed as Crown Prince. He was sent all round the country with other prominent members of the family to show the flag in that peculiar Bedouin way, which involves calling on the local sheikhs and emirs, and dispensing favours among them with an eye to the ones whose loyalty will be decisive in the future. He was good at it. He was gifted with his father's gentle concern and kindly manners, and his approach was direct and firm enough to command respect.

Naif realised that his time was running out. Talal's condition had made some improvement in Switzerland and in the small, gossip-hungry society of Amman it was now an open secret that Naif was not to succeed Abdullah. But he *was* to make one frantic bid for power.

One day in late summer Kirkbride was summoned urgently to the house of the Prime Minister, Taufiq. There he learned that the Palace Guard—the 10th Hashemite Regiment—appeared to be behaving suspiciously, and that it looked as if Naif was using them—or they were using him—to stage a takeover.

Glubb was told to act swiftly, and two other Bedouin regiments were stationed behind the palace to warn Naif off. Talal was summoned quickly from Switzerland and when he appeared, Naif left the country. The Commander of the 10th Regiment, Colonel Habes Majali, was quietly relieved of his post, and sent off as governor of Nablus police district. This did not do permanent damage to his career—Hussein later made him Army Commander-in-Chief. Indeed it has become a kind of sport in Jordan to observe how many apparent conspirators are later pardoned by Hussein, who seems unable to bear a permanent grudge against anyone. Abdullah Tell, who was convicted with Musa al Husseini and others of the murder of Hussein's grandfather, returned to Jordan and took up a civil service post in Amman with a full pardon from Hussein less than twenty years since he had been condemned to death in his absence after escaping to Egypt.

It is significant that the conspiracy against Abdullah succeeded only in avenging a number of personal feuds. There seems to have been no attempt to follow up the assassination with a bid to disrupt Jordan. But the murder did provide Hussein with a sharp warning of the dangers of having any dealings with Israel.

On the 6th of September, Hussein's father became King. There was a twenty-one gun salute, and great public rejoicing. The British sat back and sighed with relief that the crisis had passed by so peacefully. Republican stirrings in the Middle East were threatening to overthrow the established order, but Jordan was secure.

The problem was what to do with Hussein. The young prince was still only three-quarters educated, and he could not possibly go back to Alexandria : the murder of Abdullah made Egypt look an unsafe place for a Hashemite, particularly one who was now heir to the throne. Abdullah had always wanted Hussein to go to Harrow like Talal, and now that Hussein's Iraqi cousin Feisal, grandson of Abdullah's brother, was at Harrow, it seemed the obvious place for Hussein to spend his last year at public school.

Hussein himself had a lot of misgivings : at Victoria College he had been among people he could understand and communicate with quite easily. At Harrow he would be in a different world—an outcast among British boys whose English would be too fast for him. He found it difficult enough to make close friends : the prospect of trying to do so in such an alien environment made him very apprehensive.

His fears were justified. When he arrived there, he felt lost and a stranger to the complex of relationships and instincts that the other boys had developed over four full years.

He was very lonely and unhappy. Few of the other boys made any effort to befriend him; he was a quiet, unforceful person ill-equipped to thrust himself into the tightly-knit cliques of friends, which had no room for a very foreign little prince who spoke a rather strange sort of English, and was reluctant to throw himself into everything with the gusto that they did.

But if this experience made him miserable, it also toughened him. He had always been a plucky boy, but until he was exposed to Harrow, he had lived a sheltered existence; even at Victoria College there were many other boys from similar backgrounds. At Harrow, he began to develop his talent for survival in an unfriendly environment.

When he arrived at Harrow, he found himself in 'the Park', a house of 55 boys, each with his own room about ten feet long by six feet wide. Hussein's room was in a little corridor called the White Passage and his bed was made of rope and canvas; it folded up into the wall in the daytime and Hussein carved his name in the wooden frame as all the other boys did. He had to take a cold bath every morning, clean his own shoes, and press his trousers by putting them under the mattress at night. It was a long way from the warm Arab comfort of his home in Amman.

Everyone called him 'Hussein' except the House Matron, for whom he had a very special affection. Miss Audrey Miskin had a little garret room at the top of the Park; her duties were to do the boys' sewing and keep an eye on their health. Hussein used to swing into her room like a 'little monkey', and pour out his heart to her as if she were his mother. She called him 'Child', and listened patiently to all his worries, and would often massage his limbs to soothe him.

'He was a very highly strung child', Miss Miskin remembers. 'A very philosophical fellow, but a simple soul at heart. What he needed was a home. I suppose I was a sort of mother to him : his own family seemed to neglect him while he was at Harrow. He was, fundamentally, a law-abiding boy, but he did have a sense of mischief which was in turn hampered by his deep sense of duty.'

Time and again Hussein used to wander up to that little room and tell Miss Miskin about the work that awaited him in Jordan, and his worries about his father. He was growing more conscious of the illness that was eating away his father's mind and of the imminence of his own accession to Jordan's uneasy throne.

His housemaster was a Mr Stevenson, a man who chooses his words carefully, and is a respected judge of character. He thought Hussein 'a determined fellow, but limited in his academic ability.

I would not say he was successful at Harrow, but we did what we could to equip him for the scramble we knew would face him when he returned to the Middle East'.

Hussein was a strange mixture of complexes: he was intent on proving that he could do things, but was reluctant to attempt anything publicly at which he thought he would not excel. One morning he disappeared on a private cross-country run and returned, in a state of near collapse, after running for a number of hours. He was not good at games: he was never seen playing ping pong with the other boys, though he had to play rugger because it was compulsory, and he attacked the game without any sense of fear. 'He would just put his head down and go in there and fight', says Mr Stevenson.

Hussein was allowed only one special privilege. He was given leave every weekend. A large black car from the Jordanian embassy would pull up outside the Park on Sunday morning, and a forlorn little figure, wearing black tail-coat, white shirt, wing collar and striped trousers, all the trappings of a young Harrovian—would be whisked away to be treated like a Prince in the sleek high society of diplomatic Kensington. He became a close friend of Fawzi al Mulki, the Jordanian ambassador in London, who soon appreciated that Hussein's taste inclined more to fast cars and girl friends than to rugby football and table tennis. He would come back laden with packs of tasty oriental sweetmeats, which he used to share liberally with Miss Miskin.

Hussein's housemaster found the attentions of the Jordanian embassy irritating: they would fuss around Hussein, pampering him with presents and treats. There was no doubt that most of the assiduous diplomats were competing with each other for the favours of the young man who was sure to be King.

One of the things that Mr Stevenson never knew about was the car. A friend of Talal's presented Hussein with a spanking new sky-blue Rover, and the Jordanian ambassador helped find a place near Harrow where Hussein could keep it—just far enough away from the Park to elude Mr Stevenson. At a village called Sudbury, they found a garage managed by Maurice Rayner who had a passion for motor cars that Hussein instinctively felt he shared, and the two became close friends.

It was on one of his outings from Harrow that Hussein was

introduced to Dina Abdul Hamed, a distant cousin of his, at a tea party given by a friend in North West London. Dina was seven years older than he was, and studying at Girton College, Cambridge. She was petite, pretty and highly intelligent. Hussein was immediately attracted to her, and soon found himself falling in love with her. Dina, for her part, was never in love with Hussein, but she respected his position in the Hashemite family and responded to what she thought was his need for understanding, guidance and support.

Glubb came down to Harrow once and took Hussein out. He says that Hussein was not amused by Battersea Fun Fair. He did not want to go on the scenic railway or the merry-go-rounds.

'I must have misunderstood his age group, or his early introduction to public affairs in such tragic circumstances had sobered him prematurely.'* On the way back to Harrow, Glubb and Hussein visited Fortnum and Mason, and Glubb says he made up for the fact that Hussein had no tuck box at Harrow.

Hussein's housemaster had an important visitor too. A man called Geoffrey Furlonge, a high official at the Foreign Office, Head of Eastern Department, as it was known then, paid a call on Mr Stevenson in the Christmas term of 1951. Hussein knew nothing about it. It was three months after his father had become King. Furlonge had one question for Stevenson:

'Have you ever witnessed yourself, or heard tell of any occurrence that leads you to believe that Hussein is mentally unstable in any way at all?'

Stevenson was emphatic: 'Certainly not.'

Back in Jordan, Talal's condition was worsening.

On the night Queen Zein, Talal's wife and Hussein's mother, gave birth to a daughter in the Italian Hospital in Amman, her husband burst into the hospital, rushed into her bedroom and drew a knife. He shouted that he would kill Zein and the baby. Zein's life was saved by a courageous man who seized the knife from Talal just in time. Glubb sent his second-in-command, Abdul Khader Pasha, down to the hospital and Talal soon recovered himself. He was filled with horror and remorse when he realised what he had done.

* Glubb, *Soldier with the Arabs*, p. 300.

The fits were coming faster now, and the burden of being King only made them worse. The consciousness of what was happening to him made Talal lose much of his remaining confidence and he was tortured by the awareness of what he was doing to his own family.

In February 1952, Furlonge replaced Kirkbride as British ambassador in Jordan. The new ambassador was a man with a cold, clear, decisive power of judgement; he was unhampered by the affection Kirkbride had developed for Talal over many years of friendship. He was a diplomat with no personal ties to Jordan or the Hashemites. His job was to make a dispassionate review of British interests and to use his influence accordingly.

What Geoffrey Furlonge saw disturbed him. He saw a King without a real will to rule, who was beset by fits of madness that made him a danger to live with. He saw the yawning political divide in the country that threatened its stability—the Palestinians on the West Bank clamouring for free elections and more effective action against Israel, and the Jordanians on the East Bank resenting the Palestinian intrusion into their ordered existence and disinclined to risk all in another war with the Jews. The country needed strong leadership, and it patently did not have it.

Furlonge's doubts about Talal's ability to rule were sharply confirmed when he was driving past the Basman palace and noticed a small, childlike figure wandering aimlessly in the road, kicking stones with its feet. The palace guards were looking on helplessly, and as Furlonge caught up with the man, he saw a black scowl on his face that hardly faded when he recognised the British ambassador. It was King Talal.

Furlonge's judgement had been strengthened by his talk with Stevenson at Harrow, and the confidence Jordanian leaders shared with him and Glubb that Hussein was man enough for the task.

However, Talal was a popular king: his madness was not unduly aparent to those who did not know him well, and the British were already suspected of wanting to get rid of him. Talal's rantings against Britain were taken by those who did not understand, or did not want to understand their motivation to mean that he was anti-British.

The traditional tribal hierarchy, for their part, were known to be concerned about Talal's passion for reform and liberalisation. In early 1952, Talal introduced a new Constitution, which made the cabinet responsible to parliament for the first time, and reduced the powers of the King. He also pressed for an improvement in relations with other Arab states, and his government signed the Arab League's Collective Security Pact—which Abdullah had boycotted.

Talal's new political attitudes encouraged the suspicions of many Arabs that the conservative Bedouin—and the British— had a more compelling motive for removing him than their concern for his mental capacity. Moreover, suspicions were aroused by the fact that Talal was being treated regularly by a Scot, Dr Forbes Robertson, at the Hospital for Mental Diseases in Beirut. What were the British up to? They had given most of Palestine to the Jews, and now they were trying to oust the King of Jordan because they did not agree with his policies.

There was another element in the picture too. A group of young officers in the Arab Legion, taking advantage of the popular disillusion with Glubb and the Legion's British officers, started working on the King to break the British connection. Their leader was a man called Ali Abu Nuwar. He came from Salt, a town in the hills just west of Amman. He was a slender, rather dapper man, with jet-black hair and large dark eyes that stared with a hint of fanaticism at people he spoke to. He was highly articulate in Arabic and English, and spoke as if possessed with a sense of mission. Glubb reports that Ali Abu Nuwar tried to secure a secret audience with the King through Talal's barber. Glubb judged it imperative that Ali should be sent away: to Glubb and to the Jordan government of Taufiq Abul Huda, anything that would jeopardise Britain's position in Jordan would jeopardise Jordan itself. Ali Abu Nuwar was given the job of military attaché at the Jordanian embassy in Paris. But it was not the last that Glubb was to hear of him.

In May, 1952, Talal had a serious relapse and was flown to Paris for treatment. At a lunch party in Amman, held to welcome the new Pakistani ambassador, Talal had celebrated the departure of his guests by sweeping the tablecloth off the table, shattering crockery and glass: he had then struck his wife and daughter. And in Paris, Talal took to wandering alone in the streets: sometimes his family would search for him for hours.

It was a very distressing time for Hussein, who used to visit his family in Paris and Lausanne, where they occasionally spent a few days. He wrote a postcard to Miss Miskin in June:

'Dear Matron. All my greetings and respects to you and Mr and Mrs Stevenson from Switzerland—with all hopes to return once again to Harrow as things are not doing so well now. Best wishes from Hussein.'

When Hussein arrived back in Harrow after his trip, he told Miss Miskin that his father had attacked him with a knife. It was clear that things had become impossible.

The decision to remove Talal was taken in Amman in July, a few days after he returned from Europe, with no evident improvement in his condition. It was not a difficult decision to take as all the essential parties to it were in agreement. The royal family, the Jordanian Prime Minister, and the British government had already reached a consensus on his incapacity and Hussein's competence, and it only remained for Taufiq Abul Huda to translate this into action. He requested a meeting in the strictest secrecy with Glubb, whose *advice* as head of the security force was crucial and with the British ambassador whose *consent* was judged equally crucial.

On Taufiq's initiative, it was agreed that two doctors would report to the Jordanian parliament on the state of Talal's mind. Talal would be pronounced insane, and the kingdom would pass to his eldest son, Hussein. Quietly, the two men gave Taufiq their approval.

On August the 11th, the doctor's report was presented by Taufiq to a secret session of the Jordanian parliament. It was supported by evidence from three Jordanian doctors and after several hours' debate, parliament decreed that Talal was to be asked to resign, and Hussein to succeed him. The people took the decision with equanimity. It was based on the judgement of Arab doctors; the Jordanian parliament had decided on the recommendation of the Prime Minister; Glub Pasha was on leave in England at the time. Even those who believed that he and the British ambassador decided policy in Jordan, had to admit that power was transferred calmly, constitutionally.

The abdication order was taken to King Talal at the palace, and he received it without surprise.

'I had expected this,' he said. 'Please thank the Government

and the Parliament on my behalf. I pray God to bless and keep
my country and my people.'

Talal retired to Egypt. He then moved to a villa on an island
in the Bosporus off Istanbul where his family still visit him. His
illness has steadily worsened and, at the time of writing, he finds
it hard to recognise his own son—King Hussein.

IV

'MR KING OF JORDAN, SIR!'

AUGUST 1952–1953

Hussein was in Switzerland, on holiday from Harrow, when the news came. He had joined his mother, his two brothers and sister at the Beau Rivage Hotel on Lake Geneva. The weather was hot.

On the 12th of August, his mother and the rest of the family were out shopping when a page knocked at Hussein's door, and came in with an envelope on a silver salver. It was addressed to 'His Majesty King Hussein'. It was from the Prime Minister, Taufiq Abul Huda: the message was brief and to the point. Hussein had succeeded his father. He was not yet seventeen.

The plane carrying Jordan's new King touched down at Mafraq airport, and the guard of honour presented arms. Glubb Pasha stepped forward to the foot of the steps with other Jordanian leaders. The airport was ringed with troops.

A small, broad figure stepped out. He had thick, generous lips, and deep-set dark eyes that looked as if they reflected a nature full of melancholy. He stood very straight but there was a slight nervousness about him and a taut sensibility that betrayed passions held in check.

From the moment Hussein stepped out of that aircraft, he left his sheltered schooldays behind. Few people knew what to expect of him. Most of his recent school-life had been spent abroad. People's memories of him were of a rather shy, well-mannered boy, who would probably do as he was told. It did not take them long to discover they were mistaken.

But Hussein's brave composure as he emerged into the sun concealed a mind full of apprehension and haunted by memories of his unstable family life and of his unhappiness and self-consciousness at Harrow. Most vivid of all was the memory of his grandfather's murder, when in a matter of seconds the group of devoted courtiers and attendants had fled, panic stricken, from their master's side and exposed the fragility of his hold on them almost as effectively as the assassin's bullet. Anyone a quarter as human and sensitive as Hussein would have trembled on such a day. But although the abrupt assumption of responsibility after this disturbed childhood left a gap in Hussein's grounding that had a permanent effect on his maturity and judgement, he was saved by his instinctive sense of honour and discipline and by his magnetic personality. If from the day he became King his judgement sometimes faltered—in his choice of men for example —or if he occasionally gave way to youthful impulses, his essential courage, strength of character and flair for leadership soon made his weaknesses appear negligible.

Hussein made it quite clear from the outset where his interests lay. First, and last, he wanted an army, and a real air force. An army he already had, and under Glubb's management it was expanding fast. It had grown from a strength of 6,000 in 1948 to 20,000 by the end of 1952, and owed its expansion entirely to the British subsidy, which paid for the soldiers and their equipment under the Anglo-Jordan treaty. The trouble was that Britain was building up the Arab Legion as a deterrent to Communism: many Jordanians—particularly the Palestinians—thought it should direct its growing strength against Israel. Hussein himself was inspired for the moment mainly by an impulse to adventure and excitement, and by the memory of his grandfather's advice that an army which owed its strength to the King was the key to the security of the throne.

But nothing stirred Hussein's imagination so much as the idea of a strong air force. In 1952, Jordan had virtually no air force, and in the clear skies of the Middle East, an air force was the most effective demonstration of power. Hussein directed more of his energy in the course of his first two or three years as King to securing himself an air force than to any other single objective.

But for the first few months—until he came of age—he went to Sandhurst. Hussein had always dreamt of going to Sandhurst, and when the idea was put to him by his uncle Sherif Nasser, the most influential member of Hussein's family, next to his mother, and by the Prime Minister Taufiq Abul Huda, Hussein leaped at it. Talal had always told him that Sandhurst was the best training a young man could have, and Talal was a man of

FATHER AND SON: Talal was a loving father to Hussein, but Hussein's family life was soon haunted by his father's strange fits of madness. Talal used to keep a small stable of horses and taught his son to ride like his Bedouin ancestors.

GRANDFATHER AND GLUBB: King Abdullah and Glubb Pasha understood each other as Hussein and Glubb never did.

BORN OF THE DESERT: Hussein in 1945, aged 10. His Bedouin ancestry won him the constant support of the tribal sheikhs.

DEATH OF A KING:
The funeral of King Abdullah—murdered in Jerusalem in July 1951. Hussein *(extreme right)* narrowly escaped death himself when a bullet struck a medal on his chest. On his right is the Emir Naif, who contested the succession.

ASSASSIN OR PAWN?:
Colonel Abdullah Tell, pictured here in 1948 at the Dome of the Rock in Jerusalem, only a few yards from where King Abdullah was murdered. He was convicted —in his absence—for having organised the conspiracy, but still protests his innocence of the murder.

KING TALAL *(foreground)*: July 1951– August 1952. The King's deepening madness led the Prime Minister, Taufiq Abul Huda (*in the centre between Talal and Hussein*) to ask Parliament to thrust Hussein, at the age of 16, on to his father's throne.

KING HUSSEIN: August 1952 Hussein was inaugurated as King of one of the world's most unstable countries when he returned from six months' training at the British Military Academy at Sandhurst. He was 17.

judgement when he was in his right mind. Besides, Hussein was never happier than when in uniform.

Within four weeks of arriving back in Amman, Hussein had done an about-turn, and enrolled as Officer Cadet King Hussein at Sandhurst. He was given Room 109 in Inkerman Company, and his Company Commander, Major Horsfield, took him immediately to meet the Commandant. One of the Commandant's aides had already telephoned Hussein's housemaster at Harrow to ask :

'Whatever do you call this chap?'

'Hussein, of course,' said Mr Stevenson.

So 'Hussein' was what they called him. But on parade he was to be 'King Hussein', or 'King of Jordan'. And Regimental Sergeant-Major Lord, the man with one of the loudest voices on a parade ground anywhere in the world, used to take pleasure in howling out not 'King Hussein' or 'King of Jordan', but 'Mr, King of Jordan, sir!' Ten years later RSM Lord was the subject of the British Television programme, 'This is Your Life' and King Hussein flew to London specially to appear on the programme as a guest.

Hussein took to Sandhurst as everyone expected he would. He enjoyed the discipline, the adventure of the night exercises, the thrill of handling modern weapons. He had to absorb all the training they could cram into him in six months : it was a tough physical test for him, and he was not as strong as he looked. He was plagued by sinus trouble, and he was no athlete anyway.

But at Sandhurst he felt he was among friends and equals; his self confidence was growing. The old inhibitions fell away, and he threw himself into the life of the place. He chased as many girls as any other young officer cadet, and he drove cars a lot faster than any of them. Rayner was always on hand with Hussein's new 120-mile-an-hour Aston Martin, and one day Colonel Horsfield, who had taken Hussein to the Motor Show in London, was stunned to see him walk up to the stand where an enormous Lincoln was on show, and order it. It was as long as any car Hussein had seen, and it had push-button controls that made the hood go down.

Hussein's friend, Fawzi al Mulki, was still the Jordanian ambassador in London, and Hussein used to make frequent trips to London to see him. Once, another friend of Hussein's was

driving him and some other Sandhurst cadets through Knights-
bridge when the Aston Martin went into a skid : Hussein yelled
at him to jam on the brakes. The bright young cadet slammed
his foot down on the accelerator, and the car ended up on the
other side of a huge hoarding. Hussein told the driver to change
places with him and when the police arrived, they were so
delighted to have the King's autograph that they forgot about
the broken hoarding. Besides, they could hardly charge a king.

Hussein was throwing off his early shyness with quite remarkable speed. He enjoyed dancing, night clubs, and parties : he
was a good story-teller, and his College Commander Lt-Colonel
Welsh, remembers how good a mimic he was. Once Hussein was
late back from London : the ambassador had phoned Sandhurst
to say that the roads were bad and that 'His Majesty' had been
held up. This excuse was quite unacceptable to the Commandant
and Welsh was ordered to 'see Cadet Hussein suitably employed'
when he returned. The next morning, Hussein arrived shame-
faced, and Welsh said to him :

'Now, Hussein, I haven't the slightest idea what to do with
you—let's suppose the roles are reversed, and you are addressing
me : how would you tell me off?'

Hussein replied without hesitation, and with Welsh's precise
manner and voice, 'Sir, I'm going to give you the most imperial
rocket of your career !'

Welsh was delighted, and sent him packing off to London
again.

In Jordan the economic and social background against which
Hussein had to begin his rule was as awkward as any in the
world. Of his population of 1½ million, 600,000 were Palestinian
refugees, and another 450,000 were West Bank Jordanians, who
regarded Palestine, not Jordan, as their national home. Two-
thirds of Hussein's citizens were reluctant Jordanians, and a large
number of them were unemployed, living on subsistence rations
in United Nations refugee camps. They were capable, but disillusioned and despairing people, nursing their bitter hatred of
Israel and blaming Britain, America and even the Hashemites
for their position. From the early fifties onwards, they and their
cause were one of the primary moving factors in Arab politics :

in Jordan itself, politicians of opposition left-wing parties found in them a responsive audience for their militant propaganda and a rich recruiting ground for demonstations. Later their growing political frustration in Jordan, and the immovability of the Israeli presence in Palestine, provoked increasing extremism among Palestinians, and by the late 1960s their principal means of expression was no longer in terms of politics, but of violence.

The economic problems that were to face Hussein on his return from Sandhurst were no less intractable. Jordan's trade had been disrupted by the closure of its outlet to most of Palestine after the creation of the state of Israel. The rich trade in farm products, fruit and vegetables between Transjordan and Palestine collapsed with the war of 1948. And Jordan then had to feed the great influx of refugees from Israel. The country's main source of income, apart from the British subsidy, were the small phosphate and cement industries. But Jordan's budget, which amounted to £15·4 million in 1953–4, could not be balanced without the bulk of it (£10·2 million in 1953–4) being financed from outside the country.

When Hussein returned for his inauguration in the spring of 1953, his formal education was at an end. The British educational establishment had produced a young leader it could be proud of : he had all the qualities that Harrow and Sandhurst were built to foster—courage, resolution, enterprise, a measure of self-assertiveness, a good practical judgement, and the best public school manners. He persists, to this day, in calling men 'Sir'.

But his political education was limited to the intolerant Conservatism of much of the British upper middle class, and to the advice and instincts he had inherited from the patriarchal régime of his grandfather. Not surprisingly, he had little feeling for the economic and political case presented by the Left, and it was as natural for him to despise socialism and communism as it was for nearly every one of his friends at Harrow and Sandhurst. Besides, even if he *had* come into contact with the new political ideas in the Arab world that would have widened his political education, he would only have seen them as threatening his throne. And to Hussein the task of preserving his throne had nothing to do with self-preservation : it was a task that he fervently believed to be in the interests of his people.

At the same time, however, Hussein's British experience had

given him a healthy respect for British institutions. Like his father, he felt that to a degree Jordan should have political parties, a free press, and other features of that civilised democracy whose money and protection was, after all, the mainstay of his throne.

He was encouraged in these ideas by his old friend, Fawzi Al Mulki, the ambassador in London. And, soon after he returned to Amman, Hussein asked that strict disciplinarian, Taufiq Abul Huda, to move aside for a while as Prime Minister and allow Fawzi's new ideas to have a run.

It was a feature of Hussein's early career that he allowed himself to be drawn in two or more apparently opposite directions at the same time. Glubb constantly recounts how the young King would change his view from one day to the next depending on who had last been speaking to him. Until the late 1950s Hussein was impressionable, and while he was building up his political experience, he was ready to allow experiment within the limits of Jordan's patriarchal system.

Fawzi's Premiership was the first of two initiatives by King Hussein to liberalise Jordan's political system. He gave the liberals the field again in 1956. Neither of these experiments worked. In more stable times a moderate infusion of democracy might have enlivened the country by encouraging genuine participation in government by the people and the King—in partnership. But the tumult of Arab politics at that time left no place for moderation. With régimes plotting each other's downfall against the background of the Cold War and the wave of Arab nationalism sweeping the Middle East, Jordan was bound to be caught up in the frenzy. Easing restrictions on the press and political parties released forces that could not possibly work in partnership with a monarchy, which was out of step with the popular passions of the time. And Hussein had to live with the fact that most of his people were Palestinians, whose passion was for struggle with Israel—no matter what the cost.

So Fawzi's reforms unleashed discontent instead of dynamism, and the focus of the discontent was the Jordan government's attitude to Israel.

The armistice agreements of 1949 had left the border with Israel in the most inhuman muddle. Villages were split in half; even farms and orchards were bisected and the wretched Arab villagers, robbed by the armistice of half of all their property, used to creep across into Israel, to claim what they felt was rightly theirs. The Israelis, who said it was now their property, reacted sharply. Infiltrators were shot on sight: it was the only way the Israelis thought they could stop them. The Jordan government, anxious not to provoke the Israelis, also acted to stop infiltration into Israel by patrolling its side of the armistice line. But when infiltration did not stop, and when one or two Palestinian villagers took to staging the occasional reprisal raid against Israeli frontier settlements, the Israeli government adopted the policy of massive retaliation that it has never quite abandoned. The weakness of the policy was that it did more damage to the Jordan government than to the morale of the infiltrators, because each time the Israelis successfully demolished a Palestinian village, the Palestinians blamed the Jordanian government and the Arab Legion for not being there in time to help them. The Palestinians saw Hussein's army and police force acting not against Israel, but against *them*, and they were convinced that it was all a conspiracy by Glubb and his British officers in the Legion, in league with Israel. Of course it was not. Glubb was no friend of Israel's, nor were scores of British officers in the ranks of the Legion who referred contemptuously to the Israelis as the 'Jews' long after the establishment of the state of Israel, which they, like the Palestinians, regarded as a real injustice.

But Glubb was a soldier, with a practical job to do. He had long been persuaded that Israel was there to stay, whether the Palestinians liked it or not, and the Arab Legion was simply not in a position to alter the situation. It was not even in a position to defend every twist and turn of the border against raids by the Israelis who could strike at any time and in any number of places. He believed, with his old master King Abdullah, that the only hope for Jordan was to prevent infiltration so as not to provide the Israelis with the excuse to seize Arab territory. He did not doubt for a moment that the Israelis could do it, if they wanted to. Glubb's view was, by and large, accepted by the Jordanian government, most of whom were East Jordanians, who had not the deep and desperate sense of grievance that incited the Palestinians.

And what of Hussein? He knew that Glubb was right. And he remembered his grandfather's constant advice that war with Israel would be suicidal. He agreed with Glubb that incidents

along the armistice line had to be prevented so that, as the
temperature cooled over the years, the line would slowly crystal-
lise into a frontier. Although his grandfather's violent death
warned him that negotiations with Israel were out of the question,
he had inherited enough of Abdullah's realism to contemplate a
tacit acceptance of Israel as the only rational policy if Jordan
was to survive. But Hussein's judgement was governed by more
than cool logic. In spite of his British education, he was an Arab,
with the emotions of an Arab. He was fresh from the mock battles
of Sandhurst, and a part of him wanted to lead his men into
action against the common enemy. Besides, each morning he
would look out from his office in the Basman palace at what
used to be the empty hillsides south of the town, and would be
reminded by the vast new Palestinian settlements there of the
seething tempers of the refugees who clamoured daily for vengeance. Glubb found that Hussein's attitude to Israel varied
depending on the balance between his emotion and his reason at
any given time. But in general Hussein went along with the
advice of Glubb and the Jordanian government that the security
of his throne depended on preventing war with Israel, even if it
meant confrontation with the Palestinians. It may have been the
only wise choice for Hussein, but it provoked intense internal
opposition.

Through 1953 and early 1954 the Israelis staged a number
of reprisal raids that led to serious disturbances in Jordan. The
worst was in October 1953. On the night of October the 12th,
two Israeli children and their mother were killed when a hand
grenade was thrown through the window of their house in Tirat
Yehuda. It was probably the work of a freelance guerrilla group
based in Damascus, and supported by Abdullah's old enemies,
Amin Al Husseini, and King Saud of Saudi Arabia.

Two nights later the Israelis struck the Jordanian village of
Qibya, blew up forty-two houses with many of their occupants
inside, and killed a total of 66 people, three-quarters of them
women and children. A report by the UN truce observers said:

'Bullet-riddled bodies near the doorways and multiple bullet
hits on the doors of the demolished houses indicated that the
inhabitants had been forced to remain inside until their homes
were blown up over them. . . .'

An Arab Legion military report, prepared at Glubb's orders

the following day, said that 'several of the police detachment at Qibya and national guardsmen were at the time of the raid on frontier patrol duties trying to stop infiltrators going into Israel. One national guardsman lost his entire family of eleven. . . .'

The next morning, as people wandered helplessly through the wreckage, they began to ask: 'And where was the Arab Legion last night?' The question was soon taken up as a cry, and the cry became a roar of anger against the Legion, Glubb and the British officers. The government responded to popular feeling by dismissing the Legion's Brigade Commander in the area, Brigadier 'Teal' Ashton. He had sent a patrol to investigate first reports of the Israeli incursion, but he had then gone to sleep, and nobody had awakened him until it was all over.

A scapegoat had to be found: ironically, Ashton was one of the British officers most devoted to the Arab cause, and he retired to live as a recluse in Wales. He took with him his adopted son, a young Palestinian refugee he had saved from starvation.

But the sacrifice of Teal Ashton was not enough for the Palestinians. The press, freed from restraints by Fawzi al Mulki, denounced Glubb and the Legion, and demonstrations—a new phenomenon in Jordan, filled the streets of Amman. Communist agents, released from prison under Fawzi's amnesty, led the shouting against the 'Anglo-American imperialists'. Republicans in Syria and Egypt, where Colonel Nasser was coming to the fore, drew encouragement from the popular response in Jordan, and began to see in the embarrassment of its Hashemite king a possible focus for a more active foreign policy.

The Jordan government reacted to this by pressing the British to play down their links with Jordan under the Anglo-Jordan treaty: they particularly requested the British to pay the Arab Legion subsidy direct to Jordan instead of keeping it in a special Legion account in London. But the British wanted to retain control over the way their money was spent. They had not yet been shocked into realising the extent of Arab sensitivity about Western influence in the Middle East, and still thought that they could do what they liked in Jordan. Fortunately for Britain and Jordan, the crisis in the streets lasted only a few days, and order was soon restored.

Hussein was too young, and too busy flexing his muscles to be unduly concerned at the internal situation in his country. He involved himself in the business of getting to know his people with all the verve and charm of his grandfather. He had never forgotten his grandfather's account of how he had secured Trans-Jordan for the Hashemites by winning the loyalty of the Bedouin. Hussein diligently cultivated their leaders, travelling widely over the desert to visit them, feasting with them in their tents, and making himself available to them in Amman.

Once, he decided to do a test of his own popularity. He pretended to be a taxi-driver plying between Amman and Zerka, and asked people who climbed in what they thought of their King. The results of Hussein's private popularity poll were, so he says, very favourable.

But while he lavished his attention on the people of the East Bank, who felt that he was part of them, he made the Palestinians on the West Bank feel he was neglecting them. The task of integrating the two banks of the Jordan into one country was an unnatural one anyway : they had been thrown together in desperation, in the heat of war and were ill-matched; their union needed the constant encouragement and unbiased favour of a strong central leadership. Hussein had all the personal qualities for this delicate task, and his leadership was certainly strong enough, but his need for a solid political and military base made it inevitable that he would have to show a bias towards the East Bank, where his dynasty had its roots. He never won the hearts of the Palestinians. He did not often travel across the Jordan, although when he did, he worked hard to gain the people's affection. It was over a dozen years before he started building himself a residence on the West Bank, and even that was overtaken, only half-finished, by the war of 1967 and the Israeli occupation.

Cars were Hussein's big hobby, and Maurice Rayner was now set up in Amman as permanent manager of the royal 'stable' as they called it. The collection of cars Hussein had assembled at Harrow and Sandhurst had grown considerably and a Squadron Leader in the Arab Legion's tiny air force, Jimmy Clapham, was enlisted to 'hot up' some of the cars in his spare time. Whenever the Aston Martin failed to clock more than a hundred miles an hour, Hussein would ring Clapham, and ask him to tune the carburettors. Hussein later gave this car to his cousin, Feisal, who had become King of Iraq on the same day that Hussein had come of age in Jordan.

But Hussein was never left without a car himself. One day a Bristol freighter aircraft arrived from Riyadh in Saudi Arabia with a present for Hussein from his arch rival King Saud—a huge Lincoln car, with a gold-plated radiator grille. Later Hussein asked Clapham to fit it with an aero engine from one of his Chipmunk aircraft. Clapham, who was a good mechanic but also an expert in the art of the possible, firmly said it was out of the question.

Ever since his grandfather's murder, Hussein had carried a gun. He used to keep one in the dashboard pocket of the Aston Martin, and if he swung round a corner too fast, it would sometimes fly out and fall into his passenger's lap. The possibility that Hussein might be assassinated or kill himself in one of his cars was never far from the mind of his mother, Queen Zein, or the Prime Minister. But when he took to *flying*, his safety became a matter of very real concern, and they did all they could to discourage him.

It started in September 1952, when Wing Commander Fisher, then commanding Jordan's air force, flew Hussein to Jerusalem to inspect some troops. On the way back, Hussein came into the cockpit, and asked if he could try the controls. He asked so many questions and Fisher became so intent on answering them, that for some minutes they were completely lost in heavy cloud. Two days later, Glubb told Fisher that Hussein was not to be encouraged in this new interest and when Fisher took Hussein to Mafraq that afternoon and Hussein once more joined him at the controls, Fisher had to tell the King to keep it a secret. But Queen Zein got to hear of it and refused to allow Hussein to take the flying lessons he wanted.

Hussein was not to be outdone. He met the opposition from family and government head on. He said he was going to fly, and that was all there was to it. Grudgingly, his family gave their consent, but they insisted he must never be allowed to go up alone.

By June 1953, Jock Dalgleish had taken over command of the air force, and the 23rd was fixed for Hussein's first lesson. Dalgleish had been told to do all he could to discourage the young King from taking up flying, and he fairly threw the little Auster round the sky that afternoon. For an hour, he took Hussein through every twist and turn and loop the Auster could do, and

at the end of it, Hussein stumbled out feeling heartily sick. When
Dalgleish asked him casually when he would like to fly again, he
only just managed to stammer 'Tomorrow afternoon'.

All that summer, Hussein went out five, and sometimes six
days a week with Jock Dalgleish. After a few hours in the Auster,
they transferred to the larger Dove aircraft, and Hussein was soon
ready to fly solo. He was in for a shock. Dalgleish informed him
that he would never be allowed to fly by himself. Hussein was
furious; he considered he was being treated like a child, and
decided to take matters into his own hands. One afternoon, he
found the airport staff involved in investigating a slight accident
at the end of the runway. He seized the chance to leap into his
Dove and start the engines. He told the mechanic who ran up to
him that he was going to pick up the co-pilot later, and then
taxied to the end of the runway and took off. It was clear to
the airport authorities, watching his flight from the control tower,
that they could no longer stop him flying whenever he wanted
to.

Hussein and Dalgleish were up in the air, together or
separately, most of that summer. In a typical month, August,
Dalgleish's log shows that he took the King flying on all but five
days in the whole month. Hussein was soon flying jets, and in
1958 he started to learn how to fly a helicopter. He was a very
proficient pilot, and flew on many exercises with the Jordanian
air force, though he never flew in action.

His comradeship with Jock Dalgleish was a lasting one. He
would often go home with him in the evenings, after their flights,
and stay on for supper or a quick cup of tea. Dalgleish's wife,
Davina, was a warm-heated, homely person and Hussein used
to help her sometimes by making the tea while she got on with
the cooking. He would take his coat off and sit in shirtsleeves,
watching the kettle, his pistol strapped to his shoulder. He appreciated the easy, simple way they welcomed him, and they enjoyed
his company, which was never pompous, always very relaxed
and boyish.

Hussein valued the release that this British family gave him
from the more formal Jordanian life of the palace, where he
was among his own subjects. Those who knew him well in his
youth said they were not surprised to learn, years later, that
Hussein married an English girl when his Arab marriage had

failed. He was as much at home brewing a pot of tea as he was drinking goat's milk with the Bedouin.

He had a schoolboy's zest for adventure. One afternoon, he was talking to Dalgleish about Cyprus, where there was trouble between the Greeks and the Turks. Dalgleish knew Cyprus well, and recalled with pleasure the steaks at the Ledra Palace Hotel in Nicosia.

'Right,' said Hussein, 'you're on. Let's go and have one now!'

Before Dalgleish could argue with him, they were in the Dove, and flying to Cyprus. They ate two very fine steaks at the Ledra Palace—quite incognito—and then flew home.

When Glubb heard about it, he was beside himself with fury. But there was nothing he or anyone else could do about it. Hussein had by now firmly established that he took orders from no one.

V

HUSSEIN'S BALANCING ACT

1954

Three years after Hussein had escaped death in the Aqsa Mosque, he was shot at again.

It happened one evening on the lonely road from Jerash to Amman, as Hussein and Jock Dalgleish were returning from arranging a party in Jerash. They were driving a Buick, the same as one owned by Hussein's uncle, Sherif Nasser, and as they rounded a bend in deserted hill country a few miles south of Jerash, they saw Sherif Nasser's car lying with its nose in the ditch at the side of the road ahead. Hussein braked sharply, and found his uncle wandering near the car in a state of shock : nine bullets had been fired at his Buick by a carload of gunmen, who had then raced off towards Amman. Dalgleish says shots were also fired at the King's car, as it came to a stop. Incredibly, all of them were unhurt, although the cars were peppered with bullet holes. Even if the shots were meant for Hussein's uncle, a man with a passion for intrigue, who could equally have been the bandit's target, this incident reminded Hussein sharply of the fragility of his position. His once quiet little country was being caught up in the general turbulence of the Arab world. Syria was changing governments in quick succession, sometimes violently; Egypt now had a military government with a radical, aggressive foreign policy; Israeli reprisals were at their most ruthless. Hussein was fast hardening to the view of Taufiq Abul Huda and the Jordanian establishment that the country needed ruling with a strong hand and that there was no more room for democratic experiments.

And so, a year after he had begun his reforms, Fawzi al Mulki was dismissed, and the redoubtable Taufiq became Prime Minister again, for the ninth time in Jordan's history. But the opposition had had a breath of freedom, and they never ceased letting Hussein know that they wanted it back. Hussein, for his part, was engaged in a delicate balancing act : he was under pressure from four quarters—from the British government, which still coolly assumed he belonged to them, from his own friends on the East Bank who wanted rigid autocratic control, from the Palestinians who wanted the opposite, and from the growing menace of outside interference.

This meant that Hussein, who was unashamedly devoted to the British connection, for reasons both economic and sentimental, found himself in the awkward position of having to play one off against the other. For three years, from 1954 to 1957, he swayed from one side to the other—hopelessly inexperienced in the intricacies and intrigues of power politics, but managing all the same. It seemed that whichever way he went, he would be the loser, and when he finally cut the embarrassing British connection, he only left himself exposed to the full fury of the Left. A lesser man would have decided his position was, quite simply impossible, and that the place for young monarchs with shaky thrones was in Switzerland or on the Cote d'Azur—but Hussein sat tight.

The first—and central—part of the balancing act concerned relations with the British. There was, for Hussein, one fundamental fact of life : Britain paid for his army and air force, and made up the deficit in his chronically lop-sided budget. There was no one else with the ready money available, although the Americans edged tentatively into the Middle East that year (1954) with an eight million dollar aid agreement with Jordan.

But Hussein and his government were sensitive to the taunts of the Russians and others that he was nothing more than 'an outright British puppet'. The trouble was that the Anglo-Jordan treaty, under which Hussein received his aid and his arms, was not primarily intended by Britain to be a treaty committing her to defend the Arabs against Israel. It was intended to secure Britain, through her troops stationed at Aqaba and Mafraq, a foothold in the Middle East and a close Arab ally against the spread of Soviet influence. To most Arabs the treaty appeared to miss the point and to serve the interests only of the British and those who depended on them : Hussein himself was glad of the treaty, glad of the arms, and glad of the troops, but he had to make a show of wanting to reduce British influence.

In the spring of 1954, the British pressed Jordan to come to

some agreement with Israel on the explosive armistice line between the two countries. Hussein's government firmly refused to
do anything of the sort, and pointed out that Britain had not
lifted a finger to help Jordan against the numerous Israeli incur-
sions across the line into Jordan. The Jordan government went
further and demanded, as loudly as possible so that all Palestine
could hear them, that the treaty with Britain must be revised.
Hussein, his Prime Minister, and Defence Minister went to
London in a suitably pugnacious mood. But nothing came of it.
The British quietly pointed out that the treaty was a two-sided
bargain, and that the Jordanians were doing very nicely out of
it financially—or perhaps they were ready to do without the
money? So the circular process went on. Hussein and his Ministers
continued to press publicly for revision of the treaty, but privately, accepted it much as it stood.

Hussein's other problem was Glubb Pasha. He knew that Glubb
was completely loyal, and took his orders not from London, but
from Jordan. (Glubb himself goes out of his way to assert this.
'I had no official connection with the British government at all,
nor did the latter ever attempt to interfere or give orders.'*) But
Glubb was a symbol of British influence, even if he was not its
instrument, and the Palestinians and radio broadcasts from other
Arab countries were exploiting this to the full. Besides, Hussein
was coming under the increasing influence of young Jordanian
army officers, who complained to him that their opportunities
for promotion were limited by the presence of British officers, who
held most of the top posts.

The key man behind this ginger group was that ambitious and
unscrupulous young officer, Ali Abu Nuwar. Ali was anathema to
Glubb, who suspected him of conspiracy, and he had been exiled
to the Paris embassy at Glubb's suggestion in Talal's days.† He
had first met Hussein at Mafraq airport, when they were both
waiting to receive Talal back from one of his trips to Europe.
The next time they met was in Paris, when Ali was military
attaché.

Ali Abu Nuwar knew his way round Paris, and he gave Hussein
an exotic evening out on the town. Afterwards, they returned
together to the Bristol Hotel, in the rue Faubourg St Honoré,

* Glubb, *Soldier with the Arabs*, p. 420.
† See p. 44.

where Hussein was staying, and talked till four o'clock in the morning. They talked about everything, and it was not just small talk. Ali said he longed for the day when Jordan would be freed from British 'domination', when she would be closely aligned with the Arab states against Israel, and, like Fawzi al Mulki, he professed an enthusiasm for free elections and democratic institutions. Ali talked about Glubb too (though he later denied to Glubb that he had ever plotted against him), and told Hussein that the time was coming when he would need Arab officers running his army. Hussein was impressed with Ali Abu Nuwar, who was highly articulate, and had obviously thought out his arguments well. When he graduated from Sandhurst, he invited Ali to a celebration party in London. At the Dorchester Hotel in Park Lane, their political *tour d'horizon* continued.

From then on, whenever Hussein passed through Paris—and he often did—Ali was his constant companion. Glubb knew of it, but there was nothing he could do. The Arab Legion office in London helplessly perused the young military ataché's expense chits, and shrugged its shoulders. In the summer of 1954, Glubb received a personal letter from Ali assuring him of his loyalty :

'I would never intrigue against my own chief in his absence,' Ali wrote, 'I am sure that you will believe me.' Glubb immediately concluded that Ali had been doing just that : intriguing behind his back with the King. And when, a year later, Hussein asked Glubb to allow Ali to return to Amman, Glubb tried to put him off. But Hussein was adamant, and asked the Prime Minister to order Ali's return as the King's aide-de-camp. Ali returned in the autumn of 1955, and Hussein politely thanked Glubb at a lunch party, two days later, for agreeing to the posting.

Glubb found Hussein difficult to deal with on several occasions. He seemed quickly swayed and would change his mind from one day to the next. He was still not twenty, and easily influenced. After the widespread criticism of the Arab Legion for its apparent failure to stem Israeli reprisal raids, Glubb tried to get the Jordan government to endorse his strategy of defence in depth rather than along every inch of the frontier as the Palestinians demanded. But the politicians were too sensitive to Palestinian pressures to oblige, and so Glubb decided to refer it straight to the King. He took Hussein for a drive north and west to Nablus :

the King was a model of appreciative approval. He agreed, according to Glubb, to a secret meeting with him the following morning to discuss the 'Defence Plan'.

But no sooner had Glubb arrived than Hussein waved in two ADC's, some palace officials and a few others. It was clear to Glubb that every word they spoke would be all over Jordan—and that meant the West Bank as well—within a few hours. Glubb spoke for an hour, explaining the need for mutual agreement on a defence plan that would guarantee Jordan's overall security but inevitably leave the frontier with Israel open to surprise hit and run attacks. The Arab Legion just had not the forces to line the whole frontier.

The King then stood up, and took a piece of paper from his pocket.

'I do not agree with any of the plans we have heard,' he said, 'I will not surrender one hair's breadth of my country. The army will defend the demarcation line. Then we shall attack. I will sanction no withdrawal'. Hussein then went on to say he thought the army command had made several mistakes. Officer promotions were not being properly handled.

'Finally,' said the King, 'we are grateful to the General for all the work he has done, but I think now it is time for him to take a rest.'

Glubb was flabbergasted. He had never known the King quite like this before. What made it worse was that, two days later, the King was smiling, and charming as ever. He told Glubb the criticisms he had made were of no importance.

Glubb had one more try. He took Hussein on a three-day tour of the West Bank, and showed him how an Arab Legion battalion operated in defence. Again, it was a most successful outing. The King seemed to be profoundly impressed, according to Glubb, and apparently convinced that stringing the battalion along the demarcation line would have meant certain defeat in the event of an Israeli invasion. But another officer in the Legion, Brigadier Peter Young, believed that Glubb was mistaken in thinking the King favoured his plan :

'I hope I will be believed when I say that I feared then that our efforts had been in vain. If we had convinced ourselves that we had the best plan of defence, we had not convinced the King. . . . I suspect that his mind was set against the plan before the presentation began—perhaps as recently as that spring, in Paris.'*

But the growing tension between Hussein and Glubb lay beneath the surface: outwardly, for the first three years of his reign, Hussein appeared more absorbed in his flying and fast driving than in affairs of state: most of these he left to the happy partnership of his Prime Minister, the cabinet and Glubb. Nobody doubted Hussein's authority, and it was an imprudent minister who did not submit an important decision to him for approval, but effective power was in more hands than one. To most people Hussein was still a boy.

Five months after his nineteenth birthday, Hussein was married, but not before he had made the most of his freedom. Amman had been alive with rumours for some time: it was like that; gossip spread like wildfire. If the King took a pretty girl for a drive, the news would be all around town within hours. There was Flavia Tesio, the young and attractive daughter of the Italian doctor at the hospital in Amman, the same Dr Tesio who had delivered Zein's daughter a few years earlier. There was talk of marriage, but then there always was, and when Flavia was packed off to London by her parents in the winter of 1954—to a finishing school for young ladies called the Monkey Club—the rumour-mongers had to look elsewhere. They did not have long to wait.

Hussein had been fond of Dina Abdul Hamed since they first met in London on an outing from school. On a number of those trips to Europe, Hussein used to take Dina out to night clubs. Hussein's own love for Dina was encouraged by his mother, Queen Zein, who recognised Dina's keen intelligence and her Hashemite credentials—she was a great-grand niece of Sherif Hussein of Mecca.

She looked a gentle creature and was very slight, no taller than Hussein. She was not an outdoor girl: while he preferred action, she was for deliberation. They had only one thing in common— a deep pride in the Hashemite family, and it was this that made Dina readily accept when she received Hussein's letter asking for her help in preserving the dynasty and providing a focus for his people's loyalty. She was not in love with him, but believed he needed what she could give him.

* Peter Young, *Bedouin Command*, p. 109.

C

On April the 19th 1955, Hussein and Dina were married in Amman. Dina wore a grey and mauve wedding dress, and chiffon scarf. They appeared together on the balcony of the royal palace, and photographers snapped them sipping strawberry juice together. The great Arab crooner, Farad al Atrash, was there to sing for them, and there was a great public celebration. It seemed the perfect marriage. Hussein and Dina set up house in Hussein's villa just outside Amman, at Hummar, called 'Daret al Khair'— the House of Goodness, and Hussein was overjoyed at the daughter Dina bore him. They called her Aliya.

But the marriage was not to last. Dina was an intellectual, with a university education (Girton College, Cambridge and Cairo University) and a feel for the wider political thinking of the new Arab world. Moreover she talked and practised politics too— politics he did not always agree with. Hussein wanted companionship, simple, homely companionship, and he says he soon found he would not get it from Dina.

Hussein would often find Dina out when he returned home, and would be told that she was discussing affairs with the Prime Minister or other leading politicians. And Queen Zein, who had been an enthusiastic supporter of the marriage, let Hussein know of her increasing resentment that Dina was assuming too prominent a role in the royal household.

The marriage collapsed only eighteen months after the wedding. The misunderstandings between Hussein and his wife had been growing in intensity and they had found their views and their tastes increasingly in conflict. Dina went off to Cairo for a short holiday in the autumn of 1956, leaving her baby daughter in Amman. Soon after she arrived there, a letter came from the King. He said he thought it was wiser if they stayed apart and put an end to the unhappiness between them. She wrote back to ask Hussein if he would send Aliya to her, but he refused. He was angry at the publicity given to her account of their separation in the Egyptian press, and he felt it politically unwise to risk sending his daughter to Egypt.

In the next six years, Dina saw her daughter once, on a visit to Turkey. It was not until after Hussein's second marriage that he finally called on Dina one day in London, and invited her to come to Amman and see her daughter. Dina was overjoyed and since then, mother and daughter have met frequently. Dina was told privately that Hussein's new bride, Muna, had urged him to relent, but when she thanked Muna for promoting the reunion, Muna immediately said she had had nothing to do with it; His Majesty had decided of his own accord that the time had come to forget the past.

Later, in 1971, after years of campaigning for help for the Palestinian refugees, Dina finally married a Palestinian commando, with the code-name 'Salah', who had been in revolt against Hussein in September 1970, and who was, like Hussein, seven years younger than she was.

PART TWO

HUSSEIN *v* NASSER 1955–1964

VI

WHO'S FOR THE BAGHDAD PACT?

1955

It was an unfortunate coincidence that Hussein's Arab Legion were firing their first shots into crowds of civilian demonstrators in Jordanian towns at about the same time as President Nasser finally attained supreme power in Egypt.

There are few men who have reviled each other as much as King Hussein and President Nasser. Their extraordinary relationship tells much about the emotional way the Arabs decide their affairs. Although Nasser is generally considered to have used every intrigue to subvert Jordan and overthrow Hussein, he probably did not wish him dead. If Hussein had fallen, Nasser would no doubt have offered him the sanctuary he gave another Arab King whose fall was certainly welcome to him—Idris of Libya. According to Hassanein Heikal, editor of the Egyptian newspaper *Al Ahram* and one of Nasser's closest friends,* Nasser regarded Hussein with a mixture of admiration and astonishment rather than hatred. He felt that Hussein had two characters that appeared to contradict one another: Nasser would describe his feelings about Hussein in the form of a proverb—'When I hear what you say, I believe you; when I see what you do, I am dumbfounded.' But Heikal denies that Nasser ever wanted to overthrow Hussein; he says that Nasser even rejected the approaches of a revolutionary group in Jordan who asked for his approval of a coup d'état against Hussein.

In his feud with Nasser, Hussein was up against enormous odds. Nasser's militant campaign for Arab unity excited the minds of the masses throughout the Arab world and many Jordanians saw Nasser as their leader, not Hussein. Nasser's power seemed somehow born of the people, Hussein's did not. Nasser's fight to evict the British from the Middle East, in order to restore Arab dignity, was in striking contrast to Hussein's apparent wish to

* In a talk with the author in October 1971.

maintain and depend on a continuing British presence. Nasser seemed determined to pursue the war against the hated Israelis; Hussein seemed to want to hold back. Nasser's modern image made Hussein look like an anachronism.

The Russians saw all this and took advantage of it. The Americans saw much of it, but hesitated. The British saw very little of it and, partly out of a kind of myopia, partly out of loyalty, stuck with their traditional friends in the Middle East—the Hashemites. But more and more, the Hashemites looked like losers.

The autumn elections of 1954 were, according to a *Sunday Times* reporter in Amman, 'clumsily arranged to ensure the return of Abul Huda's nominees'. Hardly anyone denied that the elections were, in some measure, rigged. A number of opposition members boycotted the elections, including Said Mufti, who later became Prime Minister, and Suleiman Naboulsi, the leader of the National Socialist party—a left wing group closely in line with both the new 'Ba'ath' Arab socialist party in Syria, and the Arab socialism soon to be championed by President Nasser.

Riots broke out in a number of Jordanian towns, and the crowds were openly encouraged by the parliamentary opposition. The American Information Services Library was pelted with stones and there were the usual taunts at Glubb and the Arab Legion. But Taufiq Abul Huda, the Prime Minister, returned with a parliament in which he held 32 of the 40 seats. The Arab Legion soon restored control, but 24 people were killed and 100 injured. Hussein, for the first time, had to rely on his army's guns to silence the dissidents who, egged on from outside, were trying to stir up the people against him.

He was now caught in the rush to form rival alliances in the Middle East, and he ended where he started, caught in a stranglehold between the Right and the Left. In February 1955, Hussein was in Rome where he always stopped off to refuel and throw a coin into the Trevi fountain on his way back to Amman. Just before he left, he received word that Iraq and Turkey had signed a treaty of mutual defence aimed at Russia—the Baghdad Pact. Hussein was astonished that the British, who had promoted the idea, should want to cut Iraq off from the rest of the Arab world, without consulting the Jordanians at all. After all, Hussein's own cousin, Feisal, was king of Iraq. Only four days earlier, Anthony

Eden, soon to be Britain's Prime Minister, had met Nasser but had failed to convince him of the wisdom of the Pact. Eden saw the Pact as an extension of NATO—a frontier against Communist expansion into the Middle East. Nasser wanted a wider Arab pact which Egypt would dominate aimed as much against Israel as Russia. Nasser had pressed for Eden's backing for an Arab Defence Organisation, which Nasser said he believed would combat Soviet expansion just as well.

The following month, Nasser called on Jordan to join a security pact with Syria, Egypt and Saudi Arabia. Major Salah Salem, the Egyptian Foreign Minister, called on King Hussein. Cairo Radio attacked Hussein's cousins in Baghdad calling them 'traitors to the Arab cause', and 'cat's-paws of the imperialists'.

Hussein was not enthusiastic about a pact with Nasser. His Arab Legion intelligence officers were accumulating evidence that Egyptian embassy officials in Amman were bribing Jordanians to infiltrate Israel and cause trouble for the Jordan government, which was trying to avoid provoking the Israelis. Glubb asked the Minister of Defence in the Jordanian government, who was to visit Cairo, to mention this to President Nasser. Nasser expressed his astonishment at the reports, and said he had never heard of such a thing. He assured the Minister that he would hold an immediate enquiry. But reports of bribery continued to come into Glubb's office, and when the Prime Minister of Jordan visited Nasser in the summer of 1955, he went through the same motions : Nasser apparently gave the same helpful reply, but nothing happened. Then Nasser's radio began to attack Glubb, and Hussein, for being 'tools of the West'. The pressure was on.

But still Hussein refused to be drawn into a pact with Nasser. What mattered to him was the treaty arrangement with Britain that guaranteed the build-up of his armed forces and the balancing of his budget. Besides, Britain had just made him the promise of ten Vampire jets for his air force. Hussein saw the Arab countries round him as a flock of vultures waiting to devour Jordan. He knew that the Saudis had their eyes on Aqaba, and he feared that Israel would seize the West Bank should Jordan disintegrate. To Hussein, the British link still seemed the best key to stability, although Britain had now further provoked Nasser by joining the Baghdad Pact herself. However, Eden did assure Nasser that no attempt would be made to get other Arab countries to join.*

Hussein did his best to stay everyone's friend. At the conference of non-aligned countries at Bandung in the spring of 1955, his delegates spoke warmly of the idea of a pact with Egypt, Syria and the Saudis. But at the same time, Hussein kept his lines open to the Hashemites in Baghdad. He visited Baghdad and tried to bring them closer to Nasser's point of view. But he found that his cousin Feisal, the King, was almost powerless, and that Nuri Said, the Prime Minister and decisive power in Iraq, was totally committed to the Pact, and had no interest in establishing good relations with Nasser anyway.

Then Hussein visited Nasser. At this stage, Hussein had nothing but admiration for him. His hope was that Nasser's intention was to concentrate on the reform of Egypt and the improvement of its standard of living—not on interference in other Arab states. When the two men met, they agreed that the Baghdad Pact had been tactlessly contrived, and that Nasser should have been more closely consulted in the opening stages. But Hussein was unable to persuade Nasser to leave the Iraqis alone. At the end of the meeting, Hussein pointed out that Cairo Radio was abusing him as well as the Iraquis. Nasser again expressed amazement, and said he would look into it immediately.

But the propaganda campaign against Hussein and Glubb continued.

Then, suddenly, at the end of September 1955, the news broke that Egypt had done an arms deal with the Czechs, which meant, effectively, the Russians. Lord Trevelyan, then British ambassador in Cairo, has since made it clear that Nasser did this deal primarily to satisfy his need for armaments, which the British and Americans were reluctant to supply on any terms that he could afford. For most Jordanians, the arms deal was a triumphant slap in the face for the West. The Jordanian Parliament cabled Nasser a unanimous resolution:

'The Jordanian Chamber of Deputies congratulates you, the Soul of Arabism, and supports you in all your efforts in securing arms without any restrictions or conditions for the defence of the Arab countries.'

But Hussein saw the arms deal as the beginning of Communist

* Lord Trevelyan, *The Middle East in Revolution*, p. 56.

expansion in the Middle East, and a real threat to his own position. He reacted to it by moving in a direction that nearly ended in disaster. He pressed for more British arms and Britain asked her NATO ally Turkey, whose leaders were—conveniently— about to visit Jordan, to drop the hint that Hussein could have the extra arms if he joined the Baghdad Pact.

It all started in the closest secrecy. The President of Turkey visited Jordan : it was announced that no political subjects would be discussed, but they were—principally the possibility of Jordan joining the Baghdad Pact. It was November the 7th. Hussein, Glubb, the Prime Minister, Said Mufti, and the Turks met at Hussein's winter palace at Shuna in the Jordan valley. As they sat down, Hussein leaned over and quietly asked Glubb whether he thought Jordan could do with an army three times larger. Glubb whispered that he thought that would be lovely. Jordan at the time had one infantry division and an armoured brigade. Hussein told the Turks he could do with another two infantry divisions and a full armoured division. He also wanted economic aid to help cope with the needs of his half-million Palestinian refugees. The Turks suggested he talk direct to the British.

Hussein was excited at the prospect. Egyptian propaganda was less virulent, as it was still ignorant of what was going on. He decided to take the plunge. On the 16th of November he called in the British Ambassador, Charles Duke, and handed him a note. The Jordan government, it read, was ready to join the Pact provided it received the 'necessary backing' from Britain. Hussein felt that if he joined the Pact it would be a 'moral victory for the free world'.* He still did not see the danger.

On the 6th of December, General Templer, the British Chief of the Imperial General Staff, arrived in Amman. He had come, he said, to discuss questions concerning 'the defence of Jordan and the Arab Legion'. Trevelyan, in Cairo, was told to assure Nasser that Templer was not going to press Jordan to join the Pact. But General Templer was in no doubt about the object of his mission : to do just that. Britain wanted Jordan in the Pact, and Templer was there to secure this in exchange for re-equipping the Arab Legion as economically as possible. Templer was a tough, incisive and thoroughly determined soldier. He saw his task as a simple one—to draw up a new Jordanian order of

* *Uneasy Lies the Head*, p. 89.

battle and fit it into the framework of the Pact with Iraq and
Turkey. He and Hussein, another soldier, would be able to speak
the same language. To many, at the time, Templer seemed the
right man for the job, but it soon became clear that, through no
fault of the General's, his whole mission was misconceived and
that a soldier—and a very conspicuous one too—should never
have been chosen to do the delicate job of a diplomat.

Still Nasser stayed his hand : he had been assured that Britain
would not try to coax other Arab states into the Pact, and though
he was suspicious, he remained silent. His Commander-in-Chief,
General Abdul Hakim Amer, was in Amman at the time, pressing Jordan to join the Arab Pact. During the visit, Amer wrote
a message in the visitors' book of the Army Officers' Club at
Zerka :

'My visit to the Club, which represents the youth of the army,
gave me the impression that I am amidst the ambitious youths
who look forward to the future to raise the standard of the army
of the sister state, Jordan. This visit has increased my faith in
the Arabs and Arabism.'

Even the Russians were courting Hussein. Their ambassador in
Lebanon, Mr Kiktev, paid him a visit in October, and in
December they finally withdrew their opposition to Jordanian
membership of the United Nations.

The scene was set, and the drama began. For a week, Templer
and his aides sat at a table opposite Hussein and his cabinet.
Templer proposed to enlarge the Arab Legion with a fourth
infantry brigade, another regiment of tanks, and a medium
artillery regiment. He said the subsidy would be increased from
£10 million in 1955 to £16$\frac{1}{2}$ million in the first year, and
£12$\frac{1}{2}$ million per year from then on. In exchange, Jordan would
join the Baghdad Pact.

Hussein pressed for more, and hours of bargaining followed,
but each time agreement seemed certain, Hussein's ministers
remonstrated with him. It was clear to the British, through the
haze of cigarette smoke, that the Jordanian ministers were
divided. Some, like Hazza Majali, pressed for Jordan's accession
to the Pact. Others, like the Prime Minister, Said Mufti, and
the four Palestinian members of the cabinet, were opposed.
Templer felt that they feared the reaction that seemed inevitable :

Jordan's press was hostile, and it had given an enthusiastic welcome to General Amer's mission from Egypt.

The days dragged on, and gradually Nasser, the Saudis, and the Syrians learned what was going on. One Jordanian cabinet minister was reported to have taken a £7,000 bribe to keep Nasser informed. But, with four Palestinians in the cabinet, it was inevitable that information would leak out. Arab radio stations started up their barrage against the Pact again: the pressure on the divided government was intolerable: on the 13th of December the four Palestinians resigned and the government fell.

It was a desperate moment for Hussein. He had already offered to sign, on his own, a new agreement with Britain committing Jordan to the Pact, but Templer had wisely advised him against it. He said Hussein needed the endorsement of his cabinet on an issue as sensitive as this and Britain would only be accused of having pressed him into it behind his ministers' backs. But Hussein did not give up. He asked Hazza Majali, who was also in favour of the Pact, to form a new government, and together they declared that the new government wanted to bring Jordan into the Pact, and that the armed forces would benefit considerably as a result. There were immediate violent demonstrations in most of Jordan's towns. Templer, meanwhile, was on his way home, perfectly clear in his own mind that his mission ('my perishing mission', as he later described it to the author) had been a failure. But Whitehall, like Hussein, did not give up; a week later, *The Times* Diplomatic Correspondent reported:

'In London it still seems to be the hope that Jordan will eventually decide to join the Pact. It is believed the great majority of those who are now demonstrating against it are doing so because they have been, deliberately or otherwise, misinformed as to the implications of such a step.'

But the demonstrators were successful: Majali's government lasted five days. His position became impossible when orders he sent out to the police to disperse the crowds were countermanded by someone else. The situation was out of control. Hussein, whose highly emotional nature drove him very quickly to the depths of despair, saw himself surrounded by enemies. He saw the Communists behind all his troubles, closely in league with the

Egyptians and the Saudis, whose diplomats and agents he saw as working hand-in-glove with the opposition in Jordan. His vision of a country riddled with intrigue and subversion was supported, to a large extent, by Glubb's intelligence men, who brought him numerous reports of bribery, conspiracy, and incitement to riot. Glubb was even told that Egyptian officials openly approached police officers and told them not to disperse the mobs, assuring them that if they lost their jobs, the Egyptian government would look after them. Most of the riots started with crowds of schoolchildren, who rampaged through the streets, armed with slogans provided by their teachers.

But to suppose that Jordan's troubles at this time were entirely created by a small group of Communist and Egyptian agents would be to underestimate the widely felt revulsion and indignation among Palestinians at Hussein's and his government's policy on the Baghdad Pact. It was a feeling that was fanned and inflamed by Egyptian propaganda, but it was genuine, born of the frustration of refugees unable to recover their lands, who saw the Baghdad Pact against Communism as an irrelevance, even an obstacle, to the war that *they* wanted to fight with Israel.

On the 21st of December, Hussein dissolved parliament and asked an old friend, Ibrahim Hashim, to become caretaker Prime Minister, pending an election in the spring. But the opposition, under Suleiman Naboulsi, claimed that Hussein was acting illegally in dissolving parliament, and the Supreme Court upheld the charge on the grounds that Hussein's dissolution order had not been counter-signed by the Minister of the Interior, which of course it had not since there was no Minister of the Interior when Hussein gave the order. Further rioting broke out, and Hussein's position began to look desperate. He had only one card left to play. He called in the Arab Legion.

Glubb's men were tough and thorough in clearing the streets. They used tear gas and occasionally fired on the crowds. There were casualties and some very tight moments. A British officer, Colonel Pat Lloyd, was killed in a riot at Zerqa : he was stoned by demonstrators as he stood a few yards in front of his men, and then shot with a small pistol at point-blank range.

Hussein always wanted to be in the thick of it. He would dash off by car, with a motor-cycle escort, to investigate each incident for himself. Once, he took a look at the scenes from the air :

Dalgleish and Hussein were seen flying low over a riot in Amman : Dalgleish remembers being reproached by Ali Abu Nuwar for endangering the King's safety.

Trevelyan, British ambassador in Cairo, was told to press Nasser to reduce the tension. But Nasser now ceased denying that he had a hand in what was going on in Jordan. He said it was a purely defensive action—to stop Jordan joining a pact that would isolate Egypt. He admitted that Egypt, Syria and Saudi Arabia were offering Jordan an Arab subsidy to replace the British one. Meanwhile, Egyptian radio kept up a barrage against Glubb and the Arab Legion for crushing opposition to the Baghdad Pact.

The situation was so serious that Britain's Prime Minister, Antony Eden, flew two parachute battalions and a battalion of the Highland Light Infantry to Cyprus, and the British armoured regiment at Aqaba was ordered closer to Amman. A troop build-up on the Saudi side of the Jordan border was warned off by a British threat to defend Jordan under the Anglo-Jordan treaty.

On the 9th of January 1956, yet another Prime Minister was appointed Samir Rifai. He ordered the Arab Legion to restore order firmly, but he conceded that it was not now the government's policy to join 'any new pacts'. Curfews were imposed, and they were effective. Slowly Jordan returned to normal, and rumours of any plan to join the Baghdad Pact abruptly ceased.

Hussein knew well who had restored the position and secured his throne. On the 15th of January, he made a special broadcast in which he thanked the Arab Legion for their 'restraint', and went on :

'On this army I place great hopes for our greatest day, which will be celebrated by the whole Arab nation when our usurped rights in dear Palestine are restored.'

Hussein and Nasser had clashed for the first time, and Round One was certainly Nasser's. Hussein had been saved by his army and survived to fight Round Two. But the army had made itself even more unpopular by its action in the streets of Jordan's towns. To many it seemed an alien force, run by British officers, taking orders not from Jordan, but from their British commander, General Glubb.

VII

GLUBB GETS THE PUSH

JANUARY–MARCH 1956

The only bright spot for Hussein during that tense Christmastime was the arrival, on the 31st of December 1955, of six of the ten Vampire jet fighters from Britain. Within weeks of their arrival, he was airborne—in the pilot's seat.

During January and February 1956, after the riots in Jordan had been brought under control, tension relaxed visibly. Britain increased her economic aid and for a time Nasser eased his propaganda attacks, though the tirade against Glubb continued. One evening, after the troubles, Hussein walked into Glubb's house and had a coffee with his family. Often he invited Glubb to join him in his study at the palace : Glubb had no inkling that Hussein was anything but happy with the way the Legion was being run.

Indeed Hussein's 'coup' of March 1st was such a surprise to Glubb, Britain, and even Nasser, that many put it down at the time to the impetuous nature of the young King, who was known to take up new ideas on the spur of the moment. His natural impulsiveness may well have affected the timing of the action he took that day, but cool political calculation played the greater part in his decision. And the decision seems to have been his alone, although he was deeply influenced and closely advised by his ADC, Ali Abu Nuwar.

Hussein says his action was provoked by a number of factors :

First, Glubb was reluctant, for reasons he had often explained, to promote Arab officers *too* quickly to the top posts in the Legion. The Legion had only begun to recruit Arab officers in 1941, and the most experienced of them had now a maximum of only 15 years' service. But Hussein felt that promotion should be more rapid, and he knew that many Arab officers shared his opinion.

Second, Hussein was, as he had already explained to Glubb, in favour of a forward strategy. His reasons were not entirely cogent, based more on heroics than on military science, but that was his way, and the Arab way. Glubb's view is that Hussein seemed to be in two minds about this, swaying this way or that, depending on his audience. But Hussein is adamant that—at least at that time*—he shared the strong views of his Arab colleagues on the inadequacy of Glubb's Defence Plan.

Thirdly, Hussein was more and more aware of the age difference between Glubb and himself : nearly forty years separated them. Glubb seemed to him like a man of the Victorian era : too Conservative, too cautious. Hussein was young and excitable, an enthusiastic soldier king, anxious to command his own forces —without restriction. Glubb was in the way. What was more, Hussein believed that Glubb was interfering in Jordanian politics. Glubb strongly denies this, but Hussein says that even if Glubb did not encourage them, Jordanian leaders did turn to him or the British embassy before taking even the smallest decisions. Several leading Jordanians who were ministers during that period assert that this was the case. And an article in the British magazine *Picture Post*, at about this time, argued that Glubb was 'the uncrowned King of Jordan'.

But there was another factor, which outweighed all these, and which makes one wonder if those other factors have not been exaggerated by Hussein to add technical respectability to what was essentially a *political* decision. Hussein's action on March the 1st was a masterly political stroke : it did not destroy his links with Britain, though it shook them badly for a time, but it gained him popularity and prestige in the Arab world and, equally important, in his own army. It outflanked the nationalists who claimed that Hussein was not the master of his own army or his own country but the servant of Britain. But it was also a dangerous stroke that exposed him afterwards to conspiracies from the very officers his action had given rein.

The first among these was Ali Abu Nuwar, Hussein's ADC. Ali and his group of young officers had been deeply impressed by Nasser's takeover in Egypt and the way it had inspired the Arab world. They deny that they were working for Nasser, although there is much evidence that suggests they were in close touch with him. The overwhelming evidence of Ali's colleagues

* After the war of 1967 Hussein privately admitted that a major cause of the defeat was the forward strategy that did not allow Jordan to defend herself in depth against the Israelis on June the 5th–7th.

and contemporaries suggests that he and his group wanted eventually to follow Nasser's example and create a military republic in Jordan.

This was not how they presented their plans to the King. Hussein was given to understand that their objective was simply to free Jordan from its links with Britain and establish a close alliance with the Arab states instead.

This may even have been the limited aim of some of Ali's group at that time. But most people believe that Ali Abu Nuwar himself had his sights set higher. (It is only fair to say that Ali, at the time of writing, denies that he was ever a republican. 'I was a pure young man, without any personal ambitions,' he says, 'I was an officer who had taken an oath, and an oath is an oath.')

Glubb had no time for Ali Abu Nuwar, who was generally despised by the British officers in the Legion as a man of little professional competence. But Glubb was told by a number of his Arab officers that Ali had approached them and told them that Glubb must go.

What Glubb underestimated was the extent to which the King shared Ali's views. Just how far Hussein was actually pressed by Ali Abu Nuwar is not clear. Ali says the decision was taken by the King 'with my assistance'. Hussein says it was entirely his own decision. The strongest evidence to suggest that Hussein was under pressure is Glubb's own story. He reports talking with Hussein on the last day of February—the day before the King acted—about the gossip that occasionally went on behind his own back. There was a moment's silence, then Hussein said:

'You know, Pasha, there are people in this country who are trying to make trouble between you and me.'*

That interview with Hussein was the last time Glubb saw him in Jordan. It ended with a discussion on the arrangements for a

* *Soldier with the Arabs*, p. 422. A year before all this Glubb had told Hussein that if he ever wanted him to go, he need only ask him to resign. Glubb says that apart from the disagreement over the defence plan, there had never been any difficulty between them. Hussein denies this. He says he and Glubb had 'other arguments' as well as their *contretemps* over military strategy.

royal visit to Hebron ten days later. They parted happily, and Glubb went home. If Hussein had already planned what was to follow, he gave no such indication, neither to Glubb nor to any government ministers.

Hussein's own ministers, like Glubb, sometimes underestimated the young King's determination to be master in his own house. This was an easy mistake to make : Hussein's personality was unpredictable, and his attitude to the running of affairs was not always consistent. It was usual for him to take little interest in the details of administration, which were left to the Prime Minister and to the officials of the Diwan, the Royal Court. In these early days of his reign the Prime Minister would call on the King regularly only once a week—on Tuesday afternoons—to keep him informed of events. But Hussein changed his Prime Ministers frequently : it was usually his decision alone. And the ruling circle in Jordan was in no doubt as to where the ultimate power lay, no matter how impulsively it was exercised.

That evening, Hussein made his decision to give the world a dramatic demonstration of his power. He says he was partly provoked by two things that happened in quick succession after Glubb had left the palace. First, he had a message from his Prime Minister, Samir Rifai, to say that it was not possible to make the change in the control of the police force, that Hussein had suggested the day before. Hussein had wanted Glubb to hand over army control of the police force to the Minister of the Interior : Samir Rifai had pointed out that the British would not approve, and Hussein had angrily replied that this was a matter for Jordan—not Britain—to decide. And now Rifai was telling the King that despite his objections, it was just not possible to make the change at that time.

And, that same night, Hussein was handed a list of officers that Glubb wanted dismissed from the Legion. Among them were a number of men Hussein knew to be keen nationalists. He knew them to be ambitious too, but he did not think this a reason for sacking them. Hussein threw the list of papers on the table in his office.

'Tell Glubb Pasha I refuse to sign them !' he said angrily.

Soon after this, Bahjat al Talhouni, the King's chief of the Royal Court, found Hussein in a rage. He had scattered some documents he was working on all over the floor. As Talhouni walked in, Hussein walked out—without a word. In a room down the corridor, Hussein's aide-de-camp, Ali Abu Nuwar, was still at work.

At nine o'clock that night, Glubb's telephone rang at home. It was Ali Abu Nuwar from the palace. He asked Glubb whether he would be in Amman the following morning. Glubb replied that he would be in Zerka early in the morning, but would be back in town by noon. Ali said that the palace would get in touch with him then. He did not say why.

Later that night, orders went out that the telephone lines to houses of the Legion's British officers were to be quietly cut off the following day.

Hussein went to bed that night glad that he had decided to take no chances. He did not, he says, want to hurt Glubb's feelings, but it was most important that the blow should fall cleanly, decisively, and by surprise. He was determined that neither Britain, nor anyone else, should have the opportunity to 'try anything on'.

Early the next morning, March the 1st, while Glubb was out at Zerka addressing officers of the 1st Armoured Car Regiment, the British ambassador, Mr Charles Duke, called on the Prime Minister.

It was a routine meeting in the Prime Minister's office. A number of other ministers were there too. After a few minutes, the telephone rang. It was the King, to say he was on his way down from the palace.

As Duke left for the embassy, Hussein's car pulled up outside Rifai's office, surrounded as usual by Land Rovers carrying his armed escort. He was in uniform. Talhouni was with him, and the King had just told him, as they were driving down, that it would be one of the most important days in his life.

Hussein walked into the office, and slapped a piece of paper down on the desk in front of his Prime Minister. It said, briefly, that Glubb must be dismissed immediately.

'These are my orders,' said Hussein, 'I want them executed at once.'

Rifai, obviously concerned, asked if he could discuss the matter with his ministers, who were waiting in the next room, but Hussein insisted that Rifai summon the ministers immediately and inform them of the King's decision. Rifai did so at once in front of Hussein.

Hussein then quietly told them that he was only doing what he thought best for the country. He said he wanted them to be watchful during the next few days. He felt there would, inevitably, be some strong reaction.

He walked out of the office, leaving Talhouni with the Prime Minister. There was a brief discussion, and they decided they had no choice but to carry out Hussein's order.

'Come and see me at once,' the message read. Mr Duke did not hesitate : he was back in Rifai's office within minutes. The Prime Minister's expression told Duke he was faced with a major crisis, and that if it was to be averted, he had only a few hours. He asked the Prime Minister what he was going to do about it.

'I don't think there's anything we can do.'

'You could resign.'

'Yes, but His Majesty would only appoint another government tomorrow. All we can do is comply, and keep the situation under control,' said Rifai. And he went on to say he thought someone had probably got at the King. Hussein occasionally had ideas like this and, with luck, he would change his mind in a couple of weeks' time and invite Glubb back.*

Duke disagreed. Once Glubb had gone, there could be no coming back. Rifai said that might be, but he could see no alternative to obeying the King's order. He added that he thought it pointless to see Hussein again.

'In that case,' said the ambassador, 'do you mind if *I* see the King?'

---

* Samir Rifai's son, Zeid, disputes this account. He says his father told him, before he died, that he had immediately fully supported Hussein's action against Glubb, and never expressed the hope the King would change his mind. Hussein's uncle, Sherif Nasser, says this is nonsense and that Samir Rifai was *in tears* much of the time and deeply worried that, without Glubb, Jordan would be in jeopardy.

'I haven't told Glubb yet,' said Rifai. So Duke agreed to wait till after lunch.

On his way back from Zerka, Glubb noticed the King's car outside the Prime Minister's office, and assumed there must be a meeting of the cabinet. He had not been long back at his desk, when the Minister of Defence telephoned, asking him to come immediately to see the Prime Minister. It was just before midday.

Glubb was kept waiting a few minutes and then Samir Rifai came in from an adjoining room with the Minister of Defence. Rifai was obviously nervous. He told Glubb he was very sorry, and gave him the news as tactfully as he could. Glubb asked why. Rifai said he did not know, but he hoped it was only a temporary phase. He pointed out that he had often been dismissed as Prime Minister, and then recalled.*

Glubb said that might apply to politicians but not to him. He told Rifai not to worry and assured him that he would not cause any trouble.

Then he took a cigarette from a box on the table, and asked Rifai when he was expected to leave.

'In two hours,' said the Prime Minister.

'No, sir. I cannot,' said Glubb firmly, I have lived here for twenty-six years. Almost all my worldly possessions are here, to say nothing of my wife and children.' Rifai then suggested he might leave his family behind. But Glubb refused, and they finally agreed that he would leave at eight o'clock the following morning.

Glubb went home to tell his wife, and start their packing.

Early that afternoon, Duke rang Glubb, and asked what he was going to do.

'Pack my bags, of course!' he said.

Duke asked him if he was going to see Hussein, but Glubb replied there was no point. Duke then asked if Glubb would mind

---

* Rifai's son disputes much of Glubb's account. He has a copy of Glubb's *Soldier with the Arabs*, which belonged to his father; next to Glubb's detailed account of this conversation Samir Rifai has pencilled in words like 'Nonsense' and 'Not True' in the margin.

his seeing the King, and Glubb told him to go ahead, if he wanted to.

At two o'clock, Duke was in the King's room at the palace. The ambassador was highly indignant. He demanded an explanation and made it clear that he thought the way the blow had been delivered to Glubb was inexcusable. He told Hussein that this was not the way to treat a servant, let alone a pillar of the throne.

Hussein was a young man of twenty. He liked the British ambassador, and did not want to be unkind to him, any more than he wanted to hurt Glubb, but he was determined not to be misunderstood. He made it quite clear that he had coolly made this decision, and that it was final. He said he had no desire to hurt anyone's feelings, but that the decision had to be carried out this way to avoid bloodshed.

Duke rejected this as nonsense, saying that anyone who had told the King Glubb's dismissal could lead to bloodshed was misleading him. But Hussein was firm, and very polite. He would give no further explanation of why Glubb was dismissed, or why it was being done so speedily. Duke asked the King to stay his hand until there had been full discussions between the two governments. Anything, he thought, to play for time. But Hussein was adamant. It was precisely to avoid this kind of 'discussion' that he had acted so fast.

Duke returned to the embassy, and told his communications man to make immediate contact with London.

When Britain's Prime Minister, Antony Eden, heard the news from Duke, he was furious. He later wrote in his memoirs :

'It was meanly done, and King Hussein's explanation, that he had to act in this sudden way, in order to avoid trouble in the Legion, did not excuse him.'*

Anthony Nutting, who was one of Eden's ministers at the time, says that Eden immediately blamed Nasser. Nutting believes that Glubb's dismissal was the first of many factors that made Eden take the tough line with Nasser which ended in the Suez invasion eight months later.†

---

* Lord Avon, *Full Circle*, p. 348.
† Antony Nutting, *No End of a Lesson*.

Eden sent a personal message to Hussein and instructed his ambassador to see the King again, and protest as strongly as he could.

By coincidence, Britain's Foreign Secretary, Mr Selwyn Lloyd, was in Cairo. He was dining with President Nasser that evening. Neither of them apparently, knew anything about Glubb's dismissal until after dinner, although both sides saw pieces of paper being slipped in by aides during the evening. When Selwyn Lloyd did hear the news, he was very upset and considered cancelling an appointment with Nasser the next morning. Like Eden, he suspected that Nasser had a hand in it. And when, the next morning, Nasser congratulated him and the British government on making a very clever political move by dismissing Glubb, Lloyd thought Nasser was being intolerably sarcastic.

Whether Nasser actually knew that Glubb was to be dismissed that day is uncertain. It is possible. Contemporary witnesses say that Ali Abu Nuwar and the Egyptian military attaché in Amman were often in close touch. But, more likely, Nasser was as surprised as the British.

In Amman, Hussein had another call from Duke. Hussein says this happened at one o'clock in the morning, an hour after he had gone to bed; Duke believes it was much earlier, about 8 p.m. Again, the talk was fruitless. Hussein insisted that Glubb's dismissal was not to be taken as a blow at Britain, and was not intended to disrupt Jordan's links with Britain. Duke replied that the trouble was that this was precisely how it *was* being taken in London, and that, if the King wanted to maintain friendly relations with Britain, he should recognise that this was not the best way of going about it. All this followed Eden's instructions precisely.

Although Hussein had expected trouble from the British, he was angry at this, but he kept his composure. He wanted the British to understand that he would not change his mind. He was calm and determined.

'I believe that what I am doing is for the good of the country, and I am not going to change my mind, whatever happens.'

Duke returned to the embassy and contacted London again. Then he called on the Glubbs, and asked if there was anything he could do. Glubb replied that their only worry was that the servants would eat their pet gazelle when they left; would Mr Duke mind looking after it?

In the early hours of the morning,* Duke paid another call on the King. He wanted to make one last attempt. But Talhouni refused to awaken Hussein: Duke said he had had another important message from London: Talhouni replied that however important it was, he would not disturb the King.

The young King who had confronted the ambassador so calmly earlier that night after his apparently ruthless dismissal of Glubb was not so calm in private. He told a close friend afterwards that he wept frequently that night and thought of changing his mind, but he stuck to his decision because he knew in his heart it was right, and would be to his and Jordan's advantage.

When Glubb told the Bedouin guards at his house that he was leaving, one of them drew his revolver, and swore that he would avenge him; Glubb had to calm him down. He sent messages to British officers to quell any threat of disturbances by troops in his own support.

In the middle of the night, Glubb received a telephone call telling him to be at the airport at 6 a.m. But when he tried to leave the house, he found an armoured car outside, and was not allowed to leave till seven o'clock. Ali Abu Nuwar later claimed in an interview that Glubb had tried to escape at 6 a.m. in order to take refuge with the Royal Air Force. Ali was enjoying his revenge.

At seven, Glubb was picked up at his house by the Minister of Defence and Hussein's aide, Talhouni. Glubb was in civilian clothes. He climbed into a large black saloon car with the two men, and his wife and children followed in a second car. It was a cold wintry morning, with driving rain. The airport was ringed with troops. Duke and his wife were waiting there to see the

* Talhouni says it was at 6 a.m.

Glubbs off. An escorting armoured car pulled up near the steps of a British military aircraft, and the two cars stopped behind it. The Dukes watched Talhouni present Glubb, rather shyly, with a photograph of the King in a silver frame. Glubb read the inscription :

'With our acknowledgement of the good services and untiring exertions and with our best wishes for His Excellency General Glubb Pasha. 1/3/56. Hussein Talal.'

Glubb politely asked Talhouni to thank His Majesty.

The Glubbs said their good-byes and boarded the aircraft. As it taxied to the end of the runway, the sun appeared through the clouds, and a rainbow straddled the plane. It was thirty-two years since Glubb had first arrived in Jordan—on a camel— from Iraq.

Hussein was now free to announce the news to Jordan and as he guessed, there was widespread rejoicing all over the country, and throughout the Arab world. For those who wanted a release from what they felt was western interference in their affairs, it was a restoration of Arab dignity; for those who wanted an end to Hashemite rule, it was a useful first step towards their objective. To the British officers in the Legion, the inconceivable seemed to have happened : many of them simply did not believe the King had the power to sack Glubb.

For Hussein, the important thing now was to restore his normal friendly relations with the British government. He was lucky in the help he got from Glubb, who told Eden, on his arrival home, that he should make allowances for Hussein's personal reasons for sacking him, and do nothing drastic. Another cooling influence on Eden was Kirkbride, who happened to be on his way to Jordan to catalogue coins in the Jerusalem museum—a hobby of his. He saw Hussein and Samir Rifai, and both of them told him that the action was not intended to be anti-British. When Kirkbride returned, he was asked to attend a cabinet meeting and explain the King's point of view. Eden was apparently talking about breaking relations, and his anger was shared by most other ministers. Kirkbride begged them, one by one not to over-react. Finally he mollified them, and was sent back to Amman to explain the initial sharp British reaction to Hussein—and to return to his coins. The crisis appeared to be over: the British government, with difficulty, swallowed its pride and continued to pay its cheques in to Jordan's account.

Glubb now lives in a large rambling house in Mayfield, Sussex, full of animals and birds. He has not been back to Jordan since, though he has seen Hussein a number of times on the King's visits to London. He still believes that it was 'suicide' for Hussein to break his close links with Britain. He bears Hussein no grudge, but if you press him, he will say he does have just one regret: he has never quite forgiven Hussein for acting so sharply and without warning. He knows why Hussein felt he had to do it, but he is sad that Hussein should ever have thought that he, Glubb, might try and appeal to the army to intervene, in his support, against their own King.

VIII

HOW NASSER NEARLY WON

APRIL 1956–APRIL 1957

In the spring of 1956, the new call to Arab unity—imprecise but intoxicating—was echoing round the Middle East. It was first sounded by President Nasser of Egypt, and then taken up by nationalist groups in all other Arab countries. It meant different things to different people, but to all people it meant an end to Western domination of the Middle East, and a more aggressive attitude to Israel. It had caught the popular imagination everywhere, but it had not united Arab governments. Its effect had been to polarise the Arab world into a confrontation between those governments who wanted to use the slogans of Arab nationalism to their own advantage, and those who saw their positions threatened by it.

On the one side there was Egypt, finally free of British influence : the last British troops were leaving their Suez canal base. President Nasser's popularity was at its height. His armed forces were being lavishly equipped by the Soviet Union, and a land reform programme was being planned. Aligned with Egypt was Hussein's neighbour Syria, who had signed a Defence Pact with Egypt in October 1955—Nasser's rival to the Baghdad Pact. Syria was emerging from a series of military takeovers as a socialist state, with the strong military and economic support of the Soviet Union which was the only great power to recognise the opportunity provided by the current of Arab nationalism. The Ba'ath party in Syria was fast gaining control of the political system : it held to a more doctrinaire socialism than Nasser's and was implacably opposed to the conservative Arab states like Iraq, Jordan and Libya.

Against this new alignment was the group of states led by Iraq, who believed in the continuation of traditional policies, monarchical rule, and the support of the West against Communism. Iraq was ruled, nominally, by Hussein's young cousin,

King Feisal, but effective control was in the hands of the Prime Minister, Nuri Said. British troops were based in Iraq, and Nuri's government presided over a prosperous economy and a political system that had no room for opposition elements : Iraq supported the right wing in Syria, and tried without success to secure the election of a pro-Iraqi President in the Syrian elections of August 1955.*

The other major Arab state, Saudi Arabia, was firmly aligned with the Egyptian-Syrian group against the Hashemites. Though there was no place for socialism in the rigidly autocratic Saudi system, King Saud's age-old rivalry with the Hashemite dynasty gave him other reasons for siding with the Left.

Hussein, then, had an ally in Iraq and a traditional enemy in Saudi-Arabia, but his continuing concern was the Syrian-Egyptian campaign for Arab unity, which he found increasingly difficult to resist. In Jordan itself, he had greatly enhanced his popularity with his dismissal of Glubb. He had surprised his critics by giving rein to a new air of national self-assertion. This started in the army, after Glubb's departure. Then it moved on with Hussein's blessing, to the political field, with the success of the Left in the elections of October 1956. But Hussein soon began to lose control of this Jordanian nationalism as the forces he had unleashed, in politics and in the army, found themselves in growing conflict with his views. By April 1957 a showdown between the government and the King was inevitable. The key factors in the development of this contest, apart from Hussein himself, were the political parties in Jordan, and the composition of the army.

Before the murder of King Abdullah, political parties in Jordan were of little significance. They existed, particularly on the West Bank, but their effective power was severely curbed by the régime whose own nominees dominated parliament. After the absorption of the Palestinian West Bank by Jordan, Palestinians entered parliament and even the cabinet, but the King still retained total command. It was only after Talal's constitutional changes in 1952 that political parties began to make any headway.

On the right, and drawing their support mainly from the East Bank—the old Transjordan—were the Arab Constitutional Party

* *The Struggle for Syria*, by Patrick Seale, p. 251.

and the *Ummah* (The Nation) party. They were conservative, but their platforms were vague : what mattered was that they were on the side of the King. Further to the right were the Islamic Liberation party and the Muslim Brethren : they drew their support from the religious hierarchy.

On the left, the Communists, under the guise of the National Front Party, wanted an end to the régime and a Marxist state in Jordan. The Ba'ath party, working closely with the more influential Syrian Ba'athists advocated Arab socialism and made no secret of their call for a Jordanian republic. They wanted an end to frontiers between Arab states and to Jordan's links with Britain. The National Socialists, led by Suleiman Naboulsi, were more Jordanian in character, and advocated a constitutional monarchy in Jordan that would subscribe to socialist economic policies and alignment with other Arab states against foreign interference. The freedom of each of these parties was strictly controlled by the government under the Political Parties Laws of 1954 and 1955, which ordered a party's licence to be withdrawn 'if its object does not remain lawful, its means are not peaceful or its organisation contravenes the provisions of the Constitution', or if it contradicted any of the policies it had set out in its original programme.

The parties of the Left drew most of their support from the Palestinians, but since the union of the two halves of Jordan, many Palestinians had drifted to the East Bank, as refugees or as merchants, lawyers and teachers. The movement of people and the spread of ideas across the Jordan, encouraged by the talk from Damascus and Cairo, won support for radical policies from many East Bank people too—mainly in the towns.

However, up to the summer of 1956, and despite the presence of new ideas and a popular demand for change, Jordan was effectively ruled by a small group of conservative families, loyal to the monarchy. From 1952 onwards the cabinet had been constitutionally responsible to parliament. But the King had an absolute right to dissolve parliament and appoint his Prime Minister—a right frequently exercised by the King. No one dared challenge the oligarchy—the cabinet backed by the King— that ruled Jordan. The only effective opposition appeared in the streets.

The uniting of the two parts of Jordan had had its effect on the army by this time too. The army was in two parts : the Arab Legion, 25,000 strong, manned mostly by Transjordanian Bedouin commanded by British officers, and the National Guard, 30,000 strong, essentially a Palestinian force, less well equipped and intended for frontier duties only. But most units had some mixture of manpower. Most technical and administrative men were West Bank Palestinians or townspeople, though many of the other ranks were Bedouin. The Legion's *Base Technical Organisation*, responsible for the care and maintenance of the transport equipment and heavy weapons, was 90 per cent townsmen.

However, the fighting men in the infantry and the armoured regiments were predominantly Bedouin and almost fanatically loyal to the king : this was the tradition started by Glubb when the fighting arm of the Legion began as a desert force in the 1930s. By 1956, five of the ten infantry regiments in the Legion were Bedouin and two of the three armoured regiments. These seven Bedouin regiments were widely recognised as the spearhead of the Legion. British officers held nearly all the senior posts. But with the departure of Glubb and the immediate resignation from executive commands of all British officers, the Arabisation of the army had to move fast. And the key posts—for the first year— went mainly to non-Bedouin officers.

As a counter-balance to any threat from the growing Palestinian presence in the army, Hussein allowed his uncle, Sherif Nasser, an ambitious soldier with the popular appeal of a buccaneer, to form his own private army of Bedouin to protect the royal palace. The Royal Guard started as a battalion and soon swelled to a brigade equipped with the best weapons and armoured vehicles that Sherif Nasser could lay hands on.

And so in the spring of 1956, the King's power base—in the military and political fields—appeared secure, but the forces who were to challenge him were moving into positions of power. In May, Hussein appointed Ali Abu Nuwar to Glubb's position (after a brief period in office by Major General Radi Ennab) and Ali's cousin, Ali Hiyyari, was appointed his deputy. In June, Hussein dissolved parliament and called for free elections in the autumn. It was the chance the Left had been waiting for.

If Hussein was aware of what he was exposing himself to, he did not let it concern him too much. For the moment his position

was unassailable, as he gloried in the triumphant aftermath of
his coup against Glubb. The image of the young King who
appeared more interested in racing cars than in the business of
government had suddenly been transformed. He was greeted
everywhere with a new respect, and he was enjoying it. Never
again would a Jordanian Minister or General make the mistake
of underestimating him.

Hussein's new policy was one of cautious Jordanian
nationalism. He knew the way the Arab world was moving and
he was ready to allow himself to bend a little with it. But he
was not ready to cut free from Britain. Immediately after the
dismissal of Glubb, the leaders of Syria, Saudi Arabia and Egypt
met in Cairo and agreed to renew an offer they had made to
Hussein two months earlier. They offered to provide an Arab
subsidy to replace the £10 million a year he received from the
British on condition that he joined a defence pact with them.
Hussein had more faith in Britain's credit, and he was opposed
to a pact that excluded Iraq; nevertheless he welcomed the offer
of aid, but refused the invitation to discuss the proposed defence
pact unless all other Arab states were present as well. He suggested a wider defence arrangement to include his friends in Iraq.

In the meantime he worked strenuously to persuade the British
that he wanted to continue his links with them, despite their
anger at his dismissal of Glubb. Eden responded eventually by
swallowing his indignation and accepting that Britain's interest
would best be served by maintaining her links with Jordan, and
British aid continued although British officers were removed from
all executive posts.

Hussein then met his cousin, King Feisal of Iraq, on the 14th
of March. They discussed Hussein's new position and the ideas
he had put to the other Arabs for a pan-Arab meeting. Hussein
assured Feisal that he would not be lured into a defence arrangement that excluded Iraq.

On April the 10th, Hussein flew to Damascus for talks with
the Syrian leader, President Quwatly. They agreed, in vague
terms, on mutual co-ordination of defence policies, and closer
economic and cultural links. A similar agreement with Egypt
was signed on the 6th of May, with the Lebanon on the 22nd of
May, with Iraq on the 13th of June and with Saudi Arabia on
the 7th of September. The agreements were not as specific as

the three-power Arab defence pact which provided for a unified
military command : Hussein expressly excluded any such commitment. He hoped that this ambivalent foreign policy would satisfy
the opposition, contribute to his new-found prestige as a Jordanian Arab nationalist and, most important, allow him to go
on reaping the benefits of the British subsidy. But events left him
far behind.

On the 19th of July, the United States said it was unable to
finance the new Aswan Dam project in Egypt. Britain followed
suit with a withdrawal of her offer of funds the next day. A
week later—to the delight of the Arab world, and the fury of
the West—President Nasser retaliated by nationalising the Suez
Canal.

Through the summer, tension on the Israeli/Jordan border
increased : Palestinian guerrilla groups made raids into Israel,
and the Israelis retaliated with attacks on Jordanian towns and
frontier posts. The failure of diplomatic efforts to solve the crisis
over the Suez Canal added weight to the impression that war
was near. The British and French were already contemplating
military action against Nasser, and urged their nationals to leave
Jordan at the end of August. Israeli raids on Jordan increased in
September, and some observers saw this as an Israeli plan to force
Jordan into a pact with Egypt and Syria that would *look like* a
threat to Israel, and so provide Israel with a further pretext for
attacking Egypt.*

Hussein now sought help from three quarters. He knew he
was able to call on the British under the Anglo-Jordanian treaty.
He had his Hashemite allies in Iraq. And he was again offered
full participation in the Egypt-Syria-Saudi pact. In keeping with
his earlier policy, Hussein pressed for a wider Arab pact, and
talks began with Iraq on the one side, and Syria and Egypt on
the other.

Then on the 10th of October, the Israelis struck the Jordanian
town of Qalqilya, in reprisal for a guerrilla attack from Jordan
on two Israeli farmers. The Israeli objective was the police station
in the town. Forty-eight Jordanians were killed, including five
civilians. It was a massive operation involving Israeli artillery
and aircraft.

Hussein immediately requested air support from Britain under

* *Suez*, by Kennett Love, p. 447.

D

the treaty. The British, caught in an impossible tangle, sent none but made an urgent appeal to the Israelis, and condemned their action at the United Nations. Antony Nutting, then Minister of State at the Foreign Office in London, says that Britain then encouraged Hussein to invite Iraqi troops into Jordan, if he needed reassurance, rather than Egyptian or Syrian forces.* But the Israelis and the French objected so strongly that Britain then changed course and asked the Iraqis not to send troops to Jordan after all.

And so, on the 21st of October, with Jordanians voting in the General Election and the Palestinians clamouring for war with Israel, Hussein had the Egyptians, Iraqis and Syrians offering him troops, ostensibly to fight the Israelis. But he feared that the presence of foreign troops, particularly from Syria or Egypt, could jeopardise his own position.

The election results were an unequivocal demand for Jordan to align itself more closely with Egypt and Syria. For the first time, the parties of the Left made a significant showing, capturing 17 of the 40 seats outright. Here are the results :

Right-wing :	Islamic Liberation	1
	Muslim Brotherhood	4
Left-wing :	National Socialist	12
	National Front (Communist)	3
	Ba'ath	2
Centre :	Independent	10
	Arab Constitutional	8

Three of the Independents were known supporters of the Left, which thus had twenty supporters in the new House, exactly half of the seats, and the National Socialists had the largest single party bloc. In the old House, the opposition had held only five of the 40 seats.

The scrupulous fairness of Ibrahim Hashim's caretaker government in removing all obstacles to a free election, on the King's explicit command, had produced the first genuinely free election in Jordan's history.

But it was an election in which the Left was far more active than the Right, and in which outside interference played a major part. Cairo Radio took on the task of promoting the cause of

* Antony Nutting, *No End of a Lesson*, p. 105.

those whose platform was the ending of the Anglo-Jordanian Treaty, and the prosecution of the war with Israel in close alliance with Egypt and Syria. Ali Abu Nuwar, now a General and Hussein's Chief of Staff, made no secret of his sympathies with the Left. The Egyptian and Syrian embassies were active in publicising the rosy future that lay ahead of Jordan if she chose the Arab nationalist camp, and numerous allegations were made of Egyptian bribes to leading politicians. The Syrians, denied for the moment the opportunity of introducing troops in to Jordan, provided weapons to emphasize their solidarity with the Jordan army. The arrival of the arms consignments was announced by the Syrian ambassador in Amman only four days before the election.

Hussein himself, sensing the way opinion was moving in and around his country, gave the impression that he, too, was on the side of reform.

'I take full responsibility for the period of experiment,' he wrote six years later, 'I had felt deeply that for too long Jordanian political leaders had relied on outside help, and it was only natural that these politicians should meet with bitter opposition from younger, rising men of ambition who, like myself, thought it was time to throw off external shackles.

'I had decided therefore that younger and promising politicians and army officers should have a chance to show their mettle. I realised that many were very leftist, but I felt that even so most of them must genuinely believe in the future of their country, and I wanted to see how they would react to responsibility.'*

It was the high point of Hussein's enthusiasm for a movement that he soon began to see as a revolutionary force committed to his own removal and the institution of a republic in Jordan. For the moment he gave it every encouragement.

Three days after the electoral success of the Left, but before the formation of a new government, Hussein signed a new military pact with Egypt and Syria. Major-General Abdul Hakim Amer of Egypt was made joint commander of the forces of the three countries, and he and General Tawfiq Nizamuddin, the Syrian Chief of Staff, personally attended the opening of the new Jordanian parliament by King Hussein on the 25th of October. On the 27th of October the King invited the leader of the

* Hussein, *Uneasy Lies the Head*, p. 127.

National Socialist party, because it was the majority party, to form a government. Suleiman Nabulsi became the country's first (and last) opposition leader to be elected Prime Minister.*

It was a unique occasion. Hussein agreed to allow Naboulsi to choose his own cabinet, and Naboulsi felt that Hussein was ready for the first time to allow a Prime Minister to interpret the Constitution literally and hold himself responsible to Parliament rather than the King. Naboulsi told Hussein that his government's policy would be to end the British subsidy and seek aid and closer co-operation with the Arab states instead. Hussein readily agreed.

Two days later, the Israelis invaded Egypt, and two days after that, the British and French moved to reoccupy the Canal Zone.

The moment Hussein heard of the British involvement, he telephoned President Nasser and told him that Jordan would attack Israel. His fury at Israel, Britain and France was in striking contrast to the caution of his new Prime Minister who was too new to power and too concerned with the consolidation of his internal position to regard a military adventure with any enthusiasm. Naboulsi told the author that Hussein ordered him to attack Israel, but he refused.

'The idea was ridiculous,' Naboulsi recalls. 'We were no match for the Israelis, particularly with the British and the French involved on their side.'

Hussein's ardour was cooled in the end only by Nasser himself, who begged him not to risk Jordan's army against overwhelming odds; the military position was hopeless, Nasser said, and he had high hopes that the withdrawal of the invading forces could be obtained diplomatically. Jordan should look to her own defence in case the Israelis turned on her as well.

In the next few days, Syrian and Saudi Arabian forces entered Jordan at the government's invitation, and Hussein himself invited the Iraqis, who were also waiting at the frontier, to enter Jordan. This brought the first clash between Hussein and his new Prime Minister. Iraq was not a party to the new Jordan-Syria-Egypt pact; indeed Iraq's government was hostile to the pact and to the new policies that Naboulsi's government stood for—

* Nabulsi's socialist credentials are questioned by Kirkbride, who remembers him as a staunch conservative under Abdullah less than ten years earlier.

non-involvement in the Cold War, a firm stand against Western influence, and an end to traditional conservative policies at home. Hussein, and Iraq, made it clear to Naboulsi that the entry of Iraqi troops was a royal decision and that the Jordanian cabinet should accept it : Naboulsi replied that it was for the cabinet to make decisions like this and not the King. Naboulsi prevailed. By the end of the month all Iraqi troops had withdrawn from Jordan.

The Suez invasion was the final blow to the Anglo-Jordan Treaty. The unfortunate British ambassador in Amman, Mr Charles Duke, had to endure the contemptuous rejection of his protestations that the Anglo-French intervention was intended only to stop the fighting between Egypt and Israel. Hussein himself was appalled at the British action, although he recognised that Jordan's treaty with Britain had probably done something to deter the Israelis from launching a major attack on Jordan.

On the 20th of November the Jordanian parliament unanimously approved a report of its Foreign Relations Committee which recommended the termination of the Anglo-Jordan Treaty, the opening of diplomatic relations with the Soviet Union and the recognition of Communist China. And a week later, the Prime Minister, Mr Naboulsi, made a definitive statement of his new government's policy aims.

'The government will work in co-operation with free Arab states in order to eradicate imperialism and all its facets from the Arab homeland. . . . The government will endeavour to promote relations with free Arab countries in the political, economic and cultural fields, as a first step towards federal union. . . . The government announces that it will accept the financial aid offered by Egypt, Syria, and Saudi Arabia in order to replace the British subsidy. . . .

'The present government is determined to lead the people, under the leadership of His Majesty the King, to the path of unity, freedom, strength and honour. . . .

'The national interest requires the setting up of diplomatic, economic and cultural relations with all those countries which have sincerely stood with the Arabs in all their disputes and demands. The government is considering recommendations to establish diplomatic relations with the Soviet Union and other countries. . . .

'Since the conclusion of the Anglo-Jordan Treaty, fundamental international, internal and Arab changes have taken place rendering the treaty out of date. The government, after the acceptance of the Arab financial aid and after determining other diplomatic, international, financial and economic arrangements will terminate the treaty and will ask for the withdrawal of the British forces from and liquidation of their bases in the Jordanian lands.'*

On the 19th of January 1957, the Arab Solidarity Agreement was signed between Jordan on the one side, and Egypt, Syria, and Saudi Arabia, on the other. The three states agreed to provide Jordan with £12½ million subsidy a year for ten years. It could be automatically renewed after that period, unless one of the signatories desired to terminate it. Meanwhile negotiations began with Britain on the ending of the Anglo-Jordan treaty and, at last, on the 13th of March 1957, it was announced that British troops would be withdrawn within six months, and that the treaty was at an end.

In the meantime, relations between Hussein and the Naboulsi government had worsened. By the end of 1956, Hussein was beginning to realise that the new government and the monarchy as he understood it were simply not compatible. Each was manoeuvring to exclude the power of the other, and the government was quite patently winning the contest. At the end of December Naboulsi's cabinet allowed the Communist party to publish their newspaper, *Al Jamaheer*, banned by the Combatting Communism Act of 1953. At the same time, Hussein says that he was receiving a growing number of intelligence reports that senior army officers, including his own army chief, General Ali Abu Nuwar, were holding secret meetings with Syrian, Russian, and Egyptian officials. A number of army officers, including Sherif Nasser, resigned their commissions in protest at Ali's behaviour.

As Naboulsi went from strength to strength a conviction formed rapidly in Hussein's mind that he was the object of a conspiracy by the government, several senior officers in the army, the Soviet Union, President Nasser and Syria. He began to believe that the main short-term objective of these forces was the elimina-

* Jordan, *Chamber of Deputies Official Gazette*, 9/12/56. (Britain still had Royal Air Force units at Mafraq, and an armoured detachment at Aqaba.)

tion of the Jordanian monarchy, and its replacement with a system which, if not Communist, would be wholly dependent on Communist support. He was encouraged in these fears by the view of his own family and the more conservative elements in Jordan who saw their own positions threatened by the policies of the Naboulsi government. Now Hussein may well have exaggerated the unity and purpose of the coalition that seemed to be threatening him, but no one, at that time, could deny the momentum of republican propaganda and the growing conviction that the monarchy's days were numbered. Hussein's instinctive judgement, which had put him on the side of the radicals for the last nine months, now turned him against them, and a decisive power struggle followed between King and government.

But Hussein's position was weak. He had no precise means of knowing how thoroughly Ali Abu Nuwar had converted the army to the radical cause. It was almost certainly too late to retrieve the British subsidy, and in a confrontation with his own government, he could only be sure of external support from his Hashemite allies in Iraq. He saw the promised Arab subsidy only as a threat to his own political independence. However, the offer of help to Middle Eastern states made by President Eisenhower in January 1957—the promulgation of the Eisenhower doctrine of defence and economic aid against Communism—gave Hussein the opportunity he needed. He immediately expressed Jordan's interest in American aid, provided it was offered without conditions. At the same time, he started his own propaganda attack on 'Communist Infiltration' in the Middle East, and emphasized its threat to the Moslem religion. It is highly significant that, at about this time, King Saud of Saudi Arabia also began to be concerned at the 'religious' threat of Communism, and expressed an interest, privately at first, in American aid.*

On the 2nd of February 1957 Hussein wrote a letter to his Prime Minister, and immediately issued it to the press. It was a straight challenge to the government to abandon its policy of *rapprochement* with the Communists.

'We perceive the danger of Communist infiltration within our

---

* Naboulsi says that the American ambassador, Mr Mallory, called on him and offered Jordan $100 million if she accepted the Eisenhower Doctrine. Naboulsi replied that Jordan had only just won her independence from British economic control and that he would not now sell the country's 'precious independence' to America – even for $100 million.

Arab home,' Hussein wrote, 'as well as the danger of those who
pretend to be Arab nationalists while they have nothing to do
with Arabism. We will never allow our country to be the field
for a cold war which may turn into a destructive hot war, if the
Arabs permit others to infiltrate their ranks. . . . No gap must be
left to allow the propaganda of Communism to ruin our country.
These are our views which we convey to your Excellency as a
citizen, and as our Prime Minister. We hope that you and your
colleagues, the Ministers, will adopt an attitude which ensures
the interests of this country and stops the propaganda and agita-
tion of those who want to infiltrate through to the ranks of the
citizens. . . .'

The following day, Naboulsi, Abu Nuwar and Abdullah
Rimawi, Minister of State for Foreign Affairs, asked for an audience with Hussein, and tried to persuade him to withdraw much
of what he had said in his letter. They failed, and shortly afterwards the Jordanian chief censor banned the daily bulletin issued
in Amman by Tass, the Soviet news agency, and the Communist
newspaper *Al Jamaheer* was forced to close after only two
months. But the cabinet let it be known that there was a breach
between themselves and the King, and that they considered the
King was outreaching his constitutional powers.

Hussein then sent a message, without consulting the cabinet,
to King Saud, President Nasser, and President Quwatly of Syria.
He urged them to agree that all Arabs should fight against 'all
propaganda that belied our beliefs, faiths and religion . . .', a
clear reference to Communism. Naboulsi, when he learned of this,
immediately protested to Hussein that this sort of communication
was not part of the King's function but the cabinet's. He also
protested to Hussein that his approach to the Americans was
against the wishes of the cabinet.

The cabinet fought back at the beginning of April. Rimawi
announced that Ministers had decided at a meeting the night
before to implement parliament's request of the previous November to establish diplomatic relations with the Soviet Union,
and Naboulsi sent a delegation to the Soviet Ambassador in
Damascus to negotiate the purchase of Russian weapons for the
Jordanian forces. Hussein made it clear to Naboulsi that in view
of the new threat of Communist infiltration, he would veto any
such arrangements. For a few days, the government came near

to resigning, and Hussein says that at one stage President Nasser himself cabled Naboulsi urging him not to give in but to remain at his post, as Prime Minister. Naboulsi denies that he ever received such a cable. During this time Naboulsi's supporters demonstrated in the streets attacking Hussein's new approach to the Americans. And Egypt and Syria made clear, in radio broadcasts, their strong opposition to Hussein in his fight with his own government, and their disgust at his refusal to open friendly relations with the Soviet Union.

The clash between King and government was now almost out of control, and it was only a question of who moved first. On the 8th of April, the 1st Armoured Car Regiment surrounded Amman, and set up road blocks round the capital. Hussein immediately demanded an explanation from Naboulsi, who said it was presumably intended to secure his own, Naboulsi's resignation. Ali Abu Nuwar, for his part, explained that it was an operation to check vehicles entering and leaving Amman. Hussein demanded the withdrawal of the troops and gave Naboulsi two days to produce an explanation. The troops were withdrawn, but Naboulsi did not produce an explanation, and two days later, on the 9th, his cabinet ordered the retirement of a number of senior officials including Hussein's chief of the Royal Court, Bahjat Talhouni, and the Director of Public Security. This was the last straw : Hussein told Talhouni to demand the resignation of the government. Naboulsi consulted Abu Nuwar, who advised him to comply and finally, on the 10th of April, Naboulsi submitted his resignation to Hussein.

The government had fallen and Hussein now had to find a new one.

IX

THE ARMY DECIDES

APRIL 1957

Hussein now appeared completely isolated. He had secured Naboulsi's removal by asserting his royal prerogative and Naboulsi and his supporters believed that their forced resignation would provoke a strong reaction against the King. Hussein was, after all, dismissing Jordan's first democratically elected government because he disagreed with its policies. What followed showed that however popular Naboulsi's policies were, it was not popularity that counted but control of the army. And although Ali Abu Nuwar had now had nearly a year at the head of the army, the decisive core of it—the Bedouin element—proved loyal to the King.

Popular reaction against the dismissal of Naboulsi was not long in coming. There were immediate demonstrations in Amman and the main towns on the West Bank. The parties in the dismissed government coalition immediately distributed pamphlets calling for a continuation of 'pan-Arab' policies, and condemning the King's moves. All the leading politicians in the outgoing cabinet refused to co-operate when Dr Hussein Khalidi, a Palestinian moderate, was asked by the King to form a new cabinet on April the 11th. The next day, Hussein asked Abdel Halim Nimer, a National Socialist and former Minister in Naboulsi's cabinet, to make the attempt. But Nimer could not persuade his National Socialist colleagues to agree to a list of Ministers that the King could accept. Hussein then invited a former Prime Minister Said Mufti, to attempt the task.

In the early afternoon of Saturday, April the 13th, General Ali Abu Nuwar took the initiative. He summoned Said Mufti to an army camp just outside Amman, and confronted him in the presence of several other army leaders. Mufti was told to inform the King that the majority of the country's political and military leaders supported the idea of a government led by Nimer, but that his cabinet must be approved by them as well as by the King. Ali also told Said Mufti that unless an acceptable arrangement was reached by nine o'clock that evening, the army could not be held responsible for what might happen. Ali had now openly sided with the dismissed political leaders against the King.

At about the time that Said Mufti was reporting this to the King, a group of officers arrived from Jordan's principal army camp at Zerka with an urgent letter for Hussein. To emphasise the importance of their message, the son of the chief of the Beni Sakhr tribe of Bedouin came with them. The essence of the letter was that some units were being ordered to surround Amman, and that the commanders of these units were of doubtful loyalty to the King.

Hussein knew that the key regiments at Zerka were the infantry regiments of the Princess Aliya Brigade, commanded by Colonel Ma'an Abu Nuwar, a distant cousin of Ali Abu Nuwar's, and the 1st Armoured Car Regiment, commanded by a close friend of Ali's, Nazir Rashid. Most of the men in the Armoured Car Regiment were Bedouin, but there were a number of non-Bedouin units in the Princess Aliya Brigade.

Abu Nuwar's ultimatum—for that was how Hussein took it—still had about four hours to run, when the King had another visitor: an officer from the 1st Armoured Car Regiment, Abdul Rahman Sabila. He was brought into Hussein's private study by the King's uncle, Sherif Nasser, who had once commanded the regiment. Sabila told the King that he and his fellow officers had been summoned by Nazir Rashid, the regiment's commander at Zerka, and told to prepare to move on Amman, surround the palace and arrest the King. If there was any resistance, the regiment was ordered to use artillery. The commander then promised the regiment the 'glory' of carrying out the task of liberating their country. However, according to Sabila's report, the officers immediately met among themselves and took an oath of loyalty to Hussein: they then agreed to lie low until Sabila had consulted the King.

Hussein told Sabila to return to his regiment in Zerka, and to pretend to go along with the conspiracy until the last moment.

Hussein then sent for Ali Abu Nuwar. The evening was drawing in.

What exactly happened at Zerka that evening will probably never be satisfactorily established. After the events of the 13th of April, so many stories were told, so many charges and counter-charges were made, that the truth now lies hidden beneath a mass of conflicting evidence.

The only certainty is that in the tense political atmosphere of that weekend, suspicions were aroused among loyalist troops by the behaviour of some officers and the orders they were giving. The decisive moment came when it was learned that orders had been given to one Bedouin regiment of the Princess Aliya Brigade to prepare to move off on a three day exercise *without* weapons. Already the camp was alive with rumours of Abu Nuwar's pressure on the King, and instinct told the Bedouin Hussein was in danger. It was at this moment that rebel officers appear to have tried to launch other units—like the predominantly non-Bedouin artillery—against the Bedouin. But the suspicions of the loyalist troops had worked faster than any conspiracy, and some of the Bedouin rampaged through the camp threatening anyone they suspected, while others frantically made for Amman to find out what had happened to Hussein. It was soon utter confusion; shooting broke out, and a small number were killed or wounded.

Hussein said later that it was Ma'an Abu Nuwar who ordered one of his regiments to prepare for the exercise to keep them out of the way while others marched on the royal palace in Amman to seize the King. Ma'an says that the exercise had been planned for a long time and that it was only the announcement that it was scheduled to begin two days later, on the 15th, that aroused the suspicions of the men. When he saw the consternation the announcement caused, he immediately cancelled the exercise, but by that time he was too late to restrain the frenzied suspicions of his men. He denies he played any part in a plot against the King, and believes he was mistakenly suspected because of his distant kinship with Ali Abu Nuwar. He says the first he knew of any coup was when he was surrounded by loyalist troops in his office and accused of treachery. Ali, for his part, maintains to this day that there was never any coup against the King, but that the

King over-reacted to rumours of a plot, and staged a pre-emptive coup himself.

Ali Abu Nuwar was summoned by the King at just after seven p.m. Ali had just received a telephone call from Zerka in which he says he was first informed of the disturbances: he was told that units of the Princess Aliya Brigade were moving on Amman and that Ma'an, the Brigade's commander was beseiged in his office. Ali claims that at this time he was as astonished as the King. He admits that earlier in the day he *had* insisted that Hussein appoint a new left-wing cabinet, and that he had warned Hussein that feeling in the army and among politicians was strong. But he says he was not a party to any conspiracy.

By the time Ali walked into his study, the King was convinced that Ali was the leader of a major coup against him. Hussein and Ali give different accounts of the meeting that followed.

Hussein says he angrily asked Ali for a full explanation of the events at Zerka, but that Ali's response was stopped short by a call from Ma'an Abu Nuwar for Ali: Hussein says he then overheard Ma'an telling Ali that the situaton was out of control, and that the troops were moving on Amman, believing their King to be dead.

Hussein says he snatched the telephone from Ali, and told Ma'an he was very much alive and would come to Zerka immediately. He then told Ali to stay where he was, ran out of his study to order a car, and sent his cousin Sherif Zeid bin Shaker and another ADC to assure any advancing troops that their King was not dead but alive and in command. Hussein then changed into uniform and ordered Ali into the car with him.

Ali's version is that there was no telephone call from Ma'an, but that when Hussein told him that he thought a coup was being staged against him, Ali expressed complete astonishment and said he would go to Zerka personally to find out what was going on. He promised Hussein that he would shoot any officer commanding a unit moving against the king. It was then, according to Ali, that Hussein said he too would come to Zerka.

From then on, there is no dispute about what happened. The two men walked from the King's study, and into a grey Chevrolet. Hussein sat in front; behind him sat Ali and Sherif Nasser.

They drove off towards Zerka with Ali's own car following. At the Russeifa bridge, a few miles from Amman, they met the first lorry-load of troops. Hussein jumped out and was instantly recognised by the soldiers, who kissed him and shouted for the blood of Ali Abu Nuwar. Ali says some of them shot at him, but Hussein says the soldiers were just firing in the air in their enthusiasm. It took Hussein a few minutes to get the lorry to turn around and head back for Zerka.

When Hussein got back in the car, Ali was, he admits himself, very frightened. He told the King he thought it was clear that this was a coup against Ali Abu Nuwar, not against Hussein, and said he did not want to die: he would prefer to return to Amman. Hussein waved Ali into his staff car and told him to return to the palace and wait for him there.

When Hussein arrived in Zerka, the camp was in total confusion. There was still some firing going on, and in the darkness men were running to and fro, many of them only half-dressed, desperate to find out what was happening. No one was in command. The royal car was stopped a number of times, and as soon as Hussein was recognised, he was cheered and his car mobbed. The news that he was alive and in Zerka spread quickly through the camp, and deterred any further resistance by officers and units that were disaffected. Everywhere Hussein went he leapt out of the car, shook hands, addressed groups of men and assured them that he was safe and well. He found his cousin, Sherif Zeid, and the other ADC he had sent ahead, in the hands of some troops who refused to believe they were not conspirators. With difficulty, Hussein persuaded the men to release them. People who saw Hussein that night say he was in his element—moving excitedly among his troops like a young officer in the heat of battle, single-minded, quite fearless, communicating with his men in a simple, but highly emotional language that won instant acclaim.

By midnight the opposition had melted away. Indeed such was the confusion of that evening that most people afterwards were able to claim—quite plausibly—that they were fighting on the side of the King, because they *thought* the people they were attacking were against him. Hussein returned to Amman to find the loyal 1st Armoured Regiment had surrounded the palace. Ali Abu Nuwar was waiting in his study. Ali had had some difficulty in persuading the officers of the Armoured Regiment not to arrest him. Hussein says he found him in tears, a broken man, pleading for his life. He asked Ali what he expected to happen to him. Ali begged to be allowed to leave the country : perhaps the King could say he was going away on leave?

Hussein's first instinct was to execute the man he believed to be the leader of a conspiracy. Yet he felt pity and contempt for Ali, who had been one of his closest and most trusted favourites. To put him to death would be an impulsive act that could lead to a blood feud in the closely-knit circle of Jordan's ruling families. Besides—and more realistically—it would make a martyr of Ali, who had become the champion of the Left since the fall of Naboulsi's government. Hussein still had a political crisis on his hands. Finally, in a voice full of disgust, Hussein told him to go. The following day Ali left with his wife and family for Syria. He spent some time in Damascus and then moved on to exile in Cairo. Less than ten years later he was back in Amman—with a full pardon from Hussein, and for a time, he was the King's special representative. At the time of writing, he has returned to his old haunt, the Jordanian embassy in Paris, not as a military attaché, but as an ambassador. His cousin Ma'an was aquitted after a trial on conspiracy charges and later became a Major-General, and Chief Public Relations officer for Jordan's armed forces.

The next morning, on Sunday April the 14th, as Ali Abu Nuwar was speeding into Syria by car, Hussein took stock of his position. His palace was secured by the Armoured Car Regiment. He moved the 3rd Infantry Regiment, one of the trustworthy Bedouin units from Zerka, into Amman to control other strongpoints. A deputation of army officers confirmed the army's allegiance, and he hastened to thank the army for its loyalty 'to its King and the sacred interests of the country'. Hussein appointed Abu Nuwar's deputy, Ali Hiyyari, as army chief, in spite of his misgivings about Hiyyari's loyalty and strength of character.

The political scene was still in disarray. Said Mufti had been quite unable to form a government, and on the West Bank the streets were full of demonstrators. The staff of the main Jordanian radio station in Jerusalem were refusing to transmit, and the station in Ramallah was besieged by crowds who managed to interrupt the transmission of the King's message to his army for seventeen minutes. In the north, the brigade of some 3,000 Syrian troops, who had been there since the previous November, were in a state of alert and had actually started moving south, apparently in support of Ali Abu Nuwar. But they were 24 hours too late, and Hussein despatched a number of loyal officers from Zerka, who successfully persuaded the Syrians that it was all over.

The following day, Hussein managed to persuade Hussein Khalidi, a former minister whom he trusted, and Naboulsi, whom he did not, to form a cabinet—with Naboulsi as Foreign Minister and Khalidi in charge. The government appeared to be ready to pursue the policy of the old Naboulsi cabinet, and the new foreign minister, anxious to reassure those of his supporters who felt he was betraying them, made it clear that he still expected the new government to establish diplomatic relations with the Soviet Union.

Hussein felt more confident now that he knew he had the support of the army. The main threat was the internal political situation, and the external pressure from Syria and Egypt. On Tuesday the 16th, however, valuable support was pledged by King Saud who telephoned Hussein and placed the Saudi brigade in Jordan at his disposal. He further promised Hussein immediate payment of £5 million as the Saudi share of the annual Arab subsidy agreed that January. Egypt and Syria so far had paid nothing.

But Hussein's position remained precarious. On the 18th, he was told that Syrian troops were moving to surround Irbid and advance on Amman. He sent Ali Hiyyari, his army commander, to talk to the Syrian commander on the frontier. At the same time Hussein made a personal radio broadcast :

'We are proud of the unity of our nation and our army. This unity is our arm which we use in our struggle and which, thank God, became recently a rock on which the ambitions of foreigners will founder'. . . .

It was a characteristic piece of Hussein's rhetoric. It said very little about policy, about the economy, about the future alignment of Jordan, but it said much about the unity of the nation— although the only real unity in Jordan was now the unity between King and army.

Early on the morning of Friday the 19th, Hussein was awakened by Sherif Nasser, who told him that Ali Hiyyari had defected to Syria, presumably to join Ali Abu Nuwar. The following day, Hiyyari telephoned Hussein to say he was resigning, and at a Press Conference in Damascus, Hiyyari accused Hussein of inventing the whole idea of a plot against him in order to eliminate nationalists like himself and Ali Abu Nuwar. He claimed that the King was being aided by certain foreign military attachés and clearly implied that the Americans were involved.

Needless to say, Hussein later forgave Ali Hiyyari, just as he forgave Ali Abu Nuwar. In 1971, Hiyyari was appointed Jordanian ambassador in Cairo and the author visited him there soon afterwards : he says he resigned in 1957 because he just did not feel able to carry on; he was only 32 at the time and felt that he was being asked as a soldier to do a job that would be better done by a politician. He denies that there was any plot against Hussein in 1957, but admits that he and many other young officers did have high-spirited ideas about Arab unity.

Inside Jordan, the Left made a final bid for power. A National Congress of all left-wing parties met in Nablus on April the 22nd : 23 parliamentary deputies attended and 200 delegates from the various parties. The following day, they presented their demands to the Prime Minister in Amman, asking for federal union with Egypt and Syria, rejection of the Eisenhower doctrine, and the reinstatement of all dismissed officers. One of the deputation was a young member of the Arab Nationalist party, Doctor George Habbash, who later became the leader of one of the more extreme Palestinian Commando groups.

That night and the whole of the next day, the Cairo-based *Voice of the Arabs* broadcast the demands of the National Congress throughout Jordan, whose government radio had refused to broadcast them. Again the streets of west bank towns were filled with demonstrators, and on the evening of April the 24th, Dr Khalidi's cabinet resigned. Khalidi had promised the deputation of the National Congress that his government would consider their demands, but Hussein would not hear of it. Khalidi's position had become impossible.

In the early hours of April the 25th, Hussein appointed a cabinet that demonstrated his determination to rule with the aid of the army against any opposition : Ibrahim Hashim, the stalwart veteran of many a caretaker government, was asked to be

Prime Minister; Samir Rifai was appointed Foreign Minister. Martial law was declared, all political parties banned, and reliable army units were introduced at key points on both sides of the Jordan. Orders went out for the *Voice of the Arabs* to be jammed. Hussein told his cabinet:

'Gentlemen, we are in a race with time . . . we need control, quick and firm control. I cannot achieve it alone. It is your country and remember that many of you helped to build it. This is no time for petty argument.'*

Hussein then made a public broadcast:

'I have been patient so far in the face of propaganda and rumours, but my prestige will allow me to be patient no longer,' he said. He accused the Naboulsi government of having relations with Israel, and recalled the fact that Naboulsi had disuaded him from attacking Israel when he had wanted to at the time of the Suez invasion the previous year. He said the Naboulsi government had given the Communist party a free hand, and 'the Communist party here are brothers of the Communist party in Israel and receive instructions from them'.

That same day, the American battleship *Wisconsin* and twelve smaller ships of the US Fleet left Naples, and the aircraft carrier *Lake Champlain* hurriedly left Leghorn. The American State Department in Washington confirmed that elements of the Sixth Fleet were being moved to the eastern Mediterranean as 'a precautionary measure', and the White House announced that it considered the 'independence and integrity of Jordan' as vital.

In the next two days, Hussein's grip on the country was consolidated. Curfews ensured order in the streets, and military courts were instituted all over the country. On the 28th, Hussein flew to Saudi Arabia and cemented the new friendship and understanding between himself and King Saud. And the following day, soon after Hussein's return, the American ambassador in Amman, announced that the United States 'recognised the brave steps taken by his Majesty King Hussein and by the government and people of Jordan to maintain the integrity and independence of their nation', and was ready to advance ten million dollars in aid.

It was the evening of April the 29th. The army had restored

* Hussein, *Uneasy Lies the Head*, p. 150.

order in the streets. Hashim's government was firmly in control. Hussein had won.

But the damage to Jordan's political system was irreparable. From April 1957 onwards, there was no pretence made of democracy in Jordan. The country was ruled by a cabinet, appointed by and responsible to the King, not to parliament. The King ruled with the support of the army, and where the army's will differed from that of any portion of the people, the army had its way. From this time on, the welfare of the people depended on the benevolence of Hussein and his army. The effect of this on Jordan was to emphasize further the political rift between its two parts. Generally, the East Bank Transjordanians greeted the King's takeover with relief and satisfaction. It appeared to them likely to restore stability in the country and security for their interests. The Palestinians, on the other hand, saw the demise of the Naboulsi government as a blow to any chance they might have had of genuine participation in the running of the country. They felt it inevitable that their interests would now be less well represented to the King, and thus further neglected.

However, Hussein—at the age of 21—had demonstrated with great courage and ingenuity, his determination to preserve the rule of the Hashemites in Jordan. He had surprised many members of his own family who had more than once urged him to make the best of it and escape into exile. But the experience had hardened his earlier, broader attitude to his country's political development. Because he believed, or said he believed, his country was now the object of a Communist conspiracy, he felt forced to abandon the liberal approach of his father and adopt, without pretence, the benevolent dictatorship of his grandfather.

Hussein had firmly established himself as a formidable Arab leader: the resolution and judgement he had shown throughout the crisis were derived almost entirely from his own strength of character, not from the advice or moral support he got from anyone else. His family had certainly supported him: his mother, Queen Zein, was still very close to him, and though he had divorced Dina (in the autumn of 1956), his uncle Sherif Nasser, and his cousin Sherif Zeid were always in attendance, and he owed a lot to the dexterity of his aide, Talhouni. But he had been the undisputed leader throughout, and the victory was his alone. Hussein had been lucky, it is true, in the incompetence of his opposition. Naboulsi had tried to do too much too quickly: he had failed to dominate his cabinet and give it the cohesion it needed in its task of undermining the power of the King and assuming the authority to which it felt it had a constitutional right. Similarly, Ali Abu Nuwar, had failed to coax enough of the army's loyalty away from the King towards himself and Naboulsi: it was probably an impossible task anyway. Ali was a townsman from Salt, with a poor military reputation and the air of a subtle businessman: he was not the man to win the affection of the Bedouin in the army, particularly when his political message was hardly one to appeal to their conservative conception of society.

The question remains: did Ali and Naboulsi plan to unseat Hussein and create a republic in Jordan? Or were they just working, as they say, to bring about a more constitutional monarchy? The answer lies hidden in the devious minds of Ali Abu Nuwar and Suleiman Naboulsi. Both of them strongly deny any intention to overthrow Hussein and create a Republic. Naboulsi told the author in December, 1971 that even Nasser himself was against a change in Jordan.* But the overwhelming judgement of those who observed these events at the time was that there was a growing movement against the monarchy in Jordan, in close alliance with Syria and Egypt, and that Hussein's overthrow *was* being planned. Even if the poorly-contrived events of April the 15th were not intended to be the definitive coup, it would soon have followed, had Hussein not acted when he did.

* Naboulsi claims that on his last visit to Cairo before his resignation as Prime Minister, he was urged by Nasser to do nothing to upset the monarchy in Jordan. Nasser's last words, as he escorted Naboulsi to his car at 4 a.m. were: 'I beg you to remain on good terms with King Hussein'.

Naboulsi says that all the rumours of plots and coups against Hussein— at the time of his Premiership and later—were deliberately generated by the Palace and by the West in order to create an atmosphere of siege, which would allow the West a permanent *entrée* to Jordan as 'protectors' of the threatened Hashemite régime.

X

UNION AGAINST NASSER

MAY 1957–JULY 1958

Hussein had now declared open war on the opposition—inside and outside Jordan. But to most of the Arab World, still exulting in its snub to the West over Suez, the young King and his Bedouin tribsemen seemed an irritating anachronism. His riposte against the Left in Jordan appeared to be only a temporary reverse in the tide of history, which seemed to be moving strongly against him and his cousins in Iraq. Those, like President Nasser, who looked for the unity of the Arab world, were not intimidated by the events of April 1957 in Jordan. They were encouraged to magnify their support for the forces that opposed the King.

Hussein's main preoccupation was money. The British subsidy had come to an end: it had been a convenient source of income to Jordan since the 1920's, but it was politically impossible to continue with it, and the British had lost their drive to be involved in the Middle East after Suez. The Americans had largely replaced them and Hussein had seized upon the Eisenhower doctrine as a short-term remedy, but American aid had the same political danger as British aid, and there was no promise of permanent help from Washington. Nor could he depend on Arab aid. Relations with Syria and Egypt grew worse, rather than better, after the showdown in April. Syria was told by Hussein to remove her troops from Jordan in May, and Nasser finally broke off relations in June, after Hussein had accused the Egyptian military attaché in Amman of plotting his downfall, together with Ali Abu Nuwar and the Syrians. From then on there was no prospect of Egypt and Syria paying their share of the promised subsidy. Only the Saudis paid up.

Hussein's problem was that Jordan's economy was still chronically dependent on foreign aid. No new source of income seemed likely on the home front: a plan to harness the waters of the Yarmuk river, between Jordan and Syria, for irrigation

117

and hydro-electric schemes was held up by the hostility between
Israel, Syria and Jordan. The oil men took a desultory look at
Jordan every now and then, but soon moved on to exploit more
of the proven wealth of the Gulf. The small but growing phosphate and cement industries provided the only hope of development, in addition to the country's modest living from the land.
The last instalments of British aid had allowed Hussein's government to build a fine new tarmac road to Aqaba, and a small
modern port was being developed there. But the income from
trade was still quite inadequate to match expenditure. And Hussein looked increasingly towards the only friend he could think
of—Iraq. His Hashemite allies were at first reluctant to enter
into what looked to them like a one-sided bargain. It was to take
Hussein eight months—June 1957 to February 1958—to persuade Iraq to close ranks with Jordan.

Hussein was decisively aided in this move by developments in
Syria. The Iraqi government had never lost its ambition to control
Syria. It had, after all, been a Hashemite kingdom : for a brief
moment after the first world war, King Feisal I had ruled in
Damascus, before he was ejected by the French and set up in
Baghdad by the British. The development of Ba'athi socialism
in Syria, in shaky alliance with the Syrian Communist Party, and
with the increasing support of the Soviet Union, only encouraged
Iraq's leaders to look for an opportunity of reversing the trend
and regaining Syria for the conservatives. But the Union of Syria
with Egypt at the beginning of 1958 seemed to cement Syria
solidly into the opposite camp. It was only then that Iraq turned
to Hussein.

Syria's union with Egypt was born of the ambitions of the
Ba'ath party in Damascus, just as the break with Egypt three
years later was provoked by the frustration of these ambitions.
The Ba'athists, still a political minority in Syria in strict electoral
terms, saw a union with Nasser's Arab nationalism as their best
hope of outflanking the traditional political forces in Syria and
attaining their long-term goal of a unitary Arab socialist state.
Their call for union gained force from America's diplomatic iso-
lation of Syria in the summer of 1957, in which Hussein played a
willing part.

In spite of their opposition to the British and French intervention in Egypt in 1956, the Americans had become deeply involved

in the Middle East in the wake of the British withdrawal. On June the 29th came a further announcement of aid to Jordan, this time in the form of military equipment, and that same month the Lebanon received 15 million dollars in aid under the Eisenhower doctrine. At the beginning of August, Syria signed a major technical aid agreement with the Soviet Union, and a week later, on August the 15th, three American diplomats were expelled from Damascus. The Syrians said, with some justification, that the Americans were plotting to overthrow the Syrian government.* The Americans reacted by sending a Deputy Under Secretary in the State Department, Mr Loy Henderson, to tour the Middle East. Hussein met him in Ankara at the end of August. The effect of this visit, along with the dire warnings issuing from Washington of a Communist advance in the Middle East and the creation of a Soviet satellite in Syria, was to heighten the tension between America's friends—Turkey, Jordan, Lebanon, and Iraq—and Russia's friends—Egypt and Syria.

On the 9th of September, the Jordanian cabinet, an array of American diplomats, and 1,000 Jordanian troops assembled at Amman airport to watch the arrival of six United States Globemaster aircraft and two C119's carrying arms for the Jordanian army. Out of the planes came forty military vehicles, each mounted with the 106 millimetre recoil-less rifle, ·30 and ·50 calibre machine-guns and boxes of ammunition. The aircraft had had to fly by way of Saudi Arabia to avoid crossing Syrian or Egyptian airspace. It was the first airlift of American arms: the last British troops had left Aqaba three months earlier, and British military aid was at an end.

The encirclement of Syria was complete. On October the 13th, Egyptian troops landed at Latakia in Syria to show their solidarity with the Syrian régime, and the Syrian Ba'athis, taking advantage of this, began to work hard for a union with Egypt. It finally came on February the 1st 1958.

The internal situation in Jordan was largely under control by the end of 1957—the tight control of the army and Hussein's loyalist cabinet. The men accused of conspiring against him in April were tried in a military court. None were sentenced to death; five—including Ali Abu Nuwar and Ali Hiyyari—were sentenced to fifteen years' imprisonment. Ten year sentences were

* Seale, *The Struggle for Syria*, pp. 293–5.

imposed on twelve others. Another five were acquitted. Few of
them had to serve much of their sentences. Eight of the seventeen
convicted were outside the country anyway.

After the formation of the Egypt-Syria union, Hussein turned
his attention to Iraq. His relations with the Baghdad branch of
the family were not easy. Feisal, the King, was the same age as
he was. He and Hussein had been schoolboys together at Harrow.
But they had little in common. Hussein was the dominant character; Feisal had none of his cousin's impulsive drive and love of
adventure. He was predictable, well-mannered, and very English
in his tastes. He was unassuming and not a natural leader. Although he had come to power at the same time as Hussein, in
1953, he left most of the running of the country to his uncle,
Abdul Illah, and the Prime Minister, Nuri Said. Hussein felt
close to Feisal, but he resented the cold arrogant air of Abdul
Illah, who appeared to dictate policy to the young King. Abdul
Illah was a detached aristocrat with little feel for the political
temper of his country, and without the flair for leadership that
might have won him the support of the army. Although the Iraq
government, under his and Nuri's control, had done much for
the economy, it had lost touch with the people and, more dangerously, with the army.

When Feisal arrived in Amman on the 10th of February, the
two kings had an animated discussion about the possibilities of
a union between Jordan and Iraq. Feisal appeared ready to
accept that Hussein and he should take it in turns to be Head of
State in the new union. But when Abdul Illah arrived in Amman
two days later, he told Hussein that it was self-evident that
Iraq, with a population and area far greater than Jordan's,
should be the dominant partner. Feisal must be permanent
Head of State, and Iraq must have a majority of members in the
joint parliament. Hussein finally persuaded Abdul Illah and
Feisal to accept that the parliamentary balance should be equal,
but agreed to being Deputy Head of State.

On the 14th of February the Arab Federation was formed,
and Hussein and Feisal stood together as the flag of the Arab
Revolt was raised again. In a broadcast to Jordan, Hussein
said :

'This is the happiest day of my life, a great day in Arab history.
We are under one banner, the banner of Arabism which our

great-grandfather, Hussein Ibn Ali the Great, carried in the great Arab revolt.'

Jordan was to contribute 20 per cent of the Union budget, Iraq the other 80 per cent. The two states agreed to have a common defence policy, and to work out common foreign, economic and education policies over the next few months. The Iraqi government had its own misgivings about the economic advantages of the Union, but it saw clear political advantage in thwarting what it viewed as a new threat from the rival union between Egypt and Syria.

Although President Nasser sent a telegram to congratulate King Feisal on the achievement of the Union, the two rival groups of states were soon doing battle with each other. In Jordan, a major conspiracy against Hussein was uncovered in early July. A young officer, arrested in connection with the plot, revealed that there was to be a joint *coup d'état* against Hussein and Feisal in the middle of July. In his evidence he said that the man behind it was President Nasser. Hussein telephoned Feisal personally, warned him of the plot, and told him to send a trusted emissary to Amman so that all the information could be passed on to the Iraqi government. Feisal made the mistake of sending General Rafiq Aref, the Commander-in-Chief of the Iraqi forces, whose loyalty to the Iraqi royal family was uncertain.* Aref seemed quite unconcerned when Hussein passed on all the information to him, including the names of the conspirators, and when he left for Baghdad on the 11th of July, Aref told Hussein that it was he, Hussein, rather than Feisal, who should fear for the safety of his throne. Hussein telephoned his cousin once more on the following day to wish him a successful trip to Turkey. Feisal was due to leave early on the 14th of July for a Baghdad Pact meeting. And on the same day Hussein was expecting the arrival of troops from Iraq as part of their joint defence arrangements.

The 14th of July was the day of the revolution in Iraq, and, in spite of Hussein's warning, it caught the régime by surprise.

Iraq, as well as Jordan, had its Free Officers Group, and the régime had been naïve and unobservant not to detect it. There were many rumours of such a movement in palace circles, but they were treated with disbelief. In fact, it was highly organised, and executed its plans with ruthless efficiency. The two central

* Khadduri, *Republican Iraq*, p. 32.

figures were Brigadier Abd al-Karim Kassem and Colonel Abd al-Salam Aref. Both held commands in the Iraqi force which entered Jordan in November 1956 at Hussein's invitation to balance the Syrian and Saudi forces invited in by Naboulsi. Both Kassem and Aref were nationalists but Kassem, the leader, was not a Nasserist, nor was he a Ba'athi.

It was the government's order to Aref's brigade to move to Jordan in July 1958 that gave the revolutionaries their opportunity. The brigade was to move through Baghdad on the 14th of July. Kassem agreed with Aref that he would move his brigade into Baghdad behind Aref's in the early morning of the 14th, and that between them they would occupy the capital. They did so—with complete success. But their takeover was not bloodless.

At about five o'clock in the morning, King Feisal, Abdul Illah and other members of the royal family were roused by the sound of firing. Once they had ascertained it was a rebellion and that they had no hope of resisting, the King agreed to surrender to the officer in command of the attacking force. The officer agreed to give them safe conduct across the front courtyard, but half-way across it, he turned and fired his machine-gun, killing them all. The Prime Minister, Nuri Said, was later found killed too. A number of Jordanian officials, including the aged Ibrahim Hashim, the Deputy Prime Minister of the Union, who happened to be in Baghdad, also died in the disturbances.

The whole fabric of the Hashemite dynasty in Iraq had been destroyed and with it, Hussein's hopes of a union straddling the centre of the Arab world. It had been an artificial creation anyway, the union not of two nations, but of two branches of the same ruling family : a union that lost its meaning after a burst of machine-gun fire.

Hussein was Head of State of a Union that had suddenly ceased to exist.

XI

HUSSEIN v THE REST

Hussein first heard the news early on the morning of July the 14th. He was awakened by a telephone call informing him that his cousin was dead.

Slowly, as the day passed, and as frantic messages passed between Baghdad and Amman, the whole pathetic tale was pieced together for him. The brutal murders and the treatment of the bodies of Abdul Illah and Nuri Said, which were mutilated and displayed in public, caused Hussein deep anguish. When he heard of the death of Ibrahim Hashim and the other Jordanian officials of the Union in Baghdad, he was roused to fury and in his misery and anger, his first impulse was to invade Iraq and to restore Hashemite rule by force. Sherif Nasser was sent to Iraq at the head of an expeditionary force, and air cover was requested from Britain. A determined show of force would bring the loyal Iraqis rallying to the monarchy, the rebel army units would crumble away, and Feisal would be avenged. Jordanian forces had intervened successfully in Iraq in 1941 to restore Feisal, still a boy, and Abdul Illah as Regent, after they had been ejected by a pro-Nazi junta.

However, a sense of reality was always quick to return to Hussein after an emotional crisis, and any lingering hopes he may have had that Sherif Nasser would turn the tables on the rebels soon evaporated when he learned the full extent of the upheaval in Baghdad. The Iraqi branch of the family had been annihilated, and the rebel army, far from being the derisory force that had opposed the Arab Legion in 1941, was a modern army, fired with revolutionary fervour and apparently united in its joy at the overthrow of the monarchy. Although Hussein believed he had a legitimate title to the throne of Iraq, through the six-month-old act of union, he was not foolish enough to think he would be accepted for long even if his army could achieve a victory. Anyway, as he had expected, British air cover was politely refused, and the British did everything they could to discourage what looked to them like a suicidal military adventure in Iraq. If the situation in Baghdad had not resolved itself so quickly, he might have pursued the campaign on his own. Indeed, in a conversation with the author in 1971, he strongly asserted that he would have done, whatever the odds against him. In the event, it was hopeless. He called a cabinet meeting, and relieved many of his ministers by announcing that he was against further intervention. Sherif Nasser,* whose advance units were now 150 miles inside Iraq, was recalled to Jordan. The Union was dead.

Hussein and his ministers then took stock of the situation and it rapidly became clear that far from intervening in Iraq, their first task must be to secure Jordan. To the north, relations with Syria, now a part of Nasser's United Arab Republic, were at their worst : the Syrians had closed the frontier. To the east, they faced Iraq, a country with whom they were now virtually at war. That frontier was closed too. To the south lay Saudi Arabia where Prince Feisal, the Prime Minister had now taken over most of King Saud's powers, and was anxious to repair his relations with President Nasser. To the west lay Israel. Hussein's only access to the outside world lay through the port of Aqaba, but the tarmac road was not yet completed.

The critical need was for oil. Normally it came across Syria, in road tankers from Lebanon. This source had already been barred to Jordan. Now the road route through Iraq was barred too. The only remaining hope appeared to be by air, over Saudi Arabia. Jordan had no long-term oil storage facilities and the need was urgent. Hussein called in the American chargé d'affaires, and asked him if his government would arrange to fly in the oil at once. Hussein admits that he was desperate : at that moment it was glaringly evident to the world outside that his continued existence depended entirely on the will of Washington.

Washington was willing, and a day later the first American aircraft landed in Amman with oil from the Gulf, flown over Saudi Arabia. But within hours, the airlift stopped ; Saudi Arabia

---

* Sherif Nasser was himself recalled to Amman at 11 a.m. on the 15th. But he was not given the final order to withdraw until 11 a.m. on the 16th. Sherif Nasser was anxious to press on, and he feels that Hussein was too, but that he finally yielded to the persistent advice of Samir Rifai and Talhouni.

had raised objections. Hussein spoke personally with King Saud, but to no effect; Saud told him his government had decided not to allow overflights of oil to Jordan. He was sorry, but that was that. In a fury, Hussein told Saud that he would never forget this stand against Jordan. He then returned to the Americans and urged them to think of something quickly. They did, but it was one of the most humiliating schemes Hussein ever had to accept. Oil was flown into Jordan, over *Israeli* airspace, with the full approval of the Israeli government. It was now demonstrated to the Arab world that if *they* wanted to force the downfall of Hussein, their arch-enemy—Israel—did not. With Israel now apparently supporting Hussein, his claim to be an Arab Nationalist leader valiantly holding the front line against Zionism now began to look absurd. The fact that the deal with Israel was necessary only because the Arab states had forced him into an impossible position, was naturally overlooked by those who wanted to discredit him. And this, by now, was most of the Arab world.

On the evening of July the 14th, after President Nasser had warmly approved the revolution in Iraq and recognised Kassem's new régime there, Hussein sent urgent messages to Mr Macmillan, Britain's Prime Minister, and to President Eisenhower. He told them of his determination to maintain his position as King of Jordan, but he asked for an assurance that the United States and Britain would come to his assistance if necessary, to 'preserve the integrity and independence' of his country. By this time the Americans had responded to an appeal from Chamoun, the pro-Western President of Lebanon, to send troops to Lebanon to secure his régime. Chamoun and Hussein thought they were imminent targets for a major assault from President Nasser's new, enlarged bases in Syria, Egypt and Iraq. Hussein believed Nasser primarily responsible for the murders in Iraq. It was not yet clear—though it became so the following year—that Iraq's revolution was *not* to enlarge Nasser's empire.

Hussein's preliminary appeal to Britain and America caused agonised soul-searching in London and Washington. The trauma of the whole Suez crisis had left the British wary of having anything more to do with major military involvement in the Middle East. British troops had now evacuated all their bases in Jordan, with the termination of the Anglo-Jordan treaty. But Britain still had commitments to Kuwait and the smaller Gulf States, and she felt a strong historic and moral commitment to the welfare of the only remaining Hashemite régime, which she herself had created. More realistically, Britain depended on Middle East oil, and the conventional wisdom in London was still that the oil supply was best secured by demonstrating support, where possible, for friendly Arab régimes.

The Americans were less prompted by emotion to feel committed to Hussein, but they had already taken over from Britain the job of paying his bills and they were anxious to prevent further encroachment by the Russians. However, the clear implication throughout the diplomatic exchanges between London and Washington at this time was that any intervention in Jordan would naturally be a job for the British.*

Hussein's old friend and flying instructor, Jock Dalgleish, had been serving at High Wycombe in Buckinghamshire ever since he left Jordan in 1956, at the end of his tour of duty. It was there that he received a telephone call at 8.30 p.m. on Wednesday July the 16th.

'Are you the Dalgleish of Jordan?' asked a voice from the Ministry of Defence in London. He replied that he supposed he was, and the voice rang off, telling him to stand by for a further call.

It came at 10.30 p.m.

'How long would it take you to get ready to fly to the Middle East?'

'Half an hour,' replied Dalgleish, 'What's going on?'

'You'll find out. A car will call at eleven o'clock.'

Dalgleish was driven to a waiting Canberra bomber, which flew him to Malta, and then to Cyprus. He arrived at the large British military base at Akrotiri at seven o'clock on the Thursday morning.

Dalgleish had been alerted and despatched as part of a contingency plan following Hussein's first message to Mr Macmillan on July the 14th. But by the time Dalgleish reached Cyprus,

* Harold Macmillan, *Riding the Storm*, ch. 16

Hussein had sent a further, far more dramatic message and a full-scale operation was under way.

Late on the 16th of July, Hussein's position looked critical. The landing of American marines in the Lebanon had provoked a howl of disapproval from Syria, Egypt and Iraq, and the Jordanian government was coupled with the Lebanese in the volume of abuse from Arab radio stations. It was that evening too that Hussein says he finally uncovered the full details of a plot against him timed for the following day. He called a combined meeting of his cabinet, parliament, and the senate and got them to agree that he should make an appeal to Britain and America to send troops to Jordan.

The appeal was received in London by Mr Macmillan, just as he was about to leave the House of Commons after a debate on the Middle East. It was 10 p.m. The British cabinet met at eleven o'clock. A decision was finally made at three o'clock in the morning of the 17th. The service chiefs told Macmillan that two battalions of paratroopers were available and alerted in Cyprus: they could hold the airfield at Amman, and this would secure Hussein against any intervention by air. But supply and reinforcement would depend on the Israelis agreeing to allow overflights of their territory. And the force would be a small one ill-equipped to survive a long stay or a major attack from another country. It was a big risk.

During the discussion, Macmillan talked twice to the American Secretary of State, Mr Dulles, who promised American support for British intervention. In the end the cabinet seems to have been moved by the prospect of King Hussein suffering the same fate as his cousin. Britain—it was judged—had the power to prevent this, and Macmillan says he felt Britain's political position in the Middle East would have been gravely weakened if Jordan were absorbed by Nasser. The cabinet agreed, unanimously, at 3 a.m. to order British troops to Amman.

When Dalgleish arrived at Akrotiri at breakfast time, the first wave of the invading force was about to take off. He was met by the base station commander who told him eighteen Beverly transport aircraft would carry the first elements of 16th Parachute Brigade into Amman. They would be followed by the rest of the

2,000 men later in the day. The force commander was Brigadier
Tom Pearson. Dalgleish was to go in with the first wave.

The aircraft that were coming to Hussein's rescue had to fly,
like the American oil tankers, over Israel. As the first wave
approached the Israeli coast, they called up Tel Aviv, and
informed Israel air traffic control that they were overflying. The
Israelis sounded surprised:

'You are not cleared to overfly.'

The British commander, realising with horror that London had
not informed the Israelis, decided to risk it. Israel was twelve
miles wide at this point, and in a few minutes his aircraft would
be over Jordan.

'British task force for Amman. We have clearance,' he said.

But he had not. And, although the first wave of some 200 troops
landed in Amman minutes later, the remainder were held up in
Cyprus until after lunch, because the Foreign Office in London
had made a major blunder. Frantic communication was made
with Israel, and after a cabinet meeting in Jerusalem the Israeli
government agreed to allow the airlift over its territory, about
three hours after the first wave had already arrived.

Fortunately for the British, no opposition of any kind was
encountered by the arriving paratroopers. The airfield was quickly
occupied: the men were welcomed by the Jordanian airfield staff,
and the rest of the force arrived by evening. The situation in
Jordan appeared calm, and though the British presence for the
next few weeks remained unobtrusive, the troops were well looked
after and many of them renewed old friendships among the
Jordanian army.*

For the British troops it was easy: but not for Hussein. For
the first two or three weeks, people expected to wake up each
morning to hear that he had been assassinated. Talk of conspiracy
was everywhere. There were a number of bomb explosions, a
large number of arrests and a ruthless clamp down by Hussein's
security forces. Censorship was imposed on the press. They were
some of the most tense days the King ever had to endure.
Journalists, many of whom had to leave the country to file their

* The British government won qualified approval from Parliament, for its
action in sending troops and *The Times* Newspaper, on the 18th of July,
said: 'The sending of troops to Jordan is not only justifiable: to have failed
to do so would have been a plain dereliction of duty. Britain's ties with the
Hashemites are of a very special kind. . . '

reports, told of open public support for President Nasser and the widely held assumption that Jordan would follow Iraq into the revolutionary camp. Radio stations in Syria and Iraq called on the people almost hourly to rebel against Hussein and accused him of inviting in 'imperialist forces to save his régime in collaboration with Israel'.

And yet, incredibly, he survived. The presence of the British made outside intervention unlikely, and he could concentrate his attention on the danger of attack from within. Hussein had been deeply shaken by the discovery that one of his own personal ADCs had been involved in the plot that was betrayed earlier in July. He knew that in a political system so riddled with intrigue, and so battered from outside with propaganda and incitement to disaffection, his own survival depended on luck almost as much as on the loyalty of his security forces. His luck held, and so did his persistent courage and good humour. He had a habit, each time he felt he had averted a crisis, of wanting to joke about it with his friends—rather like a schoolboy returning from an escapade. Gradually, as the plots were revealed, as one foreign attaché after another was wheeled off to the airport to be ejected for conspiring to overthrow him, as crate after crate of Czech and Russian arms was seized on its way in from Syria— gradually, Hussein convinced people that he not *not* going to be defeated, not this time anyway.

By the end of August, the exhaustive work of the army and police had so demoralised those who were hoping for change, that the tense air of expectancy began to dissipate. British and Italian tankers began arriving at Aqaba with massive loads of oil. On the 21st of August, a United Nations resolution called on the Arab states to recognise each other's territorial integrity. In September, the United Nations Secretary General, Mr Hammarskjold, secured assurances of 'good-neighbourliness' towards Jordan from President Nasser, and in October, British forces finally withdrew. At a tea party in Amman, Hussein presented Brigadier Tom Pearson and eleven other British officers with gold watches inscribed 'King Hussein'. On November the 1st, the United Nations announced that President Nasser had lifted his blockade of Jordan and the frontier with Syria was reopened.

The crisis seemed to be over. But Hussein made the mistake of dropping his guard too quickly.

E

It was the 10th of November 1958. Hussein felt the atmosphere had relaxed enough for him to take a holiday in Europe. The first stop was to be the Beau Rivage Hotel at Lausanne, where he would meet his mother, Queen Zein, and his daughter, Aliya, for a three-week holiday. Jock Dalgleish, who had again taken up residence in Amman as Air Adviser, would help Hussein fly the Royal aircraft, a Dove. It was a small civil aircraft with a royal coat of arms on its side. Early on the 10th, the aircraft taxied out on the tarmac at Amman airport. The King, Dalgleish, Sherif Nasser, and two Jordanian pilots, who were to fly the plane home again, climbed aboard, as a group of ministers and diplomats waved their farewells. Hussein was gay and eager for a break from the strain of the last few months. There was no secret about his departure.

The Jordanian flight controllers had communicated the aircraft's flight plan to Beirut in the normal way, together with the registration number of the aircraft and the number of passengers. Jordan had been told by the United Nations ten days earlier that overflying arrangments with Syria were back to normal, and a military aircraft had flown to Cyprus over Syria only five days before. No one had any reason to think that the aircraft could not take the normal route from Amman to Beirut over Damascus, and from Beirut on to Europe. Beirut controllers had confirmed that the flight was in order.

At 8.20 a.m. with Hussein at the controls the Dove took off. It climbed to 9,000 feet and headed north-east. The air route between Amman and Damascus was not direct: pilots had to head for a point about a hundred miles south-east of Damascus known as Point Bravo, where they turned north-west for Damascus, and dropped to 8,500 feet. Point Bravo was an hour's flying time from Amman.

In half an hour, the aeroplane crossed the Syrian frontier and called Damascus. Hussein reported position and said they were just crossing the frontier near Dera'a. Damascus gave them clearance to continue. It had been cloudy when they left Amman, but it was now clearing fast. At 9.20 a.m., Hussein reached Point Bravo: he was thirty minutes flying time inside Syrian airspace. He turned north-west for Damascus and brought the plane down to 8,500. Hussein made another routine call to Damascus at Point Bravo, reporting that he was dropping altitude and would be over Damascus in about 30 minutes, and that he was heading for Cyprus by way of Beirut.

Five minutes later came the shock order from Damascus air traffic control: 'You are not cleared to overfly. You will land at Damascus.'

Hussein and Dalgleish exchanged glances. Damascus control was already giving the aircraft its landing instructions and details of weather conditions. It could be a mistake: the Syrians were not notably efficient at controlling air traffic or processing flight plans. But it did not look like that: they had been cleared at the frontier, and at Point Bravo. They assumed the worst. Hussein turned the plane sharply away to the south, and headed straight for the nearest point on the Jordanian frontier, which he reckoned was twenty minutes away.

Hussein switched to the Amman Radio channel and told them what had happened. They told him to head for home immediately and to shut down his radio to avoid his position being fixed by the Syrians. He then told Damascus he was circling, awaiting their instructions, but when he was again told to land, he said he refused to do so, and closed down his radio.

Hussein put the plane into a dive, and took it down almost to ground level to avoid detection by Syrian radar: Dalgleish says they were about six feet from the ground most of the time flying at about 200 miles an hour. Eight minutes after Hussein's refusal to land, two Syrian Mig-17 fighter aircraft approached from the direction of the Jordanian frontier, and passed overhead, at about 16,000 feet. The clouds had dispersed and the shadow of Hussein's aircraft was clearly visible against the brown Syrian desert. Within seconds, the two fighters were down at Hussein's level, racing past his right-hand wing, sweeping across his path and up overhead to dive down, apparently straight at the Dove.

Hussein handed over the controls to Dalgleish. If the Migs opened fire Hussein and his party could not survive. The Jordanian air force had only three of its twelve Vampire fighters operational at that time, and they would be outgunned by the Migs. Besides, it was too late to hope for help. All Dalgleish could do was hope to outmanoeuvre the Syrians, and pray they would not dare to fire. The Syrians did not open fire, but they did all in their power to force the Dove to the ground. Dalgleish had one big advantage over them: the Dove could alter course sharply, because of its low speed, and turn away at about 90 miles an hour. The Migs had a much wider turning circle. and tended to overshoot each time they made a run at the Dove. Once they nearly collided as they swept in on Dalgleish from opposite directions, and overshot him.

Both Hussein and Dalgleish say the attacks continued until the planes were well over the frontier. But as soon as they crossed the main road from Mafraq to Baghdad, the Syrians pulled away and headed back into their own territory. For some time Dalgleish kept the Dove just above ground level; then he climbed and flew back to Amman.

In Amman, the King was treated as a returning hero. Crowds surrounded his palace, his photographs were sold in the streets and people demanded war with Syria. The Jordan government protested to the United Nations and to the United Arab Republic. Nasser's spokesmen laughed the whole affair off as a product of the King's vivid imagination, and suggested that Hussein would be a hit in Hollywood. But the plot—if that is what it was—backfired badly. Hussein's escape, exploited to the full by his supporters, contributed to the growing legend of the young daredevil King, who refused to be beaten and who could survive the treachery of his enemies, even when he was attacked in an unarmed aircraft over foreign territory.

What really happened in Damascus that day has never been ascertained. If it was a deliberate attempt to kill Hussein, it was curiously mishandled. The Syrians left themselves only ten to fifteen minutes in which to force Hussein's plane to crash. If that was their intention, they could have intercepted him much earlier. And Dalgleish is convinced the Syrians could have found two more capable pilots.

Syria's explanation was that the plane had failed to identify itself adequately, and that it had not given the necessary notice of intention to fly over Syrian airspace. It is certainly remarkable that Hussein took the risk of flying over Syria only ten days after the end of a virtual state of war between the two countries, and that he did so after only routine clearance with the Syrian authorities—indirectly, through Beirut.

XII

THE STRUGGLE FOR STABILITY

1959–1961

The British intervention of 1958 allowed Hussein the breathing space to secure his international position by thoroughly coercing the opposition. By the end of the year, his opponents were cowed by the rigorous security measures enforced by the government of Samir Rifai, who took over from Hashim in the summer. The army was now under the command of General Habes Majali, a powerful Bedouin tribal leader, whose loyalty to the King was unquestioned.* The British deterred any major external interference, while the King's army and police effectively suppressed any remaining republican feeling in their ranks.

There was one final attempt at revolution by a group of army officers supported, apparently, by Nasser, in the spring of 1959, but the King's fast-growing intelligence system was too exhaustive for it to go undiscovered. In February, soon after Hussein left on a long tour of the United States and Europe, a Brigadier Kassim was arrested with twelve other officers on a charge of plotting to overthrow the régime. Evidence came to light which suggested that the chief military figure in the plot was General Sadek Shara, Deputy Chief of Staff and second-in-command of the army. By this time Hussein, accompanied by Shara, was in the United States and he decided to continue the tour and keep Shara close by him at all times. The coup was planned for the 15th of March, and Hussein says that Shara became more and more worried as he heard reports of the arrests in Jordan but nothing from his fellow conspirators. When the royal party reached London, Shara asked for leave to remain in Britain to undergo an urgent surgical operation. Hussein refused and insisted he return home where, on the 21st of May, he was arrested and later sentenced to death. True to style, Hussein later commuted

* Although, like many successful Jordanians, he appears to have erred as a younger man. See p. 38.

133

this to life imprisonment, and by 1971 Shara was a free man—the Director General of Hussein's passport office in Amman. He told the author in December 1971 that he had never conspired against the King in person, though he had wanted to make some changes in the Army in the interests of efficiency, and this must have led his opponents to denounce him, falsely, to the King.

With the failure of this plot, Hussein's control over the army was finally and firmly established. Even at the most critical moment of his career, in September 1970, when his country was split by civil war, the vast majority of his troops remained loyal to him, in spite of the confident predictions of his opponents that as much as half the army would desert.

But Hussein now faced an apparent change of emphasis in the tactics of those who would unseat him. Where revolution had failed, assassination might succeed. The number of direct attempts on his life now increased dramatically. Hussein had to endure another two years of intense personal danger before he was able to feel secure in his own kingdom, and even his own palace.

The attempts on his life took many forms. Most of them were alleged by the Jordanian government to have been arranged by the embassy of Nasser's United Arab Republic. Every stratagem was tried. One day Hussein was walking in the grounds of the Basman palace, and he noticed a number of dead cats. The gardens were always full of cats which strayed in from the streets of Amman, and were usually, at Hussein's order, liberally fed by palace kitchen staff. But three dead cats in one afternoon was too much : Hussein made enquiries and was astonished to hear that other members of the staff had found over a dozen dead cats in the previous two days. It turned out that one of the palace cooks, named Ahmed Na'naa, had been bribed to poison Hussein but, uncertain about the dosage needed to kill the King, he had been experimenting on the palace cats. Na'naa's confession revealed that he had been working for the Syrian secret service. Hussein later released him in response to an impassioned plea from Na'naa's young daughter.

In 1960, Hussein escaped two assassination attempts in the late summer. The Prime Minister at the time was a close friend of Hussein's, Hazza Majali, the man who had tried to take

Jordan into the Baghdad Pact in 1955. His premiership in 1955 lasted five days: in 1959 he succeeded Samir Rifai and fifteen months later on August the 29th 1960, he died violently in his own office.

It was a Monday morning. Majali was at work with a group of officials including Samir Rifai's son—Hussein's former school-friend, Zeid Rifai. At about eleven o'clock, Majali told Zeid Rifai to fetch a file from the next room. Rifai was hardly through the door, when a time bomb hidden in the Prime Minister's desk exploded: it was a powerful device, and when Rifai managed to reopen the door, he found Majali and ten officials dead.

Hussein was on his way to see his Prime Minister at the time, but had stopped briefly on the way to review the site of Amman's new University. When he heard the explosion—only a mile away to the south—Hussein considered driving straight over to investigate himself, but after some discussion with his aides, he agreed to return to the Hummar. A few minutes later a second explosion ripped apart another room, only a few yards from the office where Majali had been killed.

Hussein quickly appointed his aide, Bahjat Talhouni, Prime Minister, and persuaded most of his ministers to remain in office. Two young Syrians were later said to have planted the bombs and then escaped across the border, and the Prime Minister's Director of Information was arrested and accused of being a conspirator. But the murders were not followed by any political disturbances, and the real motive was never established.

A few weeks later, Hussein was warned of a plot to assassinate him in his palace. His security chief advised him to spend a night away, so that the building could be thoroughly checked. Hussein agreed and spent the night with the Rayners, who had often welcomed him informally as a guest. He asked Rayner to collect his clothes from the palace and some nose drops, as his sinus was troubling him.

When the nose-drops arrived, Hussein took a new bottle and asked Mrs Rayner to pour away the half-used one. It was just as well. The contents of the phial almost destroyed Mrs Rayner's sink. It was acid, presumably placed in the phial by one of the palace servants. Hussein had to dismiss all staff who had access to his bathroom. Once again he blamed the embassy of the United Arab Republic.

These attacks on Hussein and his Prime Minister drove him to such a fury against President Nasser that he seemed to those close to him to be nearing despair. He was particularly incensed at the murder of Majali, and his contempt for the treachery of the Syrians knew no bounds.

A month after Majali's death, Jordanian forces massed on the Syrian border, and Hussein was talking privately of marching on Damascus. Indeed Hussein's readiness to seize any opportunity to invade Syria and Iraq for some years after the coup of 1958 in Baghdad was one of the main headaches for the British and Americans who provided most of Jordan's aid and believed that any military adventure of this kind would destroy Jordan altogether. Baghdad was Hussein's favourite target : but his mother, Queen Zein, whose advice he still valued, constantly warned him that Damascus was the more dangerous of the two. Wisely, Hussein managed to restrain himself from attacking either. Much of Hussein's talk was probably never intended—in good Arab style—to lead to action. But in that September of 1960, he came close to giving the order to attack. Syrian and Egyptian spokesmen talked of a new 'imperialist' plot to wreck the United Arab Republic of Egypt and Syria. Hussein flew to the United Nations to tell the world how Jordan was fighting to defend herself against Communism and President Nasser.* This time he was firmly refused permission to overfly Syria, and he finally got to New York by way of Saudi Arabia and Khartoum.

When Hussein rose to speak in the General Assembly, the Russian and UAR delegations walked out of the chamber. The greater part of his speech was an open attack on both of them. He said that Jordan had chosen to take her stand with 'the free world' against Communist expansion. He said he rejected 'neutralism', and warned that there was a danger of Communist expansion 'under the guise of neutralism'. He then went on to list the attacks on Jordan by the United Arab Republic.

'We can only believe the aim of our sister Arab state was our destruction,' he said. '. . . I find considerable significance in the

---

* Hussein's feud with Nasser had now taken on the form of a permanent obsession. One friend of Hussein's says that whenever Hussein played *Consequences* at parties, he would nearly always draw pictures of President Nasser.

fact that our troubles with the United Arab Republic date from the time that I denounced the growing menace of Communism in the Arab world. Moreover, I detect a significant parallel between the tactics that have been used against Jordan and those employed by Communism all over the world.'

Hussein was criticised afterwards for making this attack on other Arab countries at the United Nations, but he felt that he would gain prestige in the West by doing so, and contribute to President Nasser's growing difficulties in the Middle East. Syria was beginning to tire of Egyptian domination and Iraq, which had begun by making overtures to Nasser in 1958, immediately after the revolution, was now at odds with him. Arab unity was as distant a prospect as ever. Indeed, it was at the United Nations that Hussein suggested to Iraq that diplomatic relations be resumed for the first time since the destruction of Hashemite rule there.

In Washington and London, Hussein's two main sources of aid, his prestige was at its height. In a world which was becoming hysterical in its condemnation of Western 'imperialism' and 'colonialism', and in which the great breakaway from empire was fast accelerating, it was refreshing to the British and American governments to have one firm advocate of their own stand against Communist expansion. The Americans were now providing financial help to Hussein on a much more permanent basis, in co-operation with the British. In 1960, the Americans contributed £18 million and the British about £3 million in aid. Jordan was able to embark on some long term economic planning. The East Ghor canal scheme would help irrigate more of the east side of the Jordan valley, and a new refinery at Zerka would ensure that Jordan's oil supply would no longer have to rely on road communications between Beirut, Baghdad and Amman, but on the less vulnerable Tapline oil pipeline from Saudi Arabia. Tourists were coming in increasing numbers to see Jerusalem, Petra and Jerash. Slowly Jordan was becoming more self-sufficient and self-confident, but there was no sign that she would ever be economically self-supporting. Exports between 1954 and 1959 increased by 44 per cent, but imports were up by more than 100 per cent. The country would clearly depend on substantial outside budgetary support for a long time to come, and since the Arab world would not pay, Hussein wasted no time in reminding the West how much he depended on them. And, for their part, Britain and America showed no sign of letting him down.

In February 1961, Hussein took a bold step. He wrote a personal letter to President Nasser, urging a restoration of sensible relations between them, an end to the propaganda battle, which had continued intermittently for five years, and even a meeting between them some time in the summer. Nasser replied favourably three weeks later, and words like 'Your Majesty' and 'My Brother' appeared liberally in the exchange of correspondence. Hussein was now preparing the ground for a period of truce with the revolutionary states in the Middle East, which were themselves in a state of disunity. When his bid for acceptance won a warm response from President Nasser, Jordan was able to enjoy a period of relative stability. It was a struggle that Hussein won by his own courage and persistence, and in the end, by confronting Nasser with the fact of Hashemite survival in Jordan against all the odds. Nasser, absorbed for the moment with his own internal problems, his personal feud with Kassem of Iraq, and the increasing restlessness in Syria, decided that this was not the time to be saddled with any revolutionary responsibilities in Jordan. He must, however, have recognised even then that the pressures from the Palestinians, who had won his support for a separate 'Palestinian entity' on the West Bank and for the creation of a Palestinian army,* would prove a more decisive political factor in the long run than the appeals of King Hussein. But for the moment he allowed the political tension between him and Jordan's King to relax.

This was a fortunate break for Hussein. It happened just when he was about to decide to marry for the second time : this time his wife was not to be an Arab princess, but an English girl, the daughter of an officer in the British army.

Hussein's love life, after his divorce from Dina in 1956, was as eventful as his political career. His passionate nature and zest for adventure and romance won him the company of many attractive girls in the Middle East and in Europe. He did not

* At the Shtura conference of foreign ministers of the Arab League in August 1960.

allow his growing preoccupation with affairs of state to rob him of the occasional chance to drive off in one of his high-powered cars from one of his palaces or embassies abroad, with a beautiful girl at his side. It was a fast, turbulent existence, but that was the way he liked to live. His name was linked with a number of women, from the German actress Barbara Valentin to the young Hashemite Princess, Hazima, and he saw Flavia Tesio again on some of his flying visits to Rome. But until 1961, there was little serious talk of marriage.

In Amman, everyone knew of the gay, informal parties the King used to give at his palace at Shuna in the Jordan valley. Sometimes the dancing would go on all night, and those who withstood the pace would end up with a picnic breakfast on the shores of the Dead Sea. The King invited as many foreigners as Jordanians to his parties: indeed, he almost preferred their company, as they were usually more relaxed and less conscious of their position than his own countrymen.

One evening, a young RAF officer brought a British girl of nineteen along as his partner to a fancy-dress party at Shuna. Her name was Toni Gardiner, the daughter of Lt-Colonel Walker Gardiner, who was Number Three in the British Military Mission to Jordan. Hussein was dressed as a pirate, and when Toni was introduced to him for the first time, she said :

'You look pretty scruffy, Your Majesty.'

Hussein fell for her immediately. It was not long before they were meeting regularly. Sometimes they met alone, sometimes Hussein would take her go-karting at Amman airport, where Maurice Rayner had introduced the sport and persuaded Hussein to become President of the Club. Hussein taught Toni to drive a go-kart and it was soon a regular date every Friday afternoon. On the way home, Hussein would often call in at the Gardiners' house for tea or an evening meal.

Toni was gentle and good-natured, without airs and ambitions —pretty, but not strikingly so, unintellectual but with a cool common sense that appealed to Hussein. She was homely and understanding, and enjoyed doing the things he did—dancing, driving, informal parties, film shows at the palace. By the winter of 1960 they were frequently seen together, and the gossip began.

The first people to show real concern were the British government. The British ambassador instructed the head of the British military mission to make discreet equiries of the Gardiners as to just what was going on.* The prospect of Britain being accused of engineering the marriage of Jordan's King with a British girl, to cement the colonialist relationship between the two countries, was one that struck horror into the hearts of British diplomats. Everything must be done to discourage it. The ambassador's first soundings produced the hopeful assessment that Toni's friendship with the King was a passing one, of little consequence. Besides it was assumed that Hussein, whose judgement was by now highly respected in London, would not commit what looked to the British very much like political suicide.

But to the surprise and chagrin of the British embassy, Hussein fulfilled their worst fears. Late in April 1961, the British ambassador was called to the Basman Palace. Hussein told him that he had decided to marry Toni Gardiner. He explained that he believed marriage would give him the settled personal life he now desperately needed. It would be a refuge from the turmoil of his public life. He had found someone who understood this need and would provide the home he wanted. Hussein assured the ambassador, who was immediately opposed to the marriage and said so, that he had weighed all the problems, but that in his judgement, the consequences would not be as serious as the British believed. The ambassador pointed out that he was concerned not with Britain's image, but with the King's, and that the marriage would provoke a wave of propaganda against him just when he seemed to have consolidated his position in the Arab world. But Hussein was adamant; he had made up his mind.

A number of government ministers, including the Prime Minister, Talhouni and the Army Commander, General Majali, urged the ambassador to do all he could to dissuade Hussein. Wasfi Tell the Jordanian ambassador in Baghdad, spoke his mind to the King himself in the strongest terms. Again, the British ambassador tried to prevail on Hussein but he was firmly rebuffed.

* A few months earlier, the previous British ambassador had warned Hussein that this mission would be withdrawn if he persisted in threatening to invade Syria. Hussein had looked unusually crestfallen on hearing this, and the ambassador was puzzled until he later heard of the news of Hussein's interest in Toni, who would presumably have left Amman with her father if the mission had been disbanded.

Hussein himself was primarily driven by his own emotions : he craved the intimate friendship that he felt only marriage would give him. And Toni Gardiner, whether the world liked it or not, was the girl he wanted to marry.

It was partly her British background and her British detachment from all the Arab feminine inhibitions and complexes that attracted him to her. The political embarrassment of her nationality was something he was prepared to live with.

Hussein had already secured the support of his mother, Queen Zein, whose advice and goodwill was still an important influence on him. His mother agreed with his own instinct : that a happy marriage was more important than the opposition it aroused. She and Hussein agreed that the only essential condition of the marriage was that Toni should become a Moslem. Hussein was delighted when Toni readily accepted that she should change her faith and adopt an Arabic name. Between them, they chose Muna al Hussein—'Hussein's wish'.

Hussein was fortunate in the coincidence of his plans for marriage with the improvement in relations with President Nasser. He decided to inform Nasser of his engagement, and face any opposition head on. It was another of those occasions when Hussein's judgement and determination proved to be right, in spite of the fears and doubts of most of those around him.

He announced his engagement on the radio on May the 1st 1961. He described Muna as a 'Muslim but not an Arab' and left her English background to a subsequent announcement. As her nationality became known in the next day or two, the attacks began :

'When Hussein said he searched for affection and warmth, he meant he did not find it among the Jordanian people,' said the Egyptian newspaper *Al Akhbar*. 'He turned towards the West to solve his family's problems as he always did when seeking the solution to his other problems.'

Hussein gave a Press Conference. Someone asked him the question that was in everyone's mind :

'Are you not afraid of the danger that might result to you from marrying a British girl ?'

'No,' said Hussein. 'I have never been afraid of anything. I have my belief in God, my belief in myself, and my belief in my people. As long as I have these three beliefs, I am confident. My only nervousness about this marriage is that it is, to a great extent, a completion of a part of my life that has been missing.'

His stand may have looked naïve, and even downright foolish to the people who heard him at the time. But it worked.

XIII

MARRIAGE AND STABILITY

1961

Hussein and Muna were married on the 25th of May, 1961.

The ceremony itself took place privately at the Zahran Palace, where Hussein's mother lived. Muna wore a pale blue linen two-piece suit, and Hussein, dark grey. The couple sat in front of a low coffee table, as a sheikh of the Moslem Sharia Court asked them in Arabic whether they took each other as man and wife.

'Na'am,' they both said, which is 'Yes' in Arabic, and everyone shouted 'Mabruk'—'congratulations'. Apart from Muna, only men were present : Mrs Gardiner, now Hussein's mother-in-law, and Queen Zein waited in another room. After the marriage a rose-petal drink was passed round, then Hussein and Muna joined the women for a drink of tea, while the men took tea separately.

After the wedding, Hussein changed into white uniform, and Muna into a splendid wedding gown of pale cream wild silk, embroidered with pearls and diamante, and they joined hundreds of guests in the main apartments of the palace. Hussein's wedding present from Britain's Queen Elizabeth was silver—a four-piece tea set. President Kennedy gave the couple a centrepiece for flowers—in gold. Later Hussein and Muna left the palace and were driven, standing up in an open car, through the crowded streets of Amman. Observers who were looking for signs of disapproval were disappointed; the cheering and waving seemed, for that one day, to be spontaneous and universal.

Once again, Hussein had confounded the pessimists.

Hussein and Muna set up home in the house at Hummar, which Hussein had had enlarged to accommodate a small family. It now had four bedrooms, and two big rooms downstairs. There was a fine view from the hilltop where the house stood and it was surrounded by orchards and open country where he and Muna could ride on horseback. In the garden was a helicopter pad, which allowed Hussein to commute in five minutes to his office, a dozen miles away, in the Basman palace in Amman. Around the boundary fence of this pastoral retreat, a ring of troops kept their permanent vigil, and one trusted soldier lived in the house itself : his name was Suleiman Mazour, and he had been Hussein's personal bodyguard since the King was a child. He came from a village south of Kerak, called Shobak, whose people traditionally supplied the rump of the King's bodyguard.

In the next few years, Hussein and Muna had four children : Abdullah, born in February 1962, Feisal, and twin girls, Zein and Aisha. Hussein's daughter Aliya, Dina's child, came to live with them as well and soon after this, Hussein allowed Aliya to visit Dina for the first time and spend holidays with her. Hussein gave his son, Abdullah, the title of Crown Prince for the first three years of his life, but in 1965 the title passed to Hussein's younger brother, Hassan, who had just left Harrow for Oxford University where he was distinguishing himself in History and Political Science.

It took Hussein 13 years as King to arrange the succession to his satisfaction. For a number of years his brother Mohamed, who was eight years older than Hassan, had held the title of Crown Prince. But Mohamed, who was judged unfit to go to Harrow, as Hussein and Hassan did, was not considered an adequate deputy. He shared Hussein's love of escapades but frequently carried this to extremes. The story is told of him that Hussein had appointed him Major-General, but one day Mohamed appeared in the uniform of a Lieutenant General.

'You can't do that,' said Hussein. 'Even *I'm* only a Lieutenant-General!' So Mohamed relented. But when Hussein next left on a foreign tour, Mohamed promoted himself Lieutenant-General again.

Most people believed Hussein was wise finally to appoint Hassan Crown Prince. Moreover, as the King's own two young sons grew up, they looked and behaved much like little English schoolboys as Jordanians. With Hassan's appointment as Crown Prince in 1965, the spotlight was conveniently removed from Abdullah and Feisal, and Hussein's immediate family could live something like a normal life. Contrary to a number of reports at the time,* Muna strongly supported Hassan's appointment as Crown Prince, and Hussein told her and a number of other close friends that there was no reason why Abdullah should not become Crown Prince when he was 18. Later, Aliya, Abdullah and Feisal went to private schools in England and returned to Amman for their holidays. And Muna, who had gladly set aside all claim to the title of Queen—or any part in the politics of Jordan—quietly and efficiently got down to the business of making a home for Hussein.

By the early 1960s, the political stability which Hussein had fought so hard to establish was beginning to bring Jordan's economy to life. British and American aid thoughtfully applied, was providing badly needed capital for the development of existing industries, like the production of potash and phosphate and the creation of new ones like oil refining. The new refinery at Zerka produced 181,000 tons of oil in 1961, and 337,000 tons in 1964. Exports of phosphate were 660,000 tons in 1964, and this had doubled by 1970. Production of cement was only 86,000 tons in 1954, but reached 316,000 tons by 1964. Smaller industries like milling, tobacco, food processing, and even the making of cardboard boxes were springing up on both banks of the Jordan. A new Jordanian middle class of industrial workers and managers, businessmen, merchants, teachers, and other professional men, was growing fast; it drew much of its dynamism from the Palestinians, both West Bank residents and refugees, many of whom forsook the grim environment of the camps and helped to build prosperous suburbs in Amman and Jerusalem. The building industry thrived, and smart stone villas matched the shabby huts of the refugees on the hills around the capital. The distinction between the Transjordanians and the Palestinians grew less sharp, with every encouragement from King Hussein. Complaints came from the West Bank, that the King favoured the development of the East Bank by establishing the new Jordan University at Amman, rather than Jerusalem, and promoting a major

---

* Suspicions were aroused when Hussein announced Hassan's appointment while Muna was away in England. But the author is satisfied that this was pure coincidence and Hussein's friends concede that Muna's absence was 'unfortunate' at that time.

irrigation scheme—the East Ghor Canal—on the east side of the Jordan valley; but the King could fairly respond that the East Bank was less developed than the West and that Amman was, after all, the capital of the country.

In the countryside, agricultural output was improved by the East Ghor Canal scheme, which was, for the moment, a substitute for the wider scheme to harness the waters of the Yarmuk and the Jordan in a major transformation of the whole pattern of the Jordan valley. The canal was to be completed by 1966 at a cost of £5 million: it would run for 40 miles down the east side of the Jordan valley and irrigate a further 30,000 acres. Jordan government loans were encouraging small farmers on the East Bank to copy the sophisticated terracing that made farms on the West Bank generally more efficient, and helped to alleviate the effects of the unpredictable climate. Wheat and barley were the main Jordanian crops, but production could vary dramatically from year to year. In a good year like 1956, the yield could be 242,000 tons of wheat; in a bad year like 1960, it could drop to 43,000 tons. But the trend was, on average, upwards; and the production of olive oil increased 16 times over between 1955 and 1964.

The Bedouin made their contribution too. By 1964, Jordan had a total of 800,000 sheep, 650,000 goats, 65,000 cattle, and 19,000 camels.

The national income of Jordan increased by 60 per cent between 1954 and 1959, and by 1966, it was more than three times the 1954 figure (1954: £51 million, 1966: £168 million). Educational facilities improved fast and by 1967, Jordan was able to boast a higher proportion of students in the population than any other Arab country except Kuwait. The new University of Jordan at Amman had 2,500 students by 1966, and 650 of them were girls.

The port of Aqaba, now joined to Amman by a fine tarmac road, began to take more of Jordan's trade which had long been robbed of its outlet through Haifa and which, until the 1960s, had to take the long and expensive route through Syria or Iraq. In 1962, 437 ships docked at Aqaba and carried cargoes of 677,000 tons: the total rose to over a million tons in 1967.

But Jordan's economy, developed under the eye of a competent civil service, still depended largely on foreign aid, as the trade figures show: by 1966, the margin of import costs over export earnings was a little more than £57 million: Jordan's exports were still only a fifth the volume of her imports. This trade deficit was partly made up by income from tourism (£12 million in 1966) and remittances from Jordanians working abroad (£13 million), but the fact remains that by the mid-sixties, Jordan needed an infusion of some £40 million a year in aid of various kinds in order to survive.

For Hussein, the five years that followed his marriage to Muna were the happiest, most tranquil years of his life. They were not free from political disturbance, as we shall see, but his main political problems seemed to be behind him, and his family life was a source of deep and growing satisfaction. He was a man of essentially simple tastes, apart from his passion for speed, and the informality and easy warmth of life at his palace constantly surprised visitors who expected it to be all extravagance and glamour. The family spent most of their time at Hummar. Later, in the autumn of 1965, they moved into a larger house they built nearby, but it was still only a family house, built of local stone, with marble floors, simple modern furniture, and magnificent views between the fruit trees towards the hills overlooking the Jordan valley. There was a playroom for the children, with built-in wall bars, and a study with dark leather armchairs in it for Hussein. In the garden they put a swimming pool, and Muna taught Hussein to swim.

Down at Shuna, in the Jordan valley, Hussein had a large riding stable. The horses, which were kept up at the Basman palace in the summer, moved down there in the winter, and the Master of the King's Horses was Santiago Lopez, a friend of Hussein's, who used to be bandleader of a London night-club. Riding became one of Muna's favourite sports: she had a fine Iraqi-Arab stallion called Jussor and she and her parents, and Abdullah and Feisal, riding Mexican ponies would make long treks in the Jordan valley. Hussein preferred riding a camel: he kept two of them in specially tall stables at Shuna. It was a common sight in the Jordan valley to see a royal riding party out for the day accompanied by one man on a camel—the King.

Down at the new port of Aqaba, Hussein built another residence—a cluster of chalets on the beach. He developed a new enthusiasm for the sea, and his love of speed made him an accomplished water-skier. He kept a fast launch there, and other boats for fishing and sailing. He was out in the Gulf of Aqaba one day in December 1965, and his boat was nearly shot up by an Israeli patrol boat doing some target practice. That same day a foal was born to one of the mares at the royal stables, and Hussein immediately named it Tracer.

Between these three places Hummar, Shuna, and Aqaba, Hussein and his family moved often, and at high speed. His helicopter allowed him to flit between any of them and his main office at the Basman in Amman, and direct telephone lines meant that he was always able to keep in touch with affairs, even from Aqaba. When he was free from work during the daytime, he would take Muna go-karting, riding, or even flying. On Friday's, the Moslem sabbath, they would go down to Shuna or Aqaba to ride or to ski, swim and fish. In the evenings, he would arrange a film show at the Basman and ask the Gardiners, the Rayners and other friends to join the family, or he would stay at home with Muna and listen to his favourite music—pop. He had no time for classical music or heavy reading : he was no intellectual, but a man of action, and if he was at home, he liked to relax his mind completely.

Hussein's idea of work was much the same : he was never happier than when he was away from his desk, visiting his troops or some new development project. He deplored paperwork. If there was a problem he had to study, he wanted it expressed to him succinctly, by word of mouth—not in a long written report. He liked to *talk* problems through. Economic and administrative detail bored him, and many an ambassador recalls the glazed look that would come over Hussein's eyes if economic affairs were under discussion. His consuming interest was the armed forces, their morale, their welfare and their equipment. He visited them regularly, and was far happier dressed in uniform than in a suit. He would spend nights with them on desert patrol, or drop out of the sky by helicopter during an exercise, and would always be one of the first at the scene of a frontier incident. In 1965, there was an Israeli raid on Jenin, and Hussein drove through the night from Aqaba to be on the scene. He arranged an emergency blood transfusion for a wounded soldier, visited the men who had been involved, and then drove back to Amman to welcome the Vice-President of India who was due on a state visit. On his way back, he was so exhausted that he dozed off at the wheel and drove his car into a wall, injuring his spine. But he was at the airport at noon to greet his guest.

The King's circle of friends and counsellors in Amman was a strange mixture. On the one hand there were his British friends— the Rayners, the Dalgleishes, and his parents in law, the Gardiners. He valued their friendship and their homeliness. During the crisis of April 1957, he had treated Maurice Rayner's house as a kind of sanctuary of understanding to which he often escaped from the worries of the palace. Then there was the group of families that made up Jordanian high society; families like the Rifais, the Talhounis and the Tells. They were the ruling establishment—some of them, paradoxically, of Palestinian extraction—energetic, intelligent, committed to the preservation of the monarchy and providing the personnel to administer the State. And finally, there was his family, Queen Zein, Sherif Nasser, his uncle, and Sherif Zeid bin Skaker, his cousin. And in the background were the Bedouin chiefs, the key to his army's loyalty, some of them related to his family, all of them close to the ear of the King.

These were the people nearest Hussein—the people who represented the main pressures and influences on him. They called him 'Sidi' ('Sire'), or 'Sayidna' ('Your Majesty'), or 'Abu Abdullah', ('Father of Abdullah'), or even 'Abby' for short. Most of the Bedouin called him 'Hussein', and 'Hussein!' was the cry that went up whenever he moved among them.

What nobody in Jordan doubted was that Hussein was in charge, that he made the decisions and that, without him, the state would collapse. Hussein listened readily to advice and had a keen feel for the important pressures on him at critical moments, but when he took a decision, it was his alone. And everyone in the ruling circle knew just how far they could go to press him. This indeed was the weakness as well as the strength of his administration. His ministers and advisers, because they were essentially appointed rather than elected, were men who did what they were told. There was little or no constructive dialogue between rulers and ruled and Jordan's politics were never enlivened with the dynamism that comes from participation : most West Bank Palestinians and many independently

minded East Bank intellectuals felt that they were ruled by an
alien, autocratic régime. A few people—very few—would go a
long way to impress their views on Hussein at the risk of dis-
pleasing him. One was Wasfi Tell, soon to become Hussein's
Prime Minister.

Another, who often went too far, was Hussein's uncle, Sherif
Nasser whose reputation for skulduggery was the gossip of
Amman.

Hussein was deeply concerned about his uncle's reputation, as
he was a valuable and powerful ally in a political crisis and a
central figure in the family. But in 1966, he decided that Sherif
Nasser had gone far enough.* Allegations were being made about
arms smuggling and other activities, and Hussein was determined
to exert his authority. Sherif Nasser's house was surrounded and
the King walked in and confronted his uncle with the news that
it was about time they understood each other. From then on,
they did.

* See *The War Business*, by George Thayer, pp. 142–3.

XIV

THE FIGHT FOR ARAB UNITY

1961–1964

From the summer of 1961, Hussein was able to sit back and watch, with some delight, the bickering among the Arab states who had been his enemies. Disunity was the dominant feature of Arab politics in the early '60s.

The collapse of Egypt's union with Syria in 1961 looked to Hussein like a gift from God. The union had been an unhappy one for some months, and Nasser's nationalisation measures in Syria in July 1961 were too much for the Syrians. A conservative régime seized power and dissolved the union : Hussein recognised it immediately. He even invited the British and American ambassadors to his office and told them he was thinking of intervening in Syria to prevent a counter-coup by President Nasser. It was apparently with some difficulty that the two men quietly counselled him to think better of it and allow the Syrians to arrange their own affairs.

This was a bad time for President Nasser. He was not on speaking terms with General Kassem of Iraq, and now his Syrian province had deserted him; he had no support from the Syrian Ba'ath party who were as disillusioned about Egyptian rule as were the right-wing in Syria. He had been on good terms with Hussein, following the exchange of letters in the spring of 1961, and, with Hussein and Saud, he supported Kuwait against the threats of General Kassem.

After the break with Syria and Hussein's obvious elation, Nasser's relations with Jordan began to deteriorate again. But he was too busy with his own problems to press actively for Hussein's downfall : he was also inclining to the more realistic view that difficult as it had been for his United Arab Republic to absorb Syria, it would be an impossible burden for it to take on another 400 miles of frontier with Israel, and a disgruntled population of Palestinians.

For Hussein, Nasser's discomfiture was an opportunity not to be missed. In a broadcast from Amman just before Christmas, he said President Nasser had disunited the Arabs by inciting one party against another. Hussein said he took pride in combating the despotism and fighting the corruption and oppression which President Nasser had brought about in Syria. And he said the day was coming when the Egyptian people would punish the despots who were gambling away the funds, resources and aspirations of their homeland.

Hussein was beginning to enjoy himself: more confident of his position at home and taking heart from the failure of Nasser to unite the Arab world, he began to adopt a stronger foreign policy. And in August 1962, he and King Saud of Saudi Arabia formed a joint military command, and decided on close co-operation in the economic and political fields. They even invited other Arab states to join with them, and talked of a combined plan to 'safeguard Arab rights in Palestine and co-ordinate policy for Arab and foreign affairs'. A month later, a dispute in the Yemen drove another wedge between Hussein and Nasser. A republican régime seized power, but the Imam fought back and soon won support from Saudi Arabia and Jordan. Nasser accepted an appeal from the republicans to send troops to their assistance.

Hussein's ambitions were aroused, and the situation appealed to his love of adventure. He saw an opportunity to flex his muscles, and he had long been itching to use his small air force, which was developing well under the professional eye of his British air adviser, Eric Bennet. Against the strong advice of at least one of his close friends, he despatched a squadron to Taiz in the Yemen to support the Imam, and to teach President Nasser a lesson. But the gesture backfired badly. The head of his air force and two of the pilots defected to Cairo, and Hussein had to send Wasfi Tell post-haste to Taiz to urge the other pilots to fly their planes home to Jordan. His first instinct had been to fly to Taiz himself. He later admitted humbly to his friends that the whole episode had been a disastrous mistake. To most of his Palestinian population, who were devoted to Nasser, the sight of their King sending his air force, not against Israel, but against Nasser and the popular revolution in the Yemen, was a further cause for deep resentment.

But Hussein could retort that he had been about to invade Israel in 1956 when Nasser, of all people, had begged him not to. Anyway, he was now confident enough of his political strength at home to indulge his wilder military fantasies abroad. More than anything else he still dreamed of marching into Baghdad to restore Hashemite rule there, and he was still trying to persuade the West to give air support to a Jordanian invasion of Iraq. But wiser counsel, gently administered, prevailed.

Behind this confident foreign policy, Jordan's domestic scene was settling down to a period of quiet development. The Prime Minister was Wasfi Tell, a powerfully built blunt-talking East Bank townsman, half Kurdish with a shock of black hair and bushy eyebrows. He was inseparable from his pipe, which he chain-smoked religiously—even when he was water-skiing. His task was to invigorate the country, which had been stunned into a sort of political inertia by the government's resolute suppression of the opposition in the late '50s. Tell promoted new men to leading positions in government and the civil service; he ordered the release of large numbers of political prisoners, and warned that they were not to be victimised. In October 1961, a new parliament of 60 members (30 from each bank) was elected; a year later, the government announced that political parties, which had been banned since 1957, would be allowed to resume their activities, provided they were not agents of outside powers. And Hussein told his government that he expected to see the electoral law amended to give women the vote.

Hussein's fortunes took a sharp turn for the worse in the spring of 1963 but the crisis was short-lived. In February 1963, General Kassem was overthrown in Iraq by Colonel Aref, who had once been his partner in ousting the Hashemites and then fallen out with him. Aref was a politician with pan-Arab leanings: he looked favourably on the idea of union with Nasser. A month later, the Ba'athis were back in Syria, and the stage seemed set for a major union between Nasser's Egypt, Syria and Iraq. Through March and the first half of April, negotiations went on in Cairo, and Jordan again began to feel isolated. Hussein and Wasfi Tell recognised the new governments in Baghdad and Damascus but they eyed the Cairo negotiations with apprehension. On the 27th of March, Hussein appointed Samir Rifai Prime Minister. This was taken by many as a conciliatory move towards the proposed union, as Wasfi Tell was not liked by Cairo. But Hussein's principal concern was to anticipate possible disturbances: if they did break out, Rifai was the man to deal with them. On April the 17th, Syria, Iraq and Egypt signed an agreement setting up a union. It was a loose agreement, providing for collective leadership to satisfy the Ba'ath and there was to be a period of 25 months before the union was to begin to come into force. Nevertheless, it was heady stuff and demonstrators were soon out in the streets of Arab capitals, including Amman, to celebrate. The demonstrations in Jordan soon turned to riots, and on April the 20th, in Jerusalem, four people were killed and thirty injured. A major demonstration in favour of union with Syria, Iraq and Egypt had begun at eight o'clock in the morning : students paraded with portraits of President Nasser, and the Jordanian flag on a public building was hauled down and replaced by one with four stars on it, to represent Jordan as part of a union of four Arab states. When the demonstrators attacked the police, a riot began. People ran screaming down the street shouting 'Nasser, Nasser!', trees were uprooted, firing began, and troops were called in.

In Amman, that evening, Samir Rifai's government was defeated in the Jordanian parliament, on a motion of no confidence. Opposition deputies called for 'another type of government, with another mentality, to enter into immediate negotiations with Cairo, Damascus and Baghdad to join the new union'. They also attacked Rifai for using troops to disperse demonstrators. The Prime Minister's answer to all this was that subversive elements had been inciting the demonstrators and that guns had been used against the police who had been trying to control the demonstrations with as little violence as possible; the government had had no choice but to call in the army in each case. But the vote went against him, and late on the evening of the 20th, he resigned.

Hussein acted firmly. He dissolved parliament, appointed his uncle Sherif Hussein bin Nasser* Prime Minister, and told the new government in a letter :

---

* Not to be confused with Hussein's other uncle, Sherif Nasser bin Jamil – see page 149. Sherif Hussein and Sherif Nasser were sometimes referred to affectionately, in private conversation, as the 'good' and the 'bad' uncle respectively.

'We are firmly confident that the manner in which members of the House withheld confidence in the Rifai government was due to personal motives and attempts to gain private advantage.'

He added that the members who had voted against Rifai were voting against the 'national interests of the country'.

Sherif Hussein's new government soon reimposed order: the army moved into the towns where the riots had broken out and curfews quickly had their effect. Hussein called a press conference and declared that the demonstrations and the parliamentary vote against Rifai were the work of 'subversive elements' which, he said, had tried to destroy the country and disrupt Jordan's relations with the Arab world. He said he welcomed the new union between Egypt, Iraq and Syria: 'We are ready to co-operate with them,' he added.

Anybody listening to Hussein at that moment, when Jordan was once more firmly under military control, would have thought that *he* was the one who was pressing for union with other Arab states, and that he and the army had been forced to act against those who had been agitating *against* union. The position, of course, was quite the reverse. Hussein had no intention of allowing Jordan to be absorbed into a union of left-wing republics that would mean the end of the monarchy, and probably also the end of Jordan's independence. This is not to say that Hussein was not an advocate of Arab unity: he had often said that he was, and he was faced with the continuing threat from Israel, which he felt could only be met by the Arabs as a united force. But Hussein's call was for an Arab unity that would *preserve* existing Arab frontiers rather than eliminate them, as the Ba'athis wanted. If there was to be unity, Hussein wanted it in a form that would allow Jordan to continue an independent monarchy: if he had a vision, it was a Gaullist vision of an *union des patries*. Hence his agreement with King Saud.

The question remains: what did Hussein's countrymen want? Was the country so infiltrated by Egyptian agents and so bombarded by Cairo's propaganda that the street demonstrators and the parliamentary majority were being beguiled into betraying their country? Or was Hussein stamping on a massive popular expression of support for union? There was no doubt among those who witnessed it that there existed a wide measure of enthusiasm for the union, particularly among the Palestinians, who made up more than half Jordan's population. The Palestinians saw the union as a means to increase the pressure on Israel, and if their choice was to be between a union that would, in their opinion, bring nearer the prospect of a liberated Palestine and one that would preserve the Hashemite kingdom of Jordan in its existing form, then the choice was easy. For most of the East Bank population, the liberation of Palestine was a goal too, but it was questionable whether the proposed union could achieve it. For them the important consideration was how much they stood to lose or gain from the union in other respects : it was something that needed to be approached cautiously, particularly in view of the sufferings of Syria under Nasser in 1958–61.

Hussein's action in April 1963, had been almost instinctive : he had seen a threat to the monarchy, he had acted sharply, and the forces of order had responded loyally and efficiently. It was a pattern Jordan had become used to. The King's power was proven and paramount.

Regrets anyone had about not joining the union were soon forgotten. It collapsed helplessly in an outburst of factional wrangling between Cairo, Damascus and Baghdad. First the Syrians broke with Nasser, and Nasserists in Syria tried to mount a coup on the 18th July. But it was defeated, and on the 23rd, Nasser was saying of Syria :

'We do not consider that the United Arab Republic is bound to the present fascist régime in Syria by any common aim. . . .'

Then Syria and Iraq had an attempt at Union on their own, but this too was doomed to failure : the Ba'athis in Iraq fell out with the President and in November Aref dismissed them from Baghdad, and, with them, hopes of union with Syria. The tripartite union that had aroused so much excitement that spring had vanished but no one doubted that the cries for unity would soon be raised again.

A new move for unity, on a rather different level, followed very quickly. President Nasser, deriving some encouragement from the fact that Syria and Iraq had failed to agree on a union between themselves, and anxious to restore his image as the leader of the Arabs, invited all Arab leaders to Cairo for a summit conference in January 1964.

Hussein eagerly accepted. His internal position was now firmly re-established. He had even felt strong enough to open diplo-

matic relations with the Soviet Union in the autumn of 1963, and
to allow Suleiman Naboulsi, who had pressed him to do this in
1957, to sit in the Jordanian senate. Hussein had a secure base
from which to make a bid for a permanent understanding with
President Nasser : it was a policy that had proved successful in
its tentative beginnings in 1961, and the time had come to con-
solidate it.*

The central issue on which an understanding had to be found
between them was the Israeli problem. The previous year, the
Israelis had announced that they proposed to draw water from
the Jordan valley to irrigate the Negev desert in the south of
Israel. They said they would draw up to the amount provisionally
agreed between them and the Arabs under the Johnston plan of
1955. An American government representative, Mr Eric Johnston, had allotted 40 per cent of the water to Israel, and 60 per
cent to the Arab states of Lebanon, Jordan and Syria, but the
agreement had never been formally accepted or signed because
the Arab states thought it would be tantamount to a recognition
of Israel.† And now the Israeli's had nearly completed their
pipeline from Lake Tiberias : there was a growing clamour from
the Arabs for some action to stop them. And it was one of the
leading topics on the agenda for the summit.

The reconciliation between Hussein and Nasser was like the
meeting of two long lost friends. Nasser met the King at the
airport and embraced him tenderly, and on their return to Cairo,
the two men walked arm in arm down the street from the Hilton
Hotel, where Hussein was staying, to the Arab League Conference
Hall. (It was the first of four meetings between Hussein and
Nasser that year : they met again privately in March and August,
and in September they both attended the second Arab summit
conference in Alexandria.)

Their minds met on the central issue. There must, they agreed,
be no war with Israel. Given the present political disunity and
the variety of Arab military commands and sources of equipment,
any involvement with Israel would be disastrous. There was pressure from the Syrians for military action to stop the diversion
of the Jordan waters by Israel, but Hussein and Nasser would

---

* For Hussein's overtures to Nasser in 1961, see p. 138.
† Failure to agree on a Jordan waters scheme had also held back Hussein's
irrigation projects. See pp. 117–118.

not hear of it. From this essentially negative, but important understanding between Hussein and Nasser, it followed that the conference had to decide what to do about the Israeli problem in
a way that *excluded*, for the moment, the use of military force
by the Arab states. And so the Conference came up with three
main proposals, which were unanimously accepted.

First, they agreed to examine ways of diverting some of the
upper tributaries of the Jordan to reduce the flow of water into
Lake Tiberias.

Second, a United Arab Command was to be set up, under the
Egyptian, Lt-General Ali Amer. His goal would be to create
a joint Arab force that would have cohesion and the freedom to
move all along the Arab front, with a full and efficient multi-
national intelligence network and full central command and control. Hussein had his doubts about this command : the delegates
talked about it with enthusiasm, but he feared that it would be
no different from any of the previous Arab joint defence arrangements. He remembered the absurdity of the war with Israel
in 1948, when his grandfather had, on paper, been the Commander-in-Chief of all Arab forces, but none of them except his
own Arab Legion had heeded him. On the other hand if there
was to be an effective defence against Israel, or indeed any
convincing offensive against Israel, Hussein knew that without
such a united command, the Arabs would never win. His worst
fears were realised three and a half years later in June 1967.

Third, it was agreed that the Palestine Liberation Organisation,
the PLO, should be formed as a basis for Palestinian resistance
against Israel's occupation of the land they claimed was theirs.
Its leader was to be Ahmed Shukairy. Hussein gave the PLO
proposal his unreserved support, but made one condition : the
PLO had to co-operate with Jordan. Hussein saw the PLO as
a useful focus for Jordan's Palestinians who had constantly
pressed for stronger action against Israel, and whose demands
had achieved wide recognition throughout the Arab world. At the
Shtura Conference in 1960, most Arab states had called for the
recognition of a 'Palestinian Entity', and although Hussein was
obviously reluctant to relinquish his hold on the West Bank of
the Jordan, he understood the need for some kind of political
settlement that satisfied the aspirations of the Palestinians. What
he now hoped was that the PLO would provide this. But he was

apprehensive about the effect of the PLO on the military balance between Israel and Jordan. He believed profoundly that Israel should not be provoked until Jordan and the other Arab armies were ready to meet the challenge. It was a lesson he had learnt from Glubb, and he insisted that the PLO's military activities should be strictly co-ordinated by the United Arab Command.

This Cairo Conference, which ended in smiles of triumph and brotherly embraces between all the Arab leaders, sowed the seeds of the disaster of 1967. It set in train the series of events that were to allow the Israelis to claim they were threatened with extinction, and it set the Arabs vying with each other to show who were the protagonists in the confrontation with 'Zionism and Imperialism'.

Hussein was caught up in the frenzy, and it involved him not only in war with Israel but with the Palestinians as well.

PART THREE

HUSSEIN v THE PALESTINIANS
1964–1972

XV

THE END OF THE FRAGILE TRUCE

1964–1966

On the 28th of May 1964, the Palestinians called a National Congress in the city of Jerusalem; 424 delegates attended, and after five days, they produced the Palestine National Charter.

This charter said that Palestine was an indivisible territorial unit, and that the establishment of Israel was entirely illegal. It said that the Palestine Liberation Organisation would have as its role the liberation of Palestine, but that it would not exercise any territorial sovereignty over the West Bank area of the Kingdom of Jordan. The charter said that the PLO would co-operate with all Arab states, and would not interfere in the internal affairs of any of them.

The PLO set itself up in Amman : its leader, Ahmed Shukairy, a rotund, inelegant man had been a Jerusalem lawyer until the war of 1948. He then became Syria's representative on the Arab League in Cairo and, after 1956, the Saudi Arabian representative at the United Nations, where he earned a reputation for hysterical language and lost many friends for the Arabs by talking of 'throwing the Jews into the sea'. His job now was to set up a Palestine Liberation Army, and he expected to get the full co-operation of Hussein.

But from the summer of 1964, the apparently warm relationship between Hussein, the Palestinians, and Nasser began to cool. Shukairy expected to be able to tax Palestinians and to conscript them for the PLO; he also expected to be allowed to distribute arms to villages on the border with Israel. Tension between Hussein and Shukairy was already evident at the second Arab summit in September 1964, and by the Casablanca summit of September 1965, it was becoming clear that a rift was inevitable. The essence of the disagreement between them was that Shukairy was acting on his own initiative and without the approval of the largely dormant United Arab Command. He was claiming that

Hussein was not living up to his obligations to the Palestinians, and was not allowing the PLO the full freedom it needed to organise. Hussein claimed that the PLO was forgetting it was pledged to respect Jordanian sovereignty.

The position was further complicated by the emergence, at the beginning of 1965, of the guerrilla organisation FATEH, the Palestine Liberation Movement, with its military arm, AL ASSIFA. This organisation developed in Damascus, independently of the more pedestrian PLO, with the encouragement of the left wing faction of the Ba'ath party in Syria who were fast gaining influence there. Salah Jedid, Yusef Zuayyen, and Nureddin Atassi were all militant radicals who believed in a military solution to the Israeli problem. Salah Jedid became Syrian Chief of Staff in December 1964, and with his backing, FATEH guerrillas started their raids into Israel. Their leader was a small unkempt figure with a round, bristly face, called Yasser Arafat.

Most of the time the FATEH guerrillas infiltrated Israel from Jordan. The long, twisting armistice line between Israel and Jordan was easy to cross without being seen, and the guerrillas scored some initial successes. Hussein acted, as he had warned he would, to try to stop the guerrillas inflaming his border with Israel. In January 1965, the Palestinians announced that King Hussein's troops had killed their first Palestinian commando, Ahmed Musa. He had been returning from a raid on the Eilaboun tunnel, part of the Israeli pipeline system, and was shot dead. Hussein made no secret of the fact that he would act to stop provocation of Israel. But still the raids went on.

The Israelis waited till May 1965. On the 25th of May FATEH guerrillas murdered six Israelis on a kibbutz, and killed a woman and two children in the town of Afula. On the 27th, the Israelis hit back, with raids on Qalqilya and Jenin. It was the news of these raids that brought Hussein speeding from Aqaba to visit the scene himself.* That same month the Syrians accused Nasser of failing to help them divert the Jordan waters, as the Arabs had agreed to do at their two summit conferences in 1964, and Israel's General Rabin warned that Israel would take action to prevent any diversion of the waters.

Nasser did not allow the pressure from Syria or the enthusiasm of FATEH to press him into war at this stage. He refused to

* See p. 148.

allow FATEH to operate from the Gaza Strip, and he told the Syrians: 'If the defence of certain countries is not possible, we cannot speak of attack, and if we talk about it, we are simply bragging and deceiving.' Nasser still had some 50,000 troops tied up in the Yemen, confronting the forces of the Imam and King Feisal, who had taken over from King Saud in Saudi Arabia in 1964. Hussein had withdrawn his recognition of the Imam of Yemen in order to show he valued his *rapprochement* with Nasser, and was now trying to arrange a settlement between Nasser and Feisal. It was at about this time too that Hussein invited Ali Abu Nuwar back from Cairo and pardoned a number of former suspected republicans in Jordan.

But Jordan's worsening relations with the PLO, and the failure of Hussein's and all other attempts to bring Nasser and Feisal to an understanding, slowly began to eat away yet again at the *entente* between Hussein and Nasser. Nasser strongly supported the PLO, and Hussein now began to suspect that Nasser was encouraging Hussein's opponents into its ranks in order to use it to to subvert the monarchy in Jordan. This naturally threw Hussein closer to his old ally Feisal, who was urging all Moslem states with traditional régimes to line up against Nasser. Feisal called it his Islamic Pact, and when Hussein showed some interest in this, during a visit to Amman by Feisal in January 1966, Nasser was furious.

It was the new government in Syria that finally forced Hussein and Nasser apart, and drove the Middle East towards war with Israel. In February 1966, the militants seized power in Damascus. They were the extreme left-wing of the Ba'ath party, and they believed in action. Salah Jedid was their leader: he was a member of the minority Alawi sect in Syria, and a passionate believer in radical socialism. All foreign assets that were still in private hands were nationalised, many supporters of the former, more moderate, Ba'athist régime were imprisoned, and extremism became the keynote of Syria's foreign policy too. Everything had to be done to encourage the Palestinian resistance, a truly popular movement, to pursue its violent campaign against Israel. Nasser had to be forced to give every assistance to the guerrillas and to all those who believed in a military solution to the Israeli presence in the Middle East. As for Hussein, he was not only against provoking Israel, but also standing in the way of progressive socialism and providing a refuge for counter-revolutionaries from Syria : he had to be overthrown.

The Syrians took over control of FATEH by the summer of 1966, and used it to increase guerrilla activity in Israel, and to subvert the régime in Jordan. They told Nasser they had no intention of attending the proposed fourth Arab summit in Algiers in September 1966, because reactionaries like Hussein and Feisal would be there too.

In July 1966, Nasser took a decisive step. He announced that he would not attend the Algiers summit either. He was moving towards Syria. They still had no diplomatic relations, but a number of factors were pushing them together into the alliance that was to challenge Israel the following year. The most important single pressure on Nasser was Syria's bid to take his place as champion of the Palestinians and chief opponent of Israel. He saw his leadership being eroded, and allowed himself to be forced to more extreme measures. He upheld the subversive campaign of FATEH. He attacked the Islamic Pact, and reopened, with all the colourful language at his command, the war of words with Hussein. By September the split was complete.

The summer of 1966, gave Hussein his last glimpse of that growing prosperity and calm which might have eventually made his country one of the happiest in the Middle East. One visiting journalist wrote in May :

'Jordan has enjoyed a remarkable spell of political tranquillity since the serious rioting and demonstratons three years ago. The benefit can be seen in the tourist boom, the well-stocked shops, the high rate of building and the newly planted fields and orchards.'*

Work on the Mukhaiber Dam on the Yarmuk river was begun after an opening ceremony by Hussein on May the 25th : this was planned to bring the same sort of transformation to Jordan's agricultural economy that the Aswan dam was already bringing to Egypt.

Hussein made a state visit to Britain. He and Muna were greeted by the Queen and Prince Philip at Victoria Station, and thirty-five London bus routes had to be diverted as the two

* Peter Mansfield in *The Guardian*, 8th May 1966.

carriages made their way to Buckingham Palace. Hussein attended a state banquet, drove a Chieftain tank in Dorset, laid a wreath on the tomb of the Unknown Soldier, and invited the Queen to make a return visit to Jordan.

But these palmy days were not to last.

Soon after his return from London, he found himself in open conflict with Egypt and Syria. He had already closed the offices of the PLO in Jordan, and told the Palestinians that they were 'no longer a movement for liberation'. He said the PLO was under the influence of Communism and had become a 'melting pot for all the discordant and displaced elements of the Arab world'. By July 1966, Hussein had Shukairy and the Syrians bitterly opposed to him, and on September the 1st, Egyptian propaganda joined in. Slowly the pressure on Hussein mounted. FATEH guerrillas filtered through Jordan and built up their attacks on Israel: the Syrian leaders held mass rallies to pour abuse on Hussein; the Russians accused Jordan of being in league with Israel and America to annihilate Syria. In October, Hussein's Prime Minister Wasfi Tell, who succeeded Sherif Hussein in 1964, warned the Syrians that if they tried to close their border to Jordan, Jordanian tanks would force it open again. Hussein now had two full armoured brigades of British and American tanks, and was waiting to receive a squadron of Starfighter aircraft from the Americans. People began to ask whether he was contemplating invasion of Syria.

Meanwhile tempers in Israel had been so aroused by the FATEH raids from Jordan that the Israeli government felt it had to act. In the five weeks beginning on October the 7th, there were six raids from Jordanian territory, four from Syria and one from Lebanon. Everyone knew that the raids were provoked and planned from Syria, and the mounting pressure for Israeli action against Syria gave the Syrian government the excuse they needed to demand a defence pact with Nasser. On November the 4th 1966, he agreed to a pact which committed him to come to Syria's aid if requested. The militancy of the Syrian régime had forced Nasser's hand.

The Israelis, who did not want to risk provoking a major war by attacking the heavily fortified Syrian frontier, decided to express their anger at FATEH activities by attacking the easier Jordan frontier instead. Their action on November the 13th nearly led to Hussein's downfall. At 5.30 in the morning a large Israeli force moved across the border and attacked the village of Samu where the Israelis said Palestinian guerrillas were being given shelter. The inhabitants of the village were bundled out into the street and the Israelis began systematically destroying their houses. While they were at work, a battalion of Jordanian soldiers raced from Hebron, and threw themselves against the invaders. But the Israelis were able to ambush the Jordanian column of lorries as it pulled into Samu, and when the Israelis finally withdrew, they left twenty-one Jordanian dead and thirty-seven wounded.

The Israelis had not intended to hurt Hussein: they had intended to provide him with an excuse to suppress Arab guerrilla activity, on the grounds that it jeopardised peace on the Israeli border. They did not bargain for the furious outcry against Hussein that swept the West Bank and was taken up by the Syrians and Egyptians. Overnight, all the pent-up grievances of the Palestinians against Hussein's régime exploded in a mass of demonstrations on the West Bank. He was accused of being unable and unwilling to defend them against Israel. He had refused to allow the Palestine Liberation Army to operate on the West Bank or arm the border villagers, and the Palestine National Guard had been absorbed into the Jordanian army—so who was there to help them? The demonstrations turned to riots, inflamed by Syrian, Egyptian and PLO propaganda: Hussein's photographs were torn to shreds, and Shukairy led an out-cry for a Palestinian Republic in Jordan, and for the immediate resignation of all Palestinians in Hussein's cabinet. The Syrians called for the overthrow of Hussein, and Egyptian-based radios called on the army to stop taking orders from the King.

Hussein's reaction was to point out that the guerrillas had precipitated the Samu raid, without co-ordinating their plans with him or with the United Arab Command, as they were pledged to. And when the Israelis had attacked, the UAC had done nothing: there had been no air cover, no reinforcements, no counter-attack. The United Arab Command had totally failed. Moreover, the Jordanian army *had* arrived promptly at the scene of the raid. The whole outburst of opposition, said Hussein, was a Communist plot to destroy Jordan.

Hussein was in fact able to restore order in the usual way,

by calling in the army, and making it clear that he was not going to tolerate anarchy in the streets. He was heartened by the support that America and Britain gave him at the United Nations, and he still hoped that Nasser would uphold his view, and the view that all the Arab states had expressed in Cairo in 1964, that Israel should not be provoked. But for most Arabs, this was no time for quiet restraint and realism. The campaign against Hussein grew. The Syrians encouraged infiltrators to attack Jordanian government installations, and according to the government, a Jordanian border guard was murdered in cold blood in his house only 400 yards from the Syrian border. Hussein was in despair at Syria. In an outburst of fury he sent the Syrian ambassador back to Damascus and refused to allow him back until February 1967.

The winter that followed was an uneasy time for Hussein. Though he had forced the Palestinians to desist from their campaign in the streets, he could do little to stop guerrilla activity and nothing to stop the growing wave of abuse against him and against Israel. But he still clung tenaciously to the belief that he had grown up with : there must be no war with Israel.

XVI

NASSER'S CHALLENGE TO ISRAEL

JANUARY–JUNE 1967

The Middle East now moved headlong into war, and it was Arab jealousies and rivalries that caused it, just as much as any real or imagined threat from Israel. The Arab states settled down to a frantic competition in brinksmanship: each wanted to prove itself the champion of the Palestinians, bolder and stronger than its Arab neighbours, readier to crush imperialism and Zionism. The pace was forced by the Syrians: they preached a violent military solution in Palestine, whipped up the FATEH, taunted Nasser until he followed them, and poured abuse and contempt on Hussein.

Only Hussein stood his ground—for the moment. He was still confident that he could control the internal situation in Jordan. But he was not now so sure about the situation on the frontier with Israel. The last thing he wanted was war with Israel when his forces were still patently inferior to hers: he would have preferred some kind of accommodation with her. But this had always been politically impossible, and now the Palestinians were baying for Israeli blood with the full support of the Arab world. He also had to face the prospect of a war breaking out when he was not prepared for it: and if war came, he feared that the Israelis would seize the West Bank. With the Arabs in their present state of disarray, Hussein had no doubt that the Israelis would play havoc with them. Hussein decided that Jordan's only hope of stability was to continue to exclude the PLO and try to control guerrilla intrusion into Israel. But he did allow arms to be distributed to frontier villages.

In the meantime, Hussein was receiving large quantities of American arms for the Jordanian army. In January 1967, a big American airlift began, and tanks rolled off American cargo ships at Aqaba. The Americans were matching the considerable shipments of Soviet arms to Egypt and Syria. Through the winter months, Hussein's Arab neighbours continued to remind him in their radio broadcasts that he had been unable to keep the Israelis out of Jordan, and condemned him for not allowing Palestinian and other troops into Jordan to attack the Israelis. This angered Hussein, and he began to revive a line of attack he had himself made on Nasser many years earlier. He asked him why, if he were so keen to get to grips with Israel, he did not dismiss the United Nations Emergency Force, which stood between Egyptian and Israeli forces in Sinai and the Gaza Strip. Amman Radio began chiding Nasser for 'hiding behind the skirts of UNEF'. And Wasfi Tell said that Nasser had made a secret agreement with Israel to keep the UNEF in Sinai in 1957 in order to avoid any Egyptian involvement in Palestine again. It was neat propaganda, but it touched sensitive Egyptian nerves and was dangerously provocative.

In February, Hussein carried his battle with Nasser even further. He withdrew his recognition from the Yemen Republican régime, and accused Nasser, who was supporting the régime, of 'massacring fellow Arabs in the Yemen'. Nasser threw back at Hussein that he was the 'Whoremonger' of Jordan.

In April, after six Syrian aircraft were shot down in a battle with Israeli fighters, Hussein's radio asked Nasser whether he had not a Defence Pact with Syria, and why, with the battle blazing periodically on Israeli's borders with Syria and Jordan, all was so quiet on Israel's border with Egypt? Hussein was playing his part in the complex of pressures that were leading towards June the 5th.

But the main pressure was still the tension between Syria and Israel, and Syria's attempt to lure Nasser into the battle. This took a decisive step forward in the second week of May. The Israelis began to warn the Syrians that this had gone far enough. They demanded that guerrilla activities, which had increased in the last few weeks despite the air battle with Syria in April, must be stopped. The Israeli Prime Minister, Mr Eshkol, delivered a strong warning to Syria to call off the FATEH or suffer the consequences. A high Israeli military source, identified by some as General Rabin, the Chief of Staff, was reported to be talking of overthrowing the Damascus government. On the 15th of May, President Nasser announced that he was proclaiming a state of maximum alert among Egyptian forces, and ordering his troops into Sinai to relieve the pressure on Syria. He said he had received intelligence reports that Israeli forces were massing near the Syrian border.

Late on the night of May the 16th, the United Nations Force was told by Nasser to leave Sinai, and two days later U Thant agreed to evacuate them. On May the 19th, Amman Radio said: 'Logic, wisdom and nationalism make it incumbent on Egypt to close the straits of Tiran. . . .' Three days later Nasser did that too, and Israel announced that this would be regarded as an act of war. Egypt was denying Israel access to her southern port of Eilat, opposite Aqaba.

Hussein heard the news with horror on the morning of May the 22nd. Up to then he and his government had been scoffing at Nasser and daring him to make a real challenge to Israel, but Jordan's jibes had only been instinctive counter-attacks to Egyptian propaganda blasts at Jordan. After all, the accepted test of any Arab country's virility was the richness of its abuse not the exercise of physical power. But now, without any consultation, or any apparent consideration of the consequences for the Arab world, Nasser had taken a step beyond abuse that Hussein immediately believed made war inevitable. Hussein says he believes Nasser did not intend the closing of the straits of Tiran to lead to war. But Hussein himself was convinced that it would, and that the war would be disastrous. The Arabs were not ready for it: there was no effective joint command, no battle plan, hardly any communication between them. Although Egypt and Syria had a defence pact, they could not, surely, hope to defeat Israel on their own. And Jordan with the most awkward frontier of the three to defend, was now exposed to Israeli attack with only Saudi Arabia as an ally. There was no certainty that Israel would respond to the closure of the straits by attacking Egypt alone, as she had in 1956. The lesson of the Samu raid suggested that Jordan might well be attacked, even if she was not responsible.

In the next two days, while the Arabs greeted Nasser's warlike moves with delight, Hussein made his decision : if there was to be a war, he would fight it too. There was no keeping Jordan out this time. It might have been possible in 1956, but it would not be in 1967. Popular resentment against him, particularly on the West Bank, would be uncontrollable if he refused to take up

Nasser's challenge to Israel. His cousin, Zeid bin Shaker, who commanded one of Hussein's tank brigades at the time, says Hussein went to war in '67 because there would have been civil war if he had not. Hussein himself says that his reasons were essentially moral ones : he felt bound by the Arab Defence Pact of 1964 that they had all signed in Cairo, and says that he simply could not stand aside while all the other Arabs fought.

Certainly, Hussein's decision to go to war was based on more than just a cool assessment of the situation. Any rational analysis would have told him that the odds were overwhelmingly against Jordan and the other Arabs, however close their alliance, and that the risk of civil war was preferable to the loss of much of his country. But like most of his best decisions, this, his worst one, was made on other grounds. It was essentially an impulsive, emotional decision, and he still feels, on looking back, that he had no alternative. Hussein did not want war with Israel but he knew, instinctively, that if there had to be a war for Palestine, Jordan, which ruled a part of Palestine, would *have* to be involved. For Hussein, it was not just a matter of expediency, it was a claim on his honour.

Once his mind was made up that he was involved, his immediate problem was defence : Hussein felt that Nasser's action would lead to an Israeli attack, and they could choose Jordan. He started to deploy his armoured units on the West Bank, and invited the Iraqis and Saudis to send troops. The Iraqis refused —for the moment; the Saudis made friendly noises, but did nothing. Hussein was frighteningly exposed. If the Israelis attacked first, he would be in serious trouble : he had a handful of Hunters to provide himself with air cover, while the Israelis could put up over 200 aircraft, and he had no allies to count on. If, on the other hand, the Arabs were to attack first, he had no idea what their plans were. He had to find out what Nasser's intentions were and, if possible, enter into an alliance with Egypt and Syria. A week earlier he would have dismissed such humiliating ideas from his mind, but he was now driven along by the conviction that he had no choice.

However, relations with Syria were virtually extinct. On May the 21st the Syrians had placed a bomb in a vehicle which exploded on the border and killed fourteen people. The Syrian ambassador had been packed off to Damascus again. Hussein would have to start with Egypt. On May the 25th, Amman radio ended its abuse of Nasser and began talking of its approval of the closing of the Straits of Tiran. Hussein sent General Amer Khammash, the Army Chief of Staff, to Cairo to find out what was going on. Khammash was to contact the headquarters of the United Arab Command, set up by the Arab states in 1964, and establish what its plans were in the event of war.

On the 18th, Khammash brought back disturbing news. He told Hussein he had tried to establish contact with the United Arab Command, but it had ceased to function. The differences between Egypt and other Arab countries had brought its activities to a complete stop. Anyway, Khammash was told, the Command had no role in the present situation, which was entirely a bilateral affair between Egypt and Syria, Khammash had tried to see Nasser, but Nasser was too busy.

Hussein had been snubbed : nobody would tell him anything— except the Egyptians who had said they were able to look after themselves. Hussein could only assume that Nasser still believed that his moves would not lead to war, and that the Israelis would not use the closing of the straits as a pretext to attack Egypt. Hussein believed that Nasser's object was to assert his prowess, to flex his muscles, to win a diplomatic victory over Israel so that he could say afterwards he had protected Syria from the Israelis and restored Egypt's position in Sinai to what it was before 1956. But Hussein's judgement was that this *would* provoke an Israeli attack. And since Hussein had already decided that if the Israelis attacked, Jordan would either be attacked herself or be morally bound to join the battle anyway, there was only one thing he could do. He summoned the Egyptian ambassador and told him he wished to meet President Nasser as soon as possible. He said he felt there was a real threat of Israeli attack on one or more Arab countries, and that Jordan wanted to play her part in meeting any attack : it was vital to co-ordinate their defences.

Late on the night of the 29th of May came Nasser's answer 'Come to Cairo as soon as you can'. The message reached Hussein at home, and he wasted no time in following it up. Soon after dawn the next morning, the King, his Prime Minister, Saad Juma, General Khammash and two other aides were at the airport. Hussein was wearing uniform, khaki battle-dress, and a cap with the emblem of his crown on it. He carried his American revolver: he had no bodyguard with him on the trip. The departure was secret: Hussein briefly went through the formality of handing over power to his brother Mohamed, in the absence of Hassan, who was at Oxford. At 7 a.m. a Jordanian airlines Caravelle, with Hussein himself at the controls, took off for Cairo. It was escorted as far as the Jordanian frontier by two Jordanian air force Hunters and then flew on alone.

Nasser was waiting at the Almaza Air Force base near Cairo, with his Prime Minister and General Ali Amer, chief of the neglected United Arab Command. Hussein handed the controls over to another pilot for the landing, disembarked quickly, and shook hands with Nasser. Nasser was reluctant to allow the photographers to take pictures until he consulted Hussein. He asked whether Hussein minded, or whether he would rather keep the whole thing a secret. Hussein said he did not mind, as people would find out soon enough. Nasser then joked about his uniform and the revolver, and Hussein explained that he had been dressed like that for a week. Nasser was wearing a suit.

Hussein felt that the welcome was a friendly one, but he sensed that Nasser was a little reserved and suspicious. Only a week earlier they had been calling each other every name they could think of. They shook hands again and kissed cheeks for the photographers. Nasser joked about arresting Hussein, and they both laughed.

As soon as they were in Nasser's black American car, they started talking business. Hussein immediately impressed on Nasser that he thought war with Israel would be a disaster for the Arabs, and that Jordan's army was not yet prepared for it. But he said that since he thought war was now likely, it was essential that their two countries work together and co-ordinate their battle plans. He said it was unthinkable that Jordan should remain outside the conflict, if any other Arab country was attacked. In the Koubbeh palace in Cairo, Hussein and Nasser were joined by Nasser's Commander-in-Chief Field Marshal Abdel Hakim Amer. Hussein suggested that the United Arab Command should be revived, but Nasser pointed out that he now had a separate and more detailed pact with Syria, and that the UAC was too broad an alliance, that covered other Arab states too. He appeared quite confident that his army, newly equipped with Russian tanks and guns, could defeat the Israelis if they attacked in Sinai. Hussein then took the plunge: with obvious enthusiasm he suggested a full-scale pact between their two countries on the lines of the Egypt-Syria alliance. Hussein asked Nasser to send for the text of the pact with Syria, and when it arrived, he took a quick look at it and told Nasser he would sign an identical one. He wanted no one to be in any doubt that Jordan would fight beside her Arab neighbours against the common enemy, however hopeless the struggle.

If Nasser was surprised by Hussein's eagerness to throw himself into a close union with his most bitter Arab enemy, he did not show it. There was only one matter Nasser wanted to clear up: Hussein had to come to terms with the PLO. Nasser surprised Hussein by summoning Ahmed Shukairy, who had been running the PLO from Gaza, since Hussein dismissed him from Jordan. Shukairy came into Nasser's drawing-room, very untidily dressed, walked up to Hussein with a broad grin and warmly greeted him as the leader of the Palestinians. He even sat down with the Jordanian delegation as Hussein signed the pact with Nasser.

After the signing, Nasser told Hussein that he would like him to take Shukairy back to Jordan in the same aircraft, to demonstrate his solidarity with the Palestinians. He even told Hussein, with a laugh, to throw Shukairy into prison if he gave any trouble, and rid Egypt of the problem. Everyone was delighted, including Shukairy.

It was decided that in the event of war, Jordanian forces would come under the command of General Abdul Moneim Riad, who was Assistant Chief of the United Arab Command. Riad was just leaving for Damascus and Baghdad, and he was asked to explain the new pact to the Iraqis and Syrians. Nasser telephoned President Aref of Iraq, told him of the pact he had signed with Hussein, and then handed Hussein the telephone. Aref told Hussein he was delighted and would do anything he could to help.

By four o'clock, Nasser had escorted Hussein out to the airport again and, with Shukairy aboard, Hussein headed for home.

It was 3.30 p.m. when Cairo Radio made the announcement of Egypt's pact with Jordan. 'This action will astound the world. Today the world shall know that the Arabs are girded for battle as the fateful hour approaches.' It was the first most Jordanians knew of Hussein's trip to Cairo: they poured into the streets

QUEEN FOR A YEAR: Hussein was only 19 when he married Dina. They had little in common except their Hashemite blood, and their differences soon became an embarrassment. They parted in 1956, soon after the birth of their daughter, Aliya.

AGAINST ALL ADVICE: Hussein married Miss Toni Gardiner, who changed her name to Muna, in May 1961. The storm that his friends expected never broke, and his second marriage was successful.

THE FIGHT FOR SURVIVAL: Hussein survived countless attempts to overthrow him—the most serious in April 1957, when Ali Abu Nuwar (*right*), then Army Commander - in - Chief, tried to turn the army against him. But Hussein outwitted him. He later pardoned Ali and appointed him Ambassador in Paris in February 1971—soon after this picture was taken.

TARGET FOR ASSASSINS: But if, by the 1960s, Hussein's control of the army became unquestioned, he was still the target for assassins. By 1966 he travelled only in a heavily armed convoy, closely watched by his devoted bodyguard—all recruited from the small village of Shobak—in Bedouin country south of Amman.

THE FIGHT FOR POWER: With the army's defeat by Israel in June 1967, Hussein's country was cut in half, and he and his generals found themselves in growing confrontation with the resentful Palestinians. Relatives, like his uncle, Sherif Nasser (*left*) and his brother, Crown Prince Hassan (*second from right*), pressed for a showdown, but Hussein restrained them.

CONCILIATION: Yasser Arafat (*left*), leader of El Fatah, and Hussein's ministers, like Abdul Moneim Rifai (*right*), made repeated attempts to reach compromise agreements through 1969 and 1970. President Nasser—through his special envoy, Hassan Sabri el Kholy (*centre*)—pressed for an understanding between the two sides, but events moved too fast for all of them.

HIJACK TO DAWSON'S FIELD: The final explosion came with the destruction of three Western airliners by extremist commandos under the noses of Hussein's army in August 1970. The PFLP blew up a VC10—followed seconds later by a TWA Boeing and a Swissair DC8. Five days later there was civil war. The fighting lasted ten days but it was indecisive and Hussein's capital was devastated.

CAIRO AGREEMENT: President Nasser's peace initiative shortly before his death in September 1970 brought a temporary end to the fighting between Hussein and the commandos. Yasser Arafat (*left*) and Hussein signed an agreement, but it did not last.

HUSSEIN AT NUMBER 10:
Hussein met the Prime Minister, Mr Heath in December 1970—three months after the civil war in Jordan. Hussein has relied on Western aid for most of his reign. In the background is Zeid Rifai, ambassador in London—a close adviser and friend of Hussein's from childhood. He was shot and wounded in the hand a year after this picture was taken.

CRUSHING VICTORY: By July 1971 the army, under the operational control of Major-General Zeid bin Shaker (*right*), and the government under Wasfi Tell (*left*), had eliminated the commandos and restored Hussein's authority throughout Jordan. Here they are seen leading a search for illegal arms. In November 1971 Tell was shot dead by four Palestinian gunmen in Cairo as an act of revenge.

HUSSEIN THE HAM: Call-sign—"Juliet Yankee One"
Hussein: "Hallo, Gulf. Hussein on the mike."
Lee Margolis, a 20 year old radio amateur of Ilford, England: "Come in, Your Majesty. . . ."

Hussein has a whole room full of radio equipment: it is an interest he shares with Muna. During the civil war of September 1970 it was his only personal contact with the outside world.

WIFE BUT NOT QUEEN: Princess Muna, formerly Miss Toni Gardiner, wanted nothing to do with the political role of a King's wife. She has remained quietly in the background, looking after their four children and the family home.

THE ROYAL FAMILY (1970): Standing (*back row, left to right*), Princess Aliya (Hussein's daughter by Dina), Princess Ferial (Mohamed's wife), Princess Muna with Aisha, Hussein with Zein, Princess Basma (Hussein's sister), Taimur (her husband), Princess Thirwat (Hassan's wife), Prince Mohamed, Crown Prince Hassan and Rahma. Standing (*front row, left to right*), Feisal (Hussein's son, born 1963), Ghazi and Talal (Mohamed's sons), Abdullah (Hussein's eldest son, born 1962). In the centre: Queen Zein, the Queen Mother.

BIRTHDAY PARTY:
for Hussein's twin daugh-
ters, Zein (*left*) and
Aisha.

ALL THE KING'S
MEN: The key to Hus-
sein's survival has been
his hold on the loyalty
of Jordan's 60,000 strong
army. Even during the
civil war of 1970, when
much of the country re-
sponded to the calls of the
commandos, very few
soldiers deserted the King.

cheering and shouting on the West Bank and in Amman, and thousands of them assembled at the airport to greet him. They saw the pact as a spectacular display of Arab unity, and they knew that the initiative had come from Hussein. They left him in no doubt that they approved. But Jordanian officials took a pace backwards when they saw Shukairy jauntily stepping off the King's aircraft : so *that* was Nasser's price !

While the wild rejoicing went on all over Jordan, the King prepared his order of battle. He had two tank brigades of his own—the 60th, commanded by Zeid bin Shaker, his cousin, and the 40th, commanded by Colonel Raken Inad Jazy. Between them they had 176 tanks : all American Pattons, except for a detachment of British Centurions deployed around Hebron. He had six infantry brigades on the West Bank, about 20,000 men altogether. His air force consisted of 22 Hunters, fighter ground attack aircraft, but six of his front-line pilots were training in America. Six of the 26 Starfighters had arrived but as Hussein had no trained pilots, he sent the aircraft to Turkey for safety.

The reinforcements he expected were one Saudi Arabian brigade, one Iraqi division, which Aref agreed to release to him following the pact with Nasser, and two Egyptian commando battalions. The Saudis telephoned on the 1st of June to say that their brigade would be arriving that same day. The others were not expected to arrive till the 3rd or 4th of June. Iraq was to provide a squadron of aircraft to be based in Jordan, and if there was a war, the Egyptians said they expected to wipe out the Israeli air force fairly quickly. Hussein ordered his tanks to stay on the East Bank of the Jordan, with small detachments placed near the frontier at Jerusalem, Hebron and Jenin. All he could do then was sit back and pray that the reinforcements would arrive before the Israelis did.

To Israel, the sight of Hussein returning triumphant from Cairo was one of the decisive factors that prompted them to go to war.* On the 1st of June, General Dayan was made Defence

---

* A friend of the mayor of Israeli Jerusalem, Teddy Kollek telephoned him on the evening of the 30th May and told him : 'Congratulations, you will soon be mayor of a united Jerusalem'.

Minister and the final decision to strike was apparently made
on the night of the 3rd/4th June.* Israel thought it imperative
to pre-empt the reinforcements which were expected to come to
Hussein's help and their assessment of the Iraqi contribution was
that it would turn Hussein's essentially defensive stance into an
offensive one. With the Iraqis and their 150 tanks poised in
the foothills near Qalqilya, the Arabs would threaten the
narrowest part of Israel. It was crucial to Israeli strategy that
this threat should be removed. Israel could only strike at Nasser's
800 tanks in Sinai if the Jordanian front remained reasonably
quiet.

On June the 1st, General Riad arrived in Amman to take up
his post. He was a respected soldier, middle-aged, experienced.
Hussein decided at the outset that Riad was to be given full
control of Jordanian forces: it was part of his agreement with
Nasser, and besides, if there was to be a defeat, as Hussein feared,
then it was essential that his enemies should be denied the opportunity of blaming the defeat on Hussein's leadership. Riad later
came in for scathing criticism from Jordanians, but never from
Hussein, who always made out that he believed Riad did his
best in the circumstances. There is no doubt that the fact that
Hussein's army was commanded by an Egyptian greatly inhibited
those who would have liked to use its quick defeat to discredit the
Hashemite régime.

June the 1st was a Thursday: it was the day the Saudis had
said their brigade would be arriving. In fact the first of their
troops, a battalion, only began to arrive at Ma'an in Southern
Jordan on June the 6th, the following Tuesday.

On Saturday the 3rd, Hussein gave a press conference at the
Basman Palace. He told the world that Iraq had now signed the
defence pact too, and that he now expected war within 48 hours.
That afternoon, the first elements of the two Egyptian commando
battalions arrived in Amman. The remainder arrived on Sunday
the 4th, but none of them were in position on the West Bank
by the morning of the 5th. The Iraqi tanks did not begin crossing
the Jordan border until the night of the 4th/5th. But Hussein
was telephoned that night to be told that he had one unexpected
bonus: a Palestinian Liberation Army battalion were asking permission to enter Jordan. A suspicious Jordanian officer on the

* Kimche and Bawly—'The Sandstorm' p. 153.

border had told the Palestinians to wait while he checked with headquarters. Hussein gave the order that they were welcome.

On the night of the 4th, Riad, Hussein and General Khammash had a meeting. They reviewed the military situation, and agreed that the reinforcements should be in place within a few days, but that the Jordanian front was still a long and exposed one. Riad made the point that the Syrians could probably hold their front with a fraction of the troops they had available. They should be able to spare a few thousand men. Hussein had his doubts about the Syrians. He would not have welcomed them in Jordan in normal times, and they had denounced the defence pact he had signed with Nasser as a betrayal of the Arab cause, but he agreed with Riad that Jordan needed reinforcements. Riad sent a message to Damascus and asked Cairo to back the request. The Syrians did not reply immediately : it was not until June the 7th that a Syrian brigade entered Jordan, but when its commander heard that Syria was under attack, he ordered his men to return home.

Hussein says he had warned Nasser on May the 30th that airports would be the first targets of any Israeli attack. That Sunday evening before he finally left military headquarters in Amman, Hussein remembers ordering a state of maximum alert at all Jordanian airports. It was past midnight when he finally got to bed.

The major defect in Hussein's and Riad's hasty preparation for war was the almost complete lack of a plan for attack or defence. Hussein's objective was to fight a defensive action, but his infantry were strung out along the frontier in a manner that gave him little defence in depth—apart from the support provided by the bulk of his two tank brigades held in reserve—and made Jordan highly vulnerable to a concentrated enemy thrust in one or two sectors—the normal Israeli tactic. Hussein's offensive plans were limited to air attack and minor raids, which could only provoke the Israelis and present them with the initiative. The anticipated arrival of the Iraqis would greatly enhance his offensive potential. But things were to move too fast for this.

Hussein must have known very well that his own military moves and the expected reinforcements from Iraq would only make the Israelis *more* likely to go to war. And he must have known too, despite his willing transfer of command to Riad, that Egyptian control of Jordan's forces would be disastrous. By the night of June the 4th, the new Egyptian commander had had three days' experience of commanding Jordan's forces. Communications with Cairo were bad enough already: the prospect of having to co-ordinate all battle orders with the Egyptian military headquarters there was an awesome one. Hussein did not have a single Jordanian liaison officer to contact in Egypt. Besides, although he had embraced Nasser only a week before, could he *really* be trusted? All his own, and his grandfather's experience must have told Hussein that Jordan could not rely on the other Arabs for her own security. Arab unity, in military or political terms was still a myth, whatever the fine words and high aspirations of those days in June 1967. Hussein's old friend and trusted adviser, Wasfi Tell, who was never afraid to speak his mind, begged him not to involve Jordan in a war with Israel. He warned the King and everyone else that Jordan was not ready to fight.

Perhaps Hussein knew and feared all this, but he was being carried away whether he liked it or not on that wave of fatal hysteria which had beguiled the Arab world into thinking it could provoke the Israelis so far and get away with it.

Before Hussein finally fell asleep that night, Israeli fighter-bomber pilots were being gently shaken awake, and their aircraft prepared for action over Egypt before dawn.

XVII

HUSSEIN'S THREE-DAY WAR

JUNE 5–7 1967

At ten minutes to nine on the morning of June the 5th 1967, Hussein was sitting down to breakfast with Muna, when the news of the Israeli attack on Egypt was telephoned to him by one of his aides. It had been announced on Cairo Radio.

Without touching his breakfast, Hussein contacted military headquarters in Amman. Yes, it was true: Israel had gone to war, but she had not attacked Jordan, Syria or the Lebanon. Yes, all Jordan's forces were on full alert, and as many aircraft as possible were airborne to avoid being caught on the ground. General Riad had just received a coded message from the Egyptian High Command. It said that Israeli planes had attacked Egyptian air bases, but that Egypt had destroyed three-quarters of them. The Egyptian air force was hitting back at targets in Israel, and forces in Sinai had taken up the attack too. Finally, the Egyptian message, which came from Field Marshal Abdel Hakim Amer, ordered General Riad to send Jordanian forces into immediate action against Israel.

Hussein ran straight to his car: he already had his uniform on; he could get some breakfast at headquarters. Suddenly all the uncertainty of the past few days had been swept away. The time for action had come and he was going to be right in the middle of it. But the difference, this time, was that Hussein was not in control. The man in command was General Riad. When Hussein arrived at army headquarters and joined Riad in the underground control centre, he found that his forces had already been ordered into action by the Egyptian General, in accordance with the orders from Cairo. Jordanian artillery was to fire on military targets in Israel, and Jordanian forces were to seize Mount Scopus, an Israeli-held outpost in Jerusalem, and the United Nations headquarters at Government House.

Hussein raised no objection. He had already taken the decision to commit Jordan to the war, and to allow Egypt overall command : if Nasser wanted him to open a second front at this critical time, then he would do so. And if Nasser was winning, as the Egyptian message suggested, then so much the better.

Riad had also warned the Jordanian air force to prepare to strike targets in Israel, but he wanted to make it a combined attack with the Syrians. The Syrians were contacted at 9 a.m. and asked to strike jointly with Jordan's Hunters, but they replied that they had not been expecting this, and that their aircraft were out on a training flight. They asked for a delay of half an hour. By 11 a.m., two hours had passed and still the Syrians prevaricated. But the Iraqis, whose fighter-bomber squadron was based at the Jordanian airfield of H3 near the Iraqi border radioed to say they were on their way to attack Israel. Riad told Hussein he felt he had no choice but to send in the Hunters, —with or without the Syrians.

If Hussein was content to leave it to Riad, his uncle, and deputy Commander-in-Chief, Sherif Nasser was not. He argued strongly with Riad that to order Jordan into a firefight without waiting for news from the Egyptian front was a disastrous mistake. A week earlier Sherif Nasser had begged Hussein to allow him to keep Jordan out of the war for the first 12 hours, or at least to wait for news, on the *Israeli* radio news, that the Egyptians had advanced to Beersheba. But Hussein, and Riad, disregarded his advice, and Sherif Nasser says he spent the rest of the war a helpless spectator.

On the Israeli side of the border, the commander was General Uzi Narkiss. He had been given strict instructions by General Dayan that the Jordanian front was to be contained, but that no attack was to be made on Jordan. The hope was that Hussein would leave Israel to fight Nasser, as he had done in 1956. Narkiss had sent many of his best troops to the Sinai front, and had placed his remaining men mainly in defensive positions. The first shelling of the Israeli sector of Jerusalem began at breakfast time on the 5th, and Narkiss assumed that the Jordanians were merely showing their solidarity with President Nasser, and that they would not mount a serious attack. But the firing did not stop and Amman Radio was saying 'The hour for revenge has come'. Israel's Prime Minister Eshkol sent a message to Hussein through the United Nations Commander in Jerusalem, General Odd

Bull. It said: 'We shall not initiate any action whatsoever against Jordan. However should Jordan open hostilities, we shall resist with all our might, and King Hussein will have to bear the consequences.'

Hussein confirms that he received this message at 11 a.m. and that he sent back this answer to General Odd Bull:

'They started the battle, and now they are receiving our reply by air.'

Between 11.30 and 12.40, Jordanian aircraft bombed the suburbs of Netanya, and Tel Aviv, and destroyed an Israeli transport plane on the ground at the airfield of Kefar Sirkin. Hussein's 155 millimetre, 'Long Tom', guns had opened up on positions well inside Israel: they had the range to reach the Mediterranean coastline.

Again and again, Narkiss asked permission to attack. It was refused at 11.30, again at 11.50 and again at 12.10. It was not until 12.30 that the Israeli air force was ordered to destroy Jordan's airfields at Amman and Mafraq, and to attack the Iraqis at H3. And at 2.30 p.m., after the Jordanians had captured Government House in Jerusalem, Narkiss was finally given the order to counter-attack.

Hussein, by this time warming to the battle, had commandeered an army jeep, and was visiting all his command posts. He spent some time, in mid-morning, at his air force headquarters studying radar reports which suggested that Israel had many more aircraft airborne than she should have. If the Egyptian report was correct, and three-quarters of them had been destroyed, what were all those 'blips' over Israel, and why were his pilots reporting so many sightings of what looked like *British* aircraft? Of course his radar could be picking up Egyptian aircraft over Israel, but it appeared that the aircraft were flying in from aircraft carriers, not far off the Israeli coast, and landing at Israeli airfields. Many of the aircraft his pilots and soldiers reported seeing were, so they said, Hunters, just like Jordan's. They could only be British.

At noon, the British, American, and French ambassadors were summoned urgently to police headquarters in Amman. They were kept waiting in a room for some minutes, and then Hussein burst through the door, white-faced, trembling with anger and waving a piece of paper at them.

'Look at this,' he said. 'This is what our radar picked up : we have detected aircraft taking off from aircraft carriers only a few miles off the Israeli coast. They flew in from there, and landed at the Israeli airfield of Megiddo.'

Hussein then told the British ambassador about the sightings of British aircraft. The King believed at that moment that it was 1956 over again, and that this time the Americans had joined the British. Both ambassadors did their best but, for the moment, Hussein was convinced of a Western plot and made no secret of his fury.

At 12.30 p.m. Hussein received his first call from Nasser. Nasser said the Egyptian air force had answered the Israeli air attack on Egypt by bombing Israel, and that his forces were now beginning a major attack on the Negev desert in Israel. He did not mention that some six hours earlier, over 300 of his aircraft had been destroyed by the Israeli air attack, and that he had no effective air force left. He was lying, and Hussein had no way of finding out the truth.

But by now it would have been too late anyway. Between 12.30 and 2.30 p.m. the Israeli air force systematically destroyed Jordan's air force and the Iraqi squadron at H3. Because they had waited two hours for the Syrians before attacking, the Jordanians had lost the chance of doing any real damage to Israel. Besides, Hussein himself admits that Jordanian intelligence was poor, and that this greatly reduced the effectiveness of their missions. Most of their aircraft were destroyed on the ground during refuelling stops and one was destroyed while trying to take off. By early afternoon, the Israelis reckoned they had knocked out 21 of Hussein's 22 Hunters. They had in fact destroyed all of them.

But the worst destruction of all occurred on the West Bank. Hussein's two tank brigades, the pride of his army, deprived of all air cover, poorly trained in the vital art of administration and logistics and hopelessly confused by their orders from Amman, were shattered in 48 hours. But they resisted bravely, and with great resourcefulness; what beat them was not Israel's armour but the merciless pounding of the Israeli air force.

The confusion started before lunch. It was before the Israelis mounted their counter-attack in Jerusalem and began to attack from the north at Jenin. Hussein's intention had been that Colonel

Jazy's 40th Brigade of 88 tanks should hold the north, while Zeid bin Shaker's 60th Brigade should hold the south. Jazy was based on the Damiya Bridge, with only 28 tanks forward near the frontier with Israel : they were placed on the heights around Jenin. This squadron guarded the natural approach for an Israeli attack from Afula and Megiddo, while the bulk of the brigade was in reserve in case the Israelis swept straight down the Jordan. The infantry was strung out fairly sparsely along the whole line of the frontier, and could do little anyway against tanks and aircraft. Zeid bin Shaker was based on Jericho, with only a detachment at Hebron and a few tanks in forward positions near Jerusalem and Ramallah. The posture was defensive, with a strong mobile reserve. The hope was that the Iraqis would soon begin crossing to the West Bank, to strengthen the front line.

This strategy was overturned just before one o'clock when Riad ordered Zeid bin Shaker's brigade to move immediately to Hebron, in order to be ready to advance on the Israeli town of Beersheba from the north as the Egyptians moved up on it from the Negev in the south. No one in Amman yet knew that the Egyptians were in headlong retreat more than 50 miles west of Beersheba. Jazy was to leave his one squadron at Jenin, and take the rest to Jericho to relieve bin Shaker. Riad hoped the exposed north flank would then soon be filled up by the Syrians. The Syrian air force had already indicated Syria's intention to fight by attacking Haifa a few minutes earlier. Again, Hussein raised no objection.

As this awkward movement began, leaving only the 28 tanks at Jenin in defensive positions, the Israelis launched their attacks on Jerusalem, at about 2.30 p.m. and on Jenin at two o'clock. At the same time, their aircraft, having completed the destruction of the Egyptian and Jordanian air forces, now turned on the Jordanian armour. As the afternoon turned to evening, Jazy's tanks drew into Jericho, and bin Shaker's moved up towards Hebron past Jerusalem, and all the time the Israeli air force pounded them. Even so, the movement was completed by evening, only to be *countermanded* by Riad that night.

The battle for Jenin, which had started soon after lunch, had gone on all afternoon without a sign of Syrian air or ground support. The squadron of Jordanian tanks held out successfully, split into three groups, and initially forced the Israelis to retire, but by evening the combined pressure from the air and from a whole Israeli tank brigade, under Brigadier Elazar, to their front and flanks, had made their position impossible. Riad made another appeal to the Syrians, without success, and Jazy drove up from Jericho to Jenin to see just how bad the situation was. Jazy was one of Hussein's best commanders : he quickly saw that if Riad did not reinforce Jenin, the West Bank would fall to Israel.

By 9 p.m. Riad had despaired of Syrian or Egyptian help for the beleaguered defenders of Jenin. He completely revised his earlier orders to the two tank commanders. He ordered 40 Brigade to move everything they could back to the north to reinforce Jenin. It took Jazy's tanks just $4\frac{1}{2}$ hours, driving through the night, and by 2 a.m. they were in position. Jazy posted most of them at the strategic crossroads called Muthallath Al Shuhada, just south of Jenin. He told one tank regiment to make for Nablus and press on to the west on the road to Tulkarm, to protect his rear. The gap had been stopped—for a few hours.

At Jerusalem, however, the Israelis were pressing forward : in the early afternoon of the 5th, they captured Government House from the Jordanians, and an Israeli armoured brigade moved round the north side of the city to relieve the besieged Israeli garrison at Mount Scopus. Israeli paratroopers, hurriedly recalled from the Sinai front, were thrown in at 2 a.m. on Tuesday the 6th, and by morning they had captured the northern part of the Arab city. The old walled city still held out. Hussein's 60th tank brigade, diverted to Hebron, then recalled to its original position when 40 Brigade was switched to the north again, struggled to hold the Jerusalem-Jericho road, mainly against air attack. One reliable independent observer told the author that 60 Brigade's misery was compounded by the fact that a large number of its tanks had run out of fuel on the road between Jericho and Hebron. Jordanian tank commanders were better at fighting than most, but had a Bedouin disdain for the duller business of maintenance. It was a facet of their training that had been sadly neglected, and one of the reasons why some experienced Jordanians felt their army was not ready for war.*

---

* The Brigade commander, Zeid bin Shaker strongly denies that any of his tanks ran out of fuel : he says only three of his tanks had to be abandoned intact when they ran into some bad ground trying to take a short cut.

Hussein never rested for a moment. He kept in constant touch with the battle from one command post or another in Amman, and that evening (the 5th), he drove out to Mafraq to visit his pilots. Fourteen of them were left. He told them to go to H3, and fight on from there in Iraqi Hunters. They were driven off in a bus, and for the next two days fought on against the Israelis, who attacked the airfield a number of times. The Jordanians say they shot down another 9 Israeli aircraft.

Hussein saw a lot of Shukairy that first day: he came into the operations room at military headquarters in Amman and remained there all through the afternoon—apparently full of confidence. But from the Tuesday morning onwards, Hussein saw nothing of him, as he had gone off to Damascus.*

That Monday night, Hussein had no time for sleep, and only time for a quick telephone call to Muna. She said everything was fine, and that he was not to worry. Abdullah and Feisal had been excitedly watching the Israeli air attacks from the terrace at Hummar.

At 4.50 a.m. on the morning of Tuesday the 6th of June, Nasser spoke to Hussein by radio-telephone. The conversation was monitored by the Israelis, and later published by them. Communications between Amman and Cairo were poor, but it was clear that they were discussing the idea of accusing the British and Americans of intervening. This is what the Israelis recorded, and the accuracy of it is confirmed by Hussein:

NASSER: 'Shall we say the US and England, or just the US?'
HUSSEIN: 'The US and England.'
NASSER: 'Does Britain have aircraft carriers?'
(Hussein's answer was indistinct, but presumably he reminded Nasser that Britain, too, had aircraft carriers, and a Royal Air Force base in Cyprus).
NASSER: 'Good. King Hussein will announce it, and I will announce it.'
HUSSEIN: 'Thank you.'
NASSER: 'Do not give up.'
HUSSEIN: 'Hello. . . . Hello, brother. Do not worry. Be strong.'

* Vance and Lauer. *Hussein: My War with Israel*, p. 104.

NASSER : 'Yes, I can hear you.'

HUSSEIN : 'Mr President, if you have something . . . or any idea at all . . . at any time. . . .'

NASSER : 'We are fighting with all our strength, and we have battles going on every front all night, and if we had problems at the beginning, it does not matter : we will overcome despite this. God is with us. Will His Majesty make an announcement on the participation of the Americans and the British?'

HUSSEIN : (Not clear).

NASSER : 'In God's name, I say that I will make an announcement and you will make an announcement and we will see to it that the Syrians make an announcement that American and British aircraft are attacking us from their aircraft carriers. We will issue an announcement; we will stress the matter, and we will drive the point home.'

HUSSEIN : 'Good. All right.'

NASSER : 'Your Majesty, do you agree?'

HUSSEIN : (Not clear).

NASSER : 'A thousand thanks. Do not give up. We are with you with all our hearts, and we are flying our planes over Israel today. Our planes have been striking at Israeli airports since the early morning.'

HUSSEIN : 'A thousand thanks. Stay well.'

Hussein still did not know what had really happened in Sinai. More than ever he thought it urgent to hold Jenin and Jerusalem, and to get the Iraqis to the front as soon as possible.

But at 6 a.m., before the Iraqis had begun crossing the Jordan, Jenin fell. The survivors of the 28 tanks, which had held the area since the day before, fell back to the Muthallath crossroads and merged with Jazy's reinforcements. There, at breakfast time, a major battle was fought. The Israelis thrust down the road from Jenin, and up from Tulkarm to crush them from both sides. Jazy claimed 27 Israeli tanks for the loss of only four of his own. But the pressure was too great. The Jordanians were outnumbered, and under pressure from the air as well, they fell back slowly towards Tubas. The Israelis tried to move in from the east, but a detachment of Jazy's force held them off 3 miles east of Zababida. By noon, it was clear that 40 Brigade could not hold on much longer.

In the south, the walled city of Jerusalem was still in Jordanian hands, but was nearly surrounded. The Israeli air force were picking off bin Shaker's tanks one by one. 60 Brigade's impossible position was made even more difficult by an order to withdraw to the East Bank of the Jordan which later was *countermanded* : bin Shaker was told to hold on at all costs.

Again, throughout Tuesday, the uncertainty about what was happening on other Arab fronts deepened the despair of Hussien's field commanders, who were being slowly, relentlessly driven back. Jazy heard a Damascus radio broadcast that day claiming that the Syrians had captured Nazareth in the north of Israel and yet there was still no sign of Syrian help for the Jordanian infantry and armour, and no relaxation in the momentum of the Israeli advance. Jordanian communications became increasingly confused, as a large number of jeep drivers failed to recharge their radio batteries overnight, and some of Jazy's tanks now ran out of fuel too.

On the East Bank the Iraqis were being attacked from the air. Hussein was greatly impressed and moved by their courage in fighting their way—against air attack all the time—down to the Jordan valley. But only a handful of vehicles actually crossed the river. All that reached Zeid bin Shaker, before his final retreat, were four Iraqi Armoured Personnel Carriers, and four anti-aircraft guns.

In Amman, it was a day of growing despair for Hussein. Early in the morning, Riad told him that they must ask for a cease-fire immediately or withdraw what was left of their forces as fast as they could to the East Bank. Hussein still clung to the hope that together, Jordan and Egypt could do something, and he assumed, after his talk with Nasser, that all was not lost on the Egyptian front. He told Riad to consult Nasser, before they decided what to do.

Riad cabled Cairo, telling the High Command that Jordan's position was desperate, and suggesting three alternatives : they could ask for a cease-fire, withdraw from the West Bank under cover of darkness that night, or fight on another day and night— till Wednesday. But Riad pointed out that if they did fight on, Jordan's army would be destroyed.

No answer came from Cairo. At 12.30, Hussein sent a message to Nasser, begging him for an urgent reply to Riad's earlier message, as his forces were suffering heavy casualties. Within minutes came a reply to Riad's message. It was from Egypt's Commander-in-Chief, Field Marshal Abdel Hakim Amer. It agreed to an immediate retreat from the West Bank, and suggested arming the civil population for a war of resistance.

But then Hussein took an extraordinary decision. He said he would not order a retreat—not just yet. He told Cairo his men would stay on the West Bank as long as they could. He was determined not to be defeated. He was also determined to retain as much ground as possible in case the Israelis agreed to a cease-fire. He sent out personal orders that his men should fight on. Hussein's emotional, impulsive nature now asserted itself in strong contrast to Riad's cold professionalism. Riad, in spite of the total collapse of his strategy, remained calm and tried to impress on the King the need to recognise the hopelessness of the situation and save what men and equipment he could. Hussein, with typical courage, but with no rational ground for hope, refused for the moment to give up. He longed to fight himself: the atmosphere of the operations room at headquarters was stifling him, driving him to despair. On the afternoon of June the 6th, and again on the 7th, he drove down to the Jordan valley. The air of battle, the suffering of his defeated army, and their pleas to him to continue the battle revived him. He was never so happy and confident as when he was moving among his men, encouraging them, sharing their fears and trying to meet their needs. It was this that had held them to him through fifteen tempestuous years.

Those who met him in the Jordan valley, during his three-day war with Israel, remember his anger more than anything else: his anger at the destruction of so fine an army, and at the treachery and weakness of his fellow-Arab governments who had failed to come to Jordan's aid, or deceived him into thinking they would.* He was unshaven, exhausted, deeply unhappy, growingly aware of the catastrophe for which he himself had been largely responsible. In the valley he saw Jazy, and warmly commended him for the way he and his men had fought. And he received a message from the hard-pressed bin Shaker urging him not to order a retreat. At one moment, two Israeli jets swooped down in an attack on the group of men and vehicles as they stood

---

* Always, when referring to June 1967, he excepts Iraq from his strictures. He says they came 'nobly, and readily' to Jordan's aid.

by Jazy's headquarters at the Damiya Bridge. Jazy leapt on Hussein, and pushed him into a trench. 'We've lost the battle,' shouted Jazy, 'but we don't want to lose you too!'

At 11 p.m. on Tuesday the 6th, the United Nations ordered a ceasefire: it was to be immediate and unconditional. The position on the West Bank was still not one of total defeat. The old city of Jerusalem was in Jordanian hands, and Jazy's men had withdrawn to Tubas. But resistance was continuing and Hussein judged it important to hold what he could until the ceasefire was effective. He discovered that Riad had ordered a retreat by all forces under cover of darkness, to the East Bank, and immediately told Riad to reverse his order. This led to more confusion: as the night went on, Jordanian troops tried desperately to counter-attack, and in Jerusalem, and around Nablus, the fighting went on until early the following morning. But by midday the following day, Jazy was forced back to the Damiya Bridge with 8 of his 88 tanks intact, and Zeid bin Shaker managed to get 40 of his tanks away from the area of Jerusalem and Jericho. One hundred and twenty-eight had been lost, and Jordan's total losses had been 6,094 dead and missing.* Late on Wednesday night, Jordan formally accepted the ceasefire: but Hussein was left with none of the West Bank. He had been totally defeated.

It was late on the Tuesday night, in an exchange of messages, that Hussein learnt the full extent of Nasser's own defeat for the first time.†

'My dear Brother King Hussein,' Nasser wrote. 'We find ourselves face to face with one of those critical moments that nations are sometimes called upon to endure. It demands courage beyond human capacity. We are fully aware of your difficult situation as at this moment our front is crumbling too.

---

* Jordan government figure. Other estimates put it much lower—at a few hundred. Many of Hussein's tank losses were due not just to their commanders' negligence referred to on page 186, but to poor refuelling facilities and the lack of recovery vehicles, which resulted in a large number of tanks having to be abandoned, some of them intact.

† Hussein later discovered from the Syrians and the Algerians that Nasser had informed *them* of the destruction of his air force on Monday the 5th of June. Hussein never brought himself to ask Nasser why he had deceived him for more than 36 hours.

'Yesterday our enemy's air force inflicted a mortal blow on us. Since then our land army has been stripped of all air support and forced to withstand the power of superior forces.

'When the history books are written, your courage and tenacity will be remembered. They will not forget the heroic Jordanian people who went straight into battle without hesitation, and with no consideration other than honour and duty.

'I think that our only chance now is to evacuate the West Bank of the Jordan tonight, and hope that the Security Council will order a ceasefire.

'The history of nations is full of reverses, victories and defeats. We must hope that the choice we are making now—even though it seems bitter—will actually be our first step forward. It is God's will and maybe something good will come of it.

'Finally, I want to tell you how much I appreciate your heroic behaviour, your strong and gallant will, and the bravery shown by the Jordanian people and their army.

'Peace be with you, and may God bless you.'

It was to this message from Nasser that Hussein again replied that he was *not* ordering a retreat. He had reversed Riad's order to withdraw after hearing that the United Nations had asked for a ceasefire. Twice during the fighting, Hussein refused to accept the necessity of withdrawal and once actually changed Riad's order to retreat into a command to hold on. His commanders were bewildered by the confusion of different orders they were receiving from Amman, which were irrelevant anyway in the face of the crushing momentum of the Israeli advance, and the inevitability of retreat.

Hussein's defeat between June the 5th and 7th is one of the saddest, and yet most characteristic episodes of his career. If he had stayed out of the fighting, just for a day or two, he would have saved the West Bank; but for Hussein such a course of action was unthinkable.* If he had accepted the disaster for what it was, a day—or even a few hours earlier, he might have salvaged

---

* According to Hussein's chief of staff, General Khammash, Hussein had no choice anyway. Contrary to the generally accepted view that Jordan began the fighting on Israel's eastern front, Khammash says he clearly recalls an early message from Jerusalem on June the 5th informing Jordanian headquarters that the *Israelis* had opened the firing.

something from the wreck of his army; but that too would have been unlike him. Given the power of Israel, the political circumstances in Jordan and the Arab world in the first half of 1967, and given, too, Hussein's own deep sense of honour, his courage and his lack of cold, prudent reason in a crisis, his involvement in the war was unavoidable, and his state of mind througout it understandable.

But, judged in cold military terms, his acceptance of Riad's _conduct_ of the war was deplorable. After making the essentially wise decision to take a defensive stance, Riad proceeded to _attack_. And instead of pressing a concentrated armoured attack that might have made some impact on Israel, he threw in a handful of infantry and, after a long delay, Hussein's tiny air force. His juggling of the armoured brigades in the Jordan valley, in full daylight, and without air cover, almost surpasses belief. And, finally, the confusion of the series of orders and counter-orders on withdrawal and cease-fire only made the misery of defeat more complete.

G

XVIII

PALESTINIANS AGAINST ISRAEL
OR HUSSEIN?

1967–1969

Hussein's anguish was terrible for his friends and advisers to behold. His spirit was broken,* he was constantly close to tears: the reality of what his country had lost was coming home to him. Jerusalem was captured: the old city had fallen quickly on the morning of the 7th, once Jordanian resistance in the rest of the city had collapsed. The Dome of the Rock, one of the sacred shrines of Islam, was lost to the Jews. Populous Arab towns like Bethlehem, Hebron, Ramallah and Nablus were now under Israeli occupation. Hussein asked himself whether he could not have fought a bit harder for them; whether he should have ordered every young Jordanian able to carry a weapon to cross the river and fight on. It would have been a hopeless and wasteful fight in the face of Israeli air power, and he soon convinced himself that there had been no alternative to defeat. He was consoled by immediate expressions of sympathy for his predicament, and admiration for the way his men had fought.† Nevertheless, his sense of shame and despair was complete.

He struggled to stop his deep voice faltering as he spoke over Amman Radio:

'We have fought with heroism and honour. One day the Arabs will recognise the role Jordan played in this war. Our soldiers have defended every inch of our earth with their precious blood. It is not yet dry, but our country honours the stain. They were not afraid in the face of the total superiority of the enemy's air

---

* General Khammash says Hussein had not slept for three nights and had consumed only tea and an endless chain of cigarettes.

† There were some exceptions: Major General Ahmed Selim, the West Bank commander, was said to have neglected his duties, and there were reports that the tank detachment at Hebron deserted.

power which surprised and destroyed the Egyptian air force, on which we were relying.

'What is done is done. My heart breaks when I think of the loss of all our fallen soldiers. They were dearer to me than my own self.

'My brothers, I seem to belong to a family which, according to the will of Allah, must suffer and make sacrifices for its country without end. Our calamity is greater than anyone could have imagined. But whatever its size, we must not let it weaken our resolve to regain what we have lost.

'If in the end you were not rewarded with glory, it was not because you were without courage, but because it was the will of God.

'May God now be with our people.'

If there was an abundance of sympathy for Hussein's distress from the world outside, and even from Israel, there were many who saw him as a pathetic figure, bewailing the misfortune that he had only brought on himself by his own rash misjudgement of the military balance and his refusal to contemplate accepting Israel's offer of non-involvement. For a few weeks he also suffered the indignation of the British and American public for his reluctance to abandon his charge that the West had provided air support for Israel.

A number of Jordanians, notably Wasfi Tell, and several senior army officers, singled out General Riad as the prime cause of their defeat, saying that he should have known better than to have accepted Cairo's account of the battle, and that, if he had left Jordan to manage her own defence, the result might have been very different. But Hussein assured Riad, when he left Jordan a few days later, that he did not feel it was his fault: he believed, like Riad, that the main cause of Jordan's defeat was the failure of the other Arabs, particularly the Syrians, to come to Jordan's help. Riad later became Egypt's Chief of Staff, and was killed by an Israeli shell on the Suez Canal in March 1969.

However deeply Hussein despised Nasser for his part in the war, and in particular for his misrepresentation of the real situation in Sinai for the first 36 hours, he never made an issue of it. Hussein met Nasser frequently over the next three years, but never charged him with treachery. Many Jordanians close to Hussein continued to talk indignantly of the 'betrayal' of Jordan by Nasser, but Hussein valued what political support he could get from Nasser too much to remind him of the past.*

The collapse of Jordan on June the 7th 1967 left Hussein with three major problems. They were as intractable as any he had had to face in the fifteen years of his reign. The first of them was the reconstruction of Jordan; her economy was shattered, her Palestinian population again unsettled, and her armour and air force largely destroyed. The second was the problem of the Israelis, who were occupying part of his territory, and demanding peace negotiations with the Arabs. And the third, and by far the most serious for him over the next few years, was the growth of Palestinian feeling first against Israel, and then against himself, which was to plunge his country into civil war. To each of these problems he applied himself with energy and ingenuity, and if, at the time of writing, he still has not fully solved any of them, the fact that he has survived them and has not been overwhelmed by them, is a remarkable tribute to his political stamina.

The most immediate problem was money. The upheaval of the war with Israel and the distortion of the map of the Middle East naturally caused the West and the Soviet Union to undertake a comprehensive reassessment of their relations with the Arabs and Israel. Hussein's worry was that the Western reassessment, particularly in America, might result in an end to American aid for Jordan. He had failed to get an immediate response from Britain and America to his request for more arms to replace his losses, and he had his doubts about financial aid too. But he was kept solvent by the decision, on the 1st of September 1967, of the richer Arab states—Kuwait, Libya, and Saudi Arabia—to provide £135 million pounds annually to the defeated countries, 'until the effects of the aggression are eliminated'. Jordan's share was to be £40 million. He was also assisted by the continuing flow of funds from Palestinians abroad, in states like Kuwait, Abu Dhabi and Libya, to their relatives in Jordan, many of whom took up residence in camps or in the towns in East Jordan after the war of June '67. His phosphate industry was unaffected; over a million tons were exported in 1967, and 1,150,000 tons in 1968. The value of Jordan's mineral output continued to rise

* See footnote to page 191.

steadily, as it was all on the East Bank. But farm output was cut substantially with the loss of the West Bank, and, with the growth of guerrilla activity and Israeli reprisals in the fertile Jordan valley, output dropped even further from 1968 onwards. In the summer of 1969, Jordan's East Ghor Canal was effectively put out of action by Israeli bombing.

The most damaging single economic effect was to the tourist industry. The increasing number of tourists who had been drawn to Jordan as the Holy Land, now went to Israel instead, and Jordan was left only with the attractions of Petra and Jerash. The Jordanians believe that if they had not lost the West Bank, their gross income attributable to tourism which was about £20 million in 1966, would have trebled by 1971,

The defeat of 1967 reduced Jordan's gross earnings by about a third. However, until the autumn of 1970, Hussein was able to balance his budget on the Arab subsidy and on Western aid, which continued again, after a short pause, in reduced quantities.

Arms were obtained from the British and Americans only after Hussein had applied considerable diplomatic pressure by threatening to buy from the Russians instead. In October 1967, Hussein visited Moscow, and when he reached London the following month, he said Jordan was seeking arms 'from any source'. Britain agreed to replace the Hunters destroyed in the war and Hussein was fortunate in finding Britain with a large number of Centurion tanks available after the conversion of her Rhine Army to Chieftains between 1967 and 1970. But the Americans were less enthusiastic and it was only Hussein's overtures to Moscow that decided them. At one stage he had virtually tied up a deal with Moscow for 130 millimetre guns, anti-aircraft guns and tanks, and was expecting a Soviet military mission to arrive in Amman within hours, when the Americans came through with an equivalent offer. Hussein readily accepted Western aid in preference to the aid he was offered by the Russians, and by 1970 he had rebuilt, and even increased the strength of Jordan's forces: he had 310 Patton and Centurion tanks, 20 Hawker Hunter and 18 Starfighter aircraft, and was installing a British 'Tigercat' missile defence system. But much of this new equipment did not arrive till 1969: the Americans did not even agree to start resupplying Jordan until the beginning of 1968: For the first year or two after the war, Jordan was virtually defenceless.

Hussein's second task was to try to win back from Israel what he had lost. He had come to recognise the need for an accommodation with Israel soon after he became King, and although he had felt unable to negotiate, there had been a tacit understanding between Israel and Jordan that the frontier should remain undisturbed. The calm was upset only when the guerrillas struck across the border, against the will of Hussein, in the mid-1950s and again from 1965 to 1967, when Hussein allowed himself, at the last moment, to abandon his previous policy. Immediately the war of 1967 was over, Hussein reverted to his well-founded conviction that the solution to the problem of Israel was not war but some form of acceptance. He immediately began urging a peace settlement with Israel that would restore all the Arab land lost in the fighting of 1967, and, in his own words, secure 'peace with justice'. He proposed a summit conference, and it was clear that Hussein was ready to go as far as the other Arabs to make sense of his relationship with Israel. But he was not prepared to take the risk on his own: he did not take up the Israeli offer of direct negotiations. Although it might well have won him back the West Bank, he judged that the political risk was too high, and the Palestinian militants, who were implacably opposed to any kind of settlement, were fast becoming the dominant political force in the Middle East.

The first Arab summit was at Khartoum, between the 29th of August and the 1st of September 1967. Hussein had already spoken to Nasser and was satisfied that he, too, was in favour of regaining his lost land by diplomatic means. The summit was boycotted by the Syrians and the Algerians, which was bad for Arab unity but hopeful for Hussein's moderate line. The important paragraph of the communiqué was this one:

'The Arab Heads of State have agreed to unite their political efforts at the international and diplomatic level to eliminate the effects of the aggression and to ensure withdrawal of the aggressive Israeli forces from the Arab lands which have been occupied since June the 5th. This will be done within the framework of the main principles by which the Arab states abide, namely, no peace with Israel, no recognition of Israel, no negotiations with it, and insistence on the rights of the Palestinian people in their own country.'

The world's immediate reaction was that the Arabs were taking

a hard line, but Hussein and Nasser both believed that this conference gave them limited scope for exploring the possibilities of a
peaceful settlement. Apparently, the *last* sentence of this central
paragraph was added mainly at the insistence of Shukairy, who
was there representing the PLO : Nasser and Hussein regarded
the *opening* sentence as the important one. This interpretation
was not the Israeli's, and it was regarded with some cynicism by
Britain's Prime Minister, Mr Wilson, when he asked Hussein
soon after Khartoum just how you could have a settlement of
any kind after saying 'No' three times. Hussein explained, with
some difficulty, that it was partly a problem of translation and
interpretation : 'No *diplomatic* recognition.' And the word used
for 'peace' meant much more than the English word for peace :
the word was 'solh' in Arabic in the communiqué, and this meant
'reconciliation', 'making up' : it was a much bigger word than
the word they did *not* use, 'salaam', which meant 'peace' as
opposed to 'war'. So Hussein explained, when we say 'No peace
with Israel' we mean something rather different from what you
might think.

'Oh, I see,' said Mr Wilson, taking his pipe out of his mouth,
'You mean : "No kissing".'

Hussein could not conceal that he regretted the intrusion of the
three 'No's' into the communiqué and made it his task to convince the West that they were not intended to be taken too
seriously. He was gratified at the success, in November 1967, of
the British-sponsored Security Council Resolution, which called
for Israeli withdrawal in return for Arab 'respect for and acknowledgement of' Israel's sovereignty, territorial integrity, political independence and 'right to live in peace within secure and
recognised boundaries free from threats and acts of force'. The
resolution, number 242, was accepted by Jordan, Lebanon and
Egypt, and rejected by Syria. Israel accepted the resolution as
a basis for negotiation.

From then on, however, in spite of the exertions of the United
Nations mediator Gunnar Jarring, little progress was made in
the drive for a settlement. The Israelis said they would only withdraw to 'secure and recognised' boundaries, but they would not
say where they proposed these should be until they could negotiate precise peace conditions with the Arabs. But the Arabs refused
to negotiate, except through the United Nations, and insisted

there was no point in going further until the Israelis promised they would withdraw all the way. And while the peace moves remained in deadlock, the Israelis quietly proceeded with public works programmes in the occupied territories on the assumption that it would be a long time before they restored them to the Arabs, if they ever did. And they complicated their bargaining position with Hussein by absorbing the Arab city of Jerusalem into the Jewish municipality, and making it clear that they would never allow the city to become divided again by returning any part of it to Hussein.

Over the next few years, the future of the West Bank became the subject of heated discussion on both sides of the cease-fire line, but nothing was decided in the absence of a peace settlement. And the line itself—along the Jordan river—slowly settled down to the status of an accepted, though unrecognised frontier. Neither Hussein nor the Israelis showed any inclination to alter it by force, and the Palestinians were unable to. The Israelis were fully occupied on the Suez Canal, and Hussein was more concerned with the defence of his frontiers against Iraq and Syria than against Israel.

However, Hussein's desire for a territorial settlement with Israel remained strong despite the pressure from the Palestinians and the diplomatic impasse. There were persistent reports of secret dealings between Hussein and the Israeli government, and of secret meetings between him and Israeli leaders. He was rumoured to have met Mr Abba Eban, the Israeli Foreign Minister, in London on a number of occasions: they both used to stay in the Dorchester Hotel, and it was suggested they deliberately allowed their visits to coincide in order to meet privately in one of their rooms. The Palestinians published a letter, which they claimed was sent by Talhouni, Hussein's Prime Minister, to the Jordanian ambassador in Rome in October 1967, asking him to suppress Italian press stories about a secret meeting between Hussein and the Israeli Prime Minister, Mr Eshkol.

Reports of a series of meetings between Hussein and the Israeli Deputy Prime Minister, Mr Allon—one of them in the Negev desert in November 1970*—were strongly denied by Hussein, but

* Two other meetings—the author has been told on very high Israeli authority—took place on an island just off the tip of the Israeli occupied Sinai peninsula. Altogether there are authoritative accounts of seven meetings between King Hussein and/or Zeid Rifai and Israeli ministers.

were treated by the Israelis in a way that convinced a number of observers in Jerusalem that the meetings had in fact taken place. The matter was raised by a member of the Israeli parliament, but the government ordered that it be struck from the record. A number of journalists' despatches, some of which asserted that they had reliable confirmation of the meetings from official Israeli sources, were heavily censored by the Israeli authorities. Colourful stories began to leak out of how the King and Allon, wearing dark glasses, met in an air-conditioned car, deep in the desert.

The truth about Hussein and Israel still remains shrouded behind a network of rumours and counter-rumours, and the sense of mystery is deliberately encouraged by the Israelis, who are reluctant to issue outright denials each time the pattern of rumours unfolds. The author raised the matter in a conversation with Mrs Golda Meir, the Israeli Prime Minister, in the spring of 1971 in her office in Jerusalem. I asked her if she had visited Amman again since her talks with Abdullah in 1948.* She replied that she had no intention of commenting. In spite of close questioning on all the rumours of conversatons between Hussein and Israeli leaders, Mrs Meir would not be drawn to say anything beyond 'No comment'. She would certainly not deny them. When I suggested that we might go on to discuss the matter 'off the record', she replied that there was no point in doing that, as she would still only be able to give non-committal replies.

The evidence from Israeli, and certainly from Palestinian sources cannot be taken as conclusive. The Israelis have their own reasons for fostering the impression that they *are* talking to leading Arabs, whether they are or not, and they have an equal interest in not going too far to embarrass or endanger the Arabs with whom they are rumoured to be holding conversations. More important is the observation of those who have been close to Hussein over the years and *none* of them has confided to the author any concrete evidence that any meetings took place. Opinions are divided : there are those who believe, instinctively, that there has been direct communication between him and the Israelis, and that this has become clear from Hussein's manner when this topic is raised in private discussion; there are others who believe that it would be suicidal for Hussein even to attempt

* See pp. 28–9.

such meetings, since one or more of his associates would *have* to be involved, and betrayal would always be possible. Hussein, it is suggested, would hardly have forgotten the lesson of Abdullah Tell, Abdullah's trusted go-between, and anyhow, would the gain of such meetings have outweighed the risk of discovery?

It is unlikely that the truth will be known in Hussein's lifetime. And, although there is a fascination in pursuing the truth, it is, to a degree, immaterial whether or not Hussein has held *direct* conversations with the Israelis. He has ample means of communicating with them indirectly, through contacts on the West Bank* and through diplomatic channels friendly to both. Any contacts he has had—direct or indirect—have had one central objective: to regain the land he lost in the war of 1967. And although it can be argued, as the Palestinians do, that Hussein's purpose has been to enlist the help of the Israelis against those Arabs who want to destroy his dynasty, it is the author's judgement that, with one possible and understandable exception†, this is a product of the fertile imagination of Hussein's opponents who have been unwilling to accept that Hussein's strength came essentially from his own resources. Besides, Hussein's record of *effective* military and diplomatic resistance to Israeli expansion is at least as good as that of any other Arab statesman or guerrilla leader. Indeed, if Hussein's own realism and determination not to provoke Israel had been the policy of the Arab world, the Arabs would not have suffered the defeat of 1967.

Hussein's third task, after the June war of 1967, was to reconcile his moderate approach to Israel with the aspirations of his Palestinian population. It proved impossible, and over the next four years relations between Hussein and the Palestinian com-

* One example, disclosed publicly in *The Times* of February the 11th 1972, was the series of discussions between Israeli politicians and the former Jordanian Defence Minister Anwar Nusseibeh, in Jerusalem. Mr Nusseibeh, a frequent visitor to Amman, denies that the talks made him an intermediary between Mrs Meir and King Hussein. The author put it to Nusseibeh, in a conversation in March 1972, that he *had* been negotiating for Hussein, and he replied—rather unconvincingly—that, on the contrary, all he had been doing was emphasizing to Mrs Meir the importance of UN resolution 242.

† See pp. 228–9 for what the author is reliably informed took place in September 1970.

mandos gradually worsened until there was a state of civil war between them.

Hussein's attitude to the Palestinian resistance movement suffered from a basic inconsistency. On the one hand he supported their aim—the liberation of Palestine : he too wanted justice for the refugees, and if they could not return home by peaceful means, he understood their demand for a guerrilla campaign designed to force the Israelis to a just settlement. He felt bound to provide them with the means of carrying on their campaign : after the defeat of '67, his troops in the Jordan valley worked together with the commandos to provide them with bases and the facilities to carry out their task.

On the other hand, he wanted to achieve what he called 'a just and lasting peace' by *diplomatic* means if he could, and he saw the violence and extremist demands of the Palestinians jeopardising his chances of achieving this. Moreover, when he saw that the commandos were producing more disruption in Jordan than in Israel, because of the vigorous retaliation by the Israelis, and the growing frustration and disorderliness of the Palestinians, he came under growing pressure from his own army and the East Bank establishment to take action to curb the anarchy in his own kingdom. He was not helped by the Egyptians and Syrians, who gave the commandos every encouragement to provoke the Israelis but refused to allow them to operate out of their own territories.

It was a return to the situation that had prevailed before the June war, except that the Palestinians were far better organised and financed *after* the war than they had been before it. By the end of 1967, it was estimated that the East Bank's pre-war refugee population of some 500,000 had increased by a further 150,000. Of these, over 90,000 were living in makeshift tented camps in the hills around Jerash and Amman. The Palestinian Liberation Organisation, which Nasser had persuaded Hussein to restore to Amman on May the 30th in the form of the ebullient Ahmed Shukairy, became active after the defeat of June the 7th in recruiting from among these newly displaced refugees. Guerrilla leaders, like Arafat of El Fateh, were able to offer pay, weapons and a sense of purpose to thousands of Palestinians : armed camps sprang up in the Jordan valley and the guerrilla campaign began.

But they were fighting against heavy odds. The Israeli frontier was no longer easy to penetrate : it ran in an almost straight line from Lake Tiberias to the Dead Sea : the Jordan flowed between the Israelis and the commandos. The expected uprising by the Arab population of the newly occupied West Bank did not take place. Even so, the commandos were able to cause substantial damage and irritation to the Israelis. In February 1968, strong Israeli retaliatory raids against Jordan caused some army leaders to press Hussein to control the commandos. The Minister of the Interior, Hassan al Khayed, said, 'Jordan is determined to strike with an iron fist those who, by their actions, would provide Israel with justification to mount further pressures against Jordan'.

Hussein was against precipitate action. He was aware of the political menace of the commandos to the stability of Jordan, but their activities were firmly supported by the mass of his Palestinian population, and by the Iraqis, who had been his close allies in the war with Israel and had still 15,000 troops stationed in Jordan, actively supporting the commando raids into Israel. His own cabinet appears to have been divided between those who thought the commandos should be curbed, and those who believed they should be enthusiastically supported. Hussein himself tended to the former view, as he feared the commandos would disrupt Jordan and frustrate hopes of a peaceful settlement with Israel; but for the moment he stayed his hand.

Then in March 1968, came the Israeli raid on the Fateh stronghold at Karameh, in the Jordan valley. A large Israeli force of tanks crossed the Jordan at dawn and headed for Karameh. They had hoped that the Jordanian army would not take part, but it did, and though the Israelis succeeded in dynamiting a number of houses in Karameh, they ran into stiff opposition from the force of commandos who had stayed there to meet them. And in the fighting with the Jordanian regular army outside the town, the Israelis lost a number of tanks, and had to delay their withdrawal in order to retrieve as many damaged tanks as they could. The details of the fighting in and around the town are now cloaked in legend, but it became the great rallying cry of the commandos, who claimed the victory as theirs, rather more loudly than the army claimed it as theirs.

For the moment, the dispute was immersed in a wave of popu-

lar rejoicing that swept Jordan. Within hours, the streets of
Amman were full of glorifying commandos who claimed that the
Israelis had now been beaten for the first time, and that the
Palestine Resistance had won the victory. A shattered Israeli tank
was dragged back to a public square in Amman, and put on
display. The funeral of the commandos killed in the battle at
Karameh turned into a massive eruption of Palestinian feeling, and
caused a rush of support to the Palestinian cause. Recruiting
flourished, and by the end of 1968 it was estimated that there
were upwards of 10,000 salaried commandos, as well as a growing mass of unofficial members of the various organisations, who
called themselves 'the militia'. Hussein himself expressed admiration for what the army and the commandos had done at Karameh, and when he was asked in the middle of all the rejoicing
if he controlled the commandos, he replied:

'I try to exert my control, but it's difficult to tell who is a
commando and who isn't. Besides, what do you expect me to do?
What should I do to a people who have lost everything—who
were driven out of their country? Shoot them? I think we have
come to the point where we are all *fedayeen*'.*

For the next few months the Palestinian voice was dominant
in Jordan. The old West Bank political parties held a meeting
in April 1968 and formed themselves into a left-wing coalition
to demand more freedom for political parties: Hussein's old
political enemy Suleiman Naboulsi was made their chairman.
Groups of commandos bombed out of their bases in the Jordan
valley, began to pull back to Amman, leaving only operational
bases in the valley. Infiltration into Israel continued, but it became daily more difficult as the Israelis strengthened their
defences along the Jordan, and sought out guerrilla bases on
the East Bank. By the autumn of 1968, Hussein's capital was
the commando stronghold that Karameh had been a year earlier,
and the pressure grew from his right-wing for action against the
more unruly of the commandos who were taking the law into
their own hands. They drove with loaded weapons through the
streets of Amman and looked more and more like a second army

---

* *Fedayeen* is the Arabic word for 'commandos'. Hussein's army Chief of
Staff at the time, General Khammash, told the author that Jordanian policy
was to encourage the commandos to cross the Jordan, but to stop them
firing across the Jordan—by force, if necessary.

within Jordan. In October, tension between the commandos and the King reached its highest point yet, and El Fateh's radio based in Cairo began to talk of a plot to destroy the Palestine Revolution from inside Jordan. It appealed to the army to stand by the movement as it had at Karameh. On November the 4th, Hussein allowed his army to strike at one guerrilla organisation, called Al Nasr (the Victory Group). Armoured cars went into action against commandos in the two big refugee camps on Jebel Ashrafiyeh and Jebel Hussein. Twenty-eight were killed, including four soldiers.

It was Hussein's first demonstration of force against the commandos, and it was temporarily effective. An agreement was made in which the commandos accepted his full authority in Jordan, but a pattern of mutual distrust was established, that deepened as the desperation and unruliness of the commandos increased, and as the reaction against them grew more indignant. As the months of 1969 passed, the uneasy relationship between Hussein and the commandos swung this way and that. In February Hussein held friendly talks with Yasser Arafat; in March Hussein made a strong bid to renew his peace moves with Israel by putting forward a six-point plan in Washington. It did little more than reiterate the Security Council Resolution 242, but it was treated by the guerrillas as a strong rejection by Hussein of their policy of violent resistance to Israel. American officials let it be known, after Hussein's talks with the newly elected President Nixon, that Hussein believed he could manage any problems he had with the commandos once a settlement had been reached with Israel. But a few months later, in August, Hussein promised the Palestinians the right to determine their own political future once the Arabs had 'ended the odious occupation and repulsed aggression'. The talk again was of war and support for the Palestinian cause.

However, as 1969 drew to a close, and the prospects of peace with Israel seemed as far away as ever, Jordan's political and military situation was becoming critical. Severe Israeli reprisals in the summer had resulted in the destruction of the East Ghor Canal, and guerrilla operations in the Jordan valley were becoming increasingly unsuccessful as the Israelis tightened their defences. The scene in Amman was now one of near anarchy, with the guerrillas controlling large parts of the city themselves.

At the end of the summer, Hussein had appointed his uncle, Sherif Nasser, Commander-in-Chief of the Jordanian army, and Rasoul Kilani Minister of the Interior. Both of them demanded a decisive showdown with the commandos, and a restoration of order on the frontier with Israel. A confrontation with the guerrillas was becoming inevitable. It was to come early in 1970.

Hussein's personal life suffered deeply from the strain of the '67 war and the years of tension that followed it. He was seldom out of uniform : he travelled everywhere with a heavy bodyguard of Bedouin troops mounted in three or four Land Rovers. He had to abandon his country retreat at Shunah only a few miles from the new Israeli front line. The palace he had begun building on the West Bank in early '67 was left abandoned by the Israelis on its solitary hilltop near Jerusalem. Life for Hussein and Muna became more strained as Jordan looked more and more like an armed camp. They still went to Aqaba for weekends, when they could. Hussein was delighted when he was telephoned during a visit to Saudi Arabia, in April 1968, with the news that he had twin daughters. They called them Zein and Aisha. But the exhilarating feeling that Hussein enjoyed before '67 of presiding over a growing economy and a stabler and more relaxed society, was gone.

His health suffered too. In 1968, he had an increasing problem with a nervous complaint in his jaw : he had been grinding down his teeth on either side. His jaw was operated on successfully in London in January 1969. And his heart was giving some cause for concern, although it never gave any serious trouble until early 1971, when he spent about two weeks in a London hospital with an irregular heart beat.

The strain of nearly 18 years on the throne of Jordan was beginning to tell.

XIX

THE HIJACK CRISIS

JANUARY–SEPTEMBER 1970

By the beginning of 1970, the restless relationship between Hussein and the Palestinian commandos had become dangerously strained. The 'Palestinian Resistance' was looking more and more like another state within Jordan. Unable to penetrate Israel's defences, and driven from their advance bases by Israeli air strikes, the guerrillas swarmed about Amman as if it were a city they had newly captured. They rejected the discipline of Hussein's laws, policed their own areas themselves, and even registered their own vehicles independently of the Jordanian authorities. They were desperate, bitter men. Israel was the prime object of their hatred, but for the moment it eluded them, and many of them turned instead on Hussein. He had refused to throw the weight of his army behind their struggle to cross the Jordan since '67. He had even obstructed them. And he was committed to a settlement with Israel that would deny them their goal—the liberation of the *whole* of Palestine.

Their dislike of Hussein's policies encouraged the commandos to feel they had the right to treat his authority with contempt. But while they despised Hussein, they could not agree among themselves what to do about him. The principal organisation, El Fateh, which had pledged itself not to interfere in the internal affairs of any Arab state, and which drew its money from Arab governments, was naturally not inclined to call for the downfall of Hussein. Indeed Arafat appears genuinely to have discouraged the prospect of a guerrilla state in Jordan, and to have worked for an understanding with the King. But others, like the Popular Front for the Liberation of Palestine, led by George Habbash, and the Popular Democratic Front, led by Naif Hawatmeh, were not so reliant on official aid and made no bones about calling for the overthrow of Hussein and his replacement by a militant

208

régime of the extreme left. They proclaimed that before Palestine could be liberated, they had to liberate Amman.

Habbash used spectacular methods. He believed there should be no frontier to the campaign of violence against Israel, and against all who supported her. His PFLP's attacks on Israeli and Western aircraft gained no support from the other commando leaders, but appealed to the imagination of many of their rank and file.

So there was no cohesion in the guerrilla movement. No less than ten organisations competed for the loyalty of the commandos; there were bitter jealousies and tensions among the various groups, and even between personalities within the groups : each group had its own ideology and its own source of finance. This left the guerrillas without any common policy, and without a disciplined command structure. There was precious little military or political liaison. When they found it convenient, all the organisations recognised Arafat's leadership of the movement; but when any of them disagreed with him, they went their own way.

So the commando leadership itself was under intense strain, and although Arafat struggled hard to maintain a working relationship with Hussein, he tended to be carried away by the growing extremism that was sweeping the commando movement irresistibly to the left.

But if the commandos were divided, so was their opposition. Many East Bank Jordanians, and most of Hussein's family expressed disgust at the behaviour of the guerrillas and begged the King to take decisive action against them. Of course there would be bloodshed, they said, but if His Majesty did not act soon, the growing dislocation of the country would only force him to act later, and the longer he waited, the greater would be the loss of life when he finally had to move. On the other hand, a number of Hussein's advisers urged him to be cautious. An all-out attack on the guerrillas would deeply offend the rest of the Arab world, which was enthusiastic about the Palestinian cause, though no doubt relieved that it was Hussein, and not they, who had to play host to the commandos. A large slice of Hussein's own budget was provided by Kuwait and Libya, who also provided generous support to the commandos. A clash with the movement that was the darling of the Arab world could

leave Hussein far more isolated economically and politically than
he had been in the '50s.

Hussein hesitated. He resented the arrogance of the commandos and their refusal to accept his and his army's authority.
He found it degrading to have to watch Arafat being received
in other Arab capitals with all the dignity of a head of state.
He was aware of the anger of much of his army and the
Jordanian establishment. But he had always been reluctant to
condone bloodshed, however necessary it appeared—to the extent
that most of his family thought he showed grave weakness. He
preferred to stay his hand and appeal to the commando leaders
to curb their wilder members and respect Jordanian law.

But his appeals were, quite patently, having no effect. With
every day that passed, the ranks of the commandos were swelled
by bands of irregular 'militia', who appeared to owe allegiance
to no one. Guns seemed to be everywhere, and gunfire was now
as common as the noise of traffic in Amman. Just before
Christmas, Princess Muna was stopped by commandos as she
was driving through Amman, and held for some time, until the
urgent appeals of the royal guard finally secured her release.

In February 1970, Hussein visited President Nasser in Cairo.
Nasser was still the undisputed leader of the Arab world, and
his public support for the commandos was therefore unequivocal.
However, Nasser, like Hussein, was working for a settlement with
Israel that would not secure the commandos' aim of a fully
liberated Palestine, and for this reason Nasser was believed
privately to sympathise with Hussein's need to curb the political
influence of the Palestinians. Nasser's problem, and Hussein's
too, was that despite any support he was able to give Hussein
privately, he was unable to do so publicly. And Hussein was in
no doubt that if he engaged in prolonged open warfare with
the commandos, Nasser would soon feel compelled to come out
against him. However, when Hussein returned to Jordan on
February 10th, he believed Nasser would give him tacit support
if he increased the pressure on the commandos, without provoking
all-out civil war.

That same day, Hussein's Minister of the Interior, Rasoul
Kilani, issued an order which was said only to revive the previous
practice in Jordan of banning the carrying or firing of weapons
in Jordanian towns and calling for the registration of all vehicles

with the Jordanian authorities. The commandos took this as a declaration of war, and outbreaks of fighting occurred at points where the commandos and the army were face to face. The order was clearly not going to be obeyed without a major struggle, and at a meeting between Hussein and the commando leaders at the house of the Prime Minister, Talhouni, the King was persuaded to 'freeze' his Minister's order and the commandos promised, in return, to try to curb the spirits of their members. But no one doubted that the commandos had won a political victory, and at a Press Conference on the 14th of February, Hussein was on the defensive. He said that an 'unfortunate error' had been made 'due to a misunderstanding'.

'Frankly,' he said, 'we had not expected such a reaction to our government's ban on the carrying of arms. Perhaps there was a lack of communication.' He said the government did not want to stop the commandos possessing weapons: it was just that everyone felt the need for an 'organised situation'. The Minister's order would be put into 'cold storage'.

Ten days later Kilani was dismissed.

The commandos had won the day. Hussein had tested their resolve and found, to his consternation, that they would fight desperately to preserve their freedom in his cities. He had, it was true, secured assurances from Arafat, but both of them knew, by this time, that their demands were irreconcilable. Hussein either had to live with the license of the commandos, or extinguish it by force. His only consolation was that, although Syria and Iraq immediately condemned his attempt to take firm action as a move to 'liquidate' the commando movement altogether, Nasser remained silent.

The uneasy truce between Hussein and the guerrillas lasted, with minor interruptions, for four months.

On the 9th of July 1970, Hussein's chief aide at the palace, Zeid Rifai, was awakened early by the sound of gunfire. He called the Chief of Security and Hussein's cousin, Zeid bin Shaker, now commanding the key armoured division near Amman, and was told that the commandos were firing on the Intelligence Headquarters in Amman. Rifai dressed and since his driver had not yet arrived, drove himself to the area of the shooting. As he drove westwards, he found himself caught in a cross-fire where the commandos were firing across the road towards the Intelligence Building. Rifai accelerated, swerved past two wrecked cars and drove to a nearby house, where he telephoned Hussein and urged him to stay in the safety of the Hummar Palace until he arrived.

When Rifai joined the King, and told him that the Intelligence Building was under fire, Hussein immediately wanted to go to the scene. Rifai begged him not to, but Hussein said, no, he had to go and see for himself. They agreed that the safest route would be to take the northern road in from the Hummar by the Suweilih crossroads rather than the direct route into Amman.

Quickly, a motorcade was assembled : three armoured Land Rovers in front, then the King's car, a Mercedes, and finally three more armed Land Rovers. Hussein sat in the front seat, on the driver's right, and in the back seat sat Zeid Rifai and the army commander, Sherif Nasser. Each of them carried a G3 automatic German rifle, fully loaded.

As the leading Land Rover approached the Suweilih cross-roads, its driver noticed that the Army Command Post there was deserted. But the wooden barrier was, as usual, lowered across the road to Amman. The cars stopped one behind the other as they rounded the corner, and two soldiers stepped out of the leading vehicle to raise the barrier.

At that moment a barrage of machine-gun fire opened up on them from some high ground to the right. Most of the fire came from a heavy machine-gun—a 50 millimetre Russian gun, nicknamed Doshka by the Arabs—but there was light and sub-machine-gun fire as well. The first soldier was killed almost instantly : the other dropped to the ground wounded. Then the firing turned on the rest of the motorcade and the soldiers returned the fire. Some of them darted out of their vehicles and took cover behind a low bank which ran along the right-hand side of the road, with a small ditch by it.

Hussein stayed in his seat : his first reaction was to utter the word 'Igh' under his breath, an Arabic ejaculation that means something like 'Shame on you!' Then, he thrust his gun from the car window and, along with the two in the back seat, fired back at the commandos. For what seemed like two minutes, they fired from this exposed position in the car, and then Rifai looked at Hussein and said :

'Sir, please get out of the car and make for the roadside.'

Hussein appeared to be only half aware that he was being spoken to; he had a kind of distant look on his face, as he loosed off round after round at the slope to his right. Rifai and Sherif Nasser kicked open the back door, and again called more urgently to Hussein to get out. Finally, almost reluctantly, he stopped firing, opened his door and ran across with them to the ditch. When he reached it, Rifai leapt on top of him, and was almost beaten to it by the Major in charge of the King's escort, who had the same idea. Hussein said afterwards that between them they had done more damage to him than the commandos. But he was safe. The guards continued firing, and when the fight ended, the King's men claimed eight dead commandos for the loss of one soldier killed and four wounded. Hussein returned to the Hummar Palace and was surrounded by his royal guard, who embraced him passionately one after the other, weeping with relief at his escape. Palace officials say they received messages from all the commando organisations, including the PFLP, denying all responsibility for the attempt on the King's life.

The news of the attack on Hussein swept through the army like an angry bushfire. They already had provocation enough to launch themselves against the guerrilla strongholds in Amman : this was the last straw. The Bedouin, particularly, were unable to contain their fury, and for thirty-six hours there were clashes between the army and the commandos. The commandos claimed that the army shelled the large Wahdat and Al Husseini refugee camps in Amman, and that hundreds were killed and wounded. The Popular Front for the Liberation of Palestine seized 58 foreigners in two of Amman's leading hotels and said they would hold them hostage until the shelling stopped, and even blow up the hotel if they had to.

On the evening of June the 10th, a ceasefire was arranged, but it collapsed quickly the following morning, and El Fateh now matched the PFLP's challenge to Hussein by issuing one of their own. They said that Hussein must dismiss four leading advisers, and in particular his army commander, Sherif Nasser, and the Armoured Division commander, Zeid bin Shaker. El Fateh claimed that these two men were ordering troops to attack commando positions and that Hussein was being advised by them and by Rasoul Kilani and Wasfi Tell to eliminate the Palestinian Resistance Movement altogether. Still Hussein hesitated. The army, and his family,* clamoured for immediate action against the commandos. Many of them were exasperated at his unwillingness to act, but they recognised, some of them reluctantly, that he must make the decision, and he alone. Hussein's Prime Minister, Talhouni, wavered : like Hussein, he was not eager to be responsible for the order that could lead to wide-scale bloodshed. There was also the problem of the hostages.

On top of all this, the commandos surrounded the house of Zeid bin Shaker's mother, and when his sister, Jozah, climbed on to the roof to see what was going on, she was hit in the throat and chest by commando machine-gun fire. They were already firing at a guard on the roof, and probably did not intend to hit her, but she fell back into the arms of her mother and died almost instantly. Hussein's fury and grief—Jozah was, like Zeid, his cousin—inclined him to react drastically, but, according to a close friend of both Hussein's and bin Shaker's, Zeid bin Shaker urged the King not to allow Jozah's death to decide him one way or the other, and offered to resign his command, as the commandos demanded, if that would remove the King's dilemma.

At this stage it appears that Talhouni and some of his ministers pressed the King to have another try at an accommodation with the Palestinians, and Hussein reluctantly agreed. Sherif Nasser and Zeid bin Shaker were relieved of their commands. General Mashour Haditha, a man known to be acceptable to the commandos, was appointed Commander-in-Chief. In return, the commandos released the hostages.

Hussein's conciliatory policy was too much for some of his enraged soldiers. The day after the dismissal of Sherif Nasser, General Haditha's car came under fire in a suburb of Amman. There were mutterings among army units known to be devoted to the two dismissed officers, and some of them were reported moving on Amman to crush the guerrillas whether the King liked it or not. The King had to call for restraint and obedience among his troops, and for a few days there was speculation in Amman that right-wing elements in the army were plotting a

* "The family", when a political matter was at issue, never included Princess Muna. She recognised throughout that her task was to make a home for Hussein, not to give him political advice. She was out of the country at this time anyway with her elder son, and young Prince Feisel, aged 6, who was badly shaken by the attempt on his father's life was sent off to London to join Muna and Abdullah.

coup against Hussein, and his new Commander-in-Chief. Sherif Nasser's presence in Jordan was obviously embarrassing for Hussein, and they agreed between them that he should leave the country for a while. But at a press conference on the 17th of June, Hussein went out of his way to praise the two men he had dismissed, and said the army had acted with restraint and dignity.

Hussein was trying to restore the shaky balance between army and commandos, whose leaders appeared to be doing their bit to maintain some order in the streets of Amman. On the 26th of June, Hussein asked a well-known advocate of reconciliation, Abdul Moneim Rifai, the brother of Samir Rifai, who was now dead, to take over the premiership from Talhouni, and the following day, a committee of Arab officials arrived from Algeria, Tunisia, Sudan, Egypt and Libya, at Hussein's invitation, to help bring the two sides in Jordan together. In two weeks, an apparently sincere effort by both sides brought the agreement of July the 10th, which was signed by Rifai, Arafat and representatives of the five-nation committee. Under it, the government agreed to recognise the commandos 'Central Committee', to allow free movement within Jordan, and to accept the presence of the militia as well. In return, the commandos agreed to disband their bases and arms depots in Jordanian cities and to stop carrying their weapons in towns. For a brief moment, Hussein thought he could look forward to an understanding with the commandos and a return to stability in Jordan. Rifai believed that Hussein genuinely favoured reconciliation with the Commandos; he noticed that the King was deeply distressed each time new incidents threatened to upset the agreement.

The new understanding lasted a month. At the beginning of August, Hussein and Nasser accepted the American proposals for a ceasefire in the Middle East to allow the United Nations mediator to pursue his search for a settlement in an atmosphere of calm. Hussein's cautious state of open warfare with Israel across the Jordan was at an end, and so was any vestige of common purpose with the commandos. Until then Hussein's army and the Palestinians had been fighting a desultory war with Israel: Hussein had been reluctant to risk reprisals by forcing the pace, and he had accepted the outlines of a settlement, under the UN resolution, that was quite unacceptable to the commandos, but, in the absence of progress towards any settlement, his army and the commandos had been pointing their guns across the Jordan in a fragile alliance with each other. However, when Jordan and Egypt ordered a ceasefire, the alliance evaporated. The commandos saw the ceasefire as a threat to their aim of winning back the whole of Palestine by force, and they believed that if they did not react vigorously against it, their political influence in the Arab world would be eroded. They felt betrayed by Nasser, and believed that Hussein's acceptance of the ceasefire demonstrated his determination to attack not Israel, but the Palestinian resistance. Their mistake was that instead of throwing themselves against Israel in order to provoke a collapse of the ceasefire they allowed the extremists among them to drag the movement more and more into an open confrontation with Hussein.

Throughout August, the PFLP and the PDFLP took the lead. They called repeatedly for the overthrow of Hussein and raised the temperature in Amman to such a level that the capital was in a constant state of crisis. Fighting broke out almost daily; agreements were quickly made between government and commandos, and as quickly broken. As the confrontation gathered pace, the drift of the commandos back to Amman from the Jordan valley area quickened too. There were differences and even clashes between the Fateh and the two extremist groups, but the whole movement could not avoid being dragged into the struggle that began to take on the appearance of civil war.

On September the 1st, Hussein drove to the airport to greet his daughter Aliya: he took the back road from the Hummar, and as his car was turning a bend, heavy firing opened up on his motorcade from houses to the right of the road. This time, the cars did not stop: they accelerated fast, and when they had rounded the bend, they all pulled into the side. Hussein and his bodyguards leapt out, firing again for all they were worth, and jumped into a ditch at the side of the road. Again, Hussein escaped with his life, because the ambush was hopelessly mismanaged. The guerrillas had not been close enough to the road to strike decisively in the first few seconds.

Hussein was still smarting under this attack, when the guerrillas staged their most spectacular coup of all. On the evening of September the 6th, two large passenger airliners, one Swiss and the other American, touched down at the desert airstrip of

Dawson's Field, a few miles north-east of Zerka on the road to Mafraq. The planes carried 310 passengers and crew between them, 127 of them women and children. They had been hijacked as they were leaving airports in Europe. Another attempt to hijack an El Al Boeing over London failed, when the two hijackers were overpowered, and a fourth plane, a Pan American Jumbo Jet was hijacked to Cairo and blown up at the airport there three minutes after landing.*

The men who excitedly surrounded the two captive aircraft at Dawson's Field, who attempted to seize the El Al aircraft and destroyed the Jumbo were commandos of the PFLP.

But the Popular Front's leader, George Habbash, was away studying 'revolutionary' tactics in North Korea. It was the Front's second-in-command, Wadi Haddad, who had conceived the plan, and was now putting it into effect. His intention was to force the West to recognise the desperation of the commando movement. He was determined to show that the Palestinians could make their demands felt, if they were ready to use extreme methods, and strike where the West and Israel were most vulnerable. On the evening of September the 6th, the Popular Front announced that, if seven commandos held in prisons in Western Europe and several more held in Israel were not released within seven days, they would blow up the aircraft with the passengers inside them. Three days later, they added one more aircraft, a British VC 10 with 115 passengers and crew on board.

The Popular Front's action was not applauded by Arab governments : it was, privately, condemned. The guerrilla movement was immediately split : some, like Arafat, believed that the PFLP's action could do no good to the commando cause and would only reduce their already failing prestige : others admired the daring of the Popular Front and called on the PLO Central Committee to approve their action. For some days the movement was badly divided. Arafat attempted to impose his control on the extremists, but he was unable or unwilling to be firm enough, and although most of the hostages had been released by September the 12th, fifty-four remained in the hands of the PFLP, with the full approval of Arafat's Central Committee which endorsed

* For details of the hijacking and the events of the following three weeks that led up to the death of Nasser on the 29th of September, see *Leila's Hijack War*, by the author and David Phillips.

the Front's demands to the West and Israel on the 10th of September. On the 12th, the remaining hostages were removed from the aircraft and taken off to hiding places in Amman and North Jordan, where they were kept throughout the fighting of the next few days. All of them were released before the end of the month : they were well treated by the guerrillas, and not one was injured.

Hussein thought the hijackings were the 'shame of the Arabs'. But for those seven days, from the 6th to the 12th of September, he was powerless to take any action. His tanks surrounded Dawson's Field, and his army commander, General Haditha, tried to negotiate the release of the hostages with the guerrillas. But the Front had little to say to Haditha, except to warn him to keep his men off the airfield : they were too busy negotiating with the Red Cross, who were representing western governments, and with their own colleagues on the Central committee. Meanwhile, more and more units of the army were taking independent action against pockets of commandos. The troops—particularly the Bedouin—were unable to contain their fury at the commandos' activities. Many officers came to Hussein and pressed him to act, if he did not want to lose complete control of his army. Fighting broke out almost hourly. Agreements between the two sides lost all meaning. The trouble was that no one was in command— on either side. Those who saw Hussein during the first fortnight of September saw a man struggling with his own indecision, fighting off the pressure from his generals and his family for decisive action, straining to retain some sort of middle position that would keep his line open to the commandos without forfeiting his army's affection. Hussein claims that he often went out himself to restrain his troops from falling on the commandos. He says that one day after the hijacking his brother, Prince Mohamed, and his cousin, Sherif Zeid, went to try to stop a column of 155 millimetre guns moving up to shell Amman. After a few minutes Sherif Zeid telephoned Hussein at the Hummar to say that they were unable to stop the infuriated troops pressing on towards Amman; would His Majesty please come and try to influence them in person?

Hussein says he drove down to a crossroads south of Hummar, and attempted to stop the advancing artillery column. But they would not stop even for him : one shouted 'You get out of the way.' Another, says Hussein, fixed a grenade on the end of his rifle and pointed it at himself, saying: 'Get out of the way, or I will shoot myself. We had faith in you, we had love for you, but we are losing it.' It took Hussein three hours to persuade his men to trust him to try to find a solution that would not mean open civil war.

By the night of the 14th of September, the country was close to anarchy. Abdul Moneim Rifai, the Prime Minister, and Yasser Arafat worked late into the night hammering out yet another agreement between them, which would guarantee the commandos certain rights in Jordan and allow them bases outside the towns from which to attack Israel. The following day, at noon, Rifai took this latest agreement to the King. If it was not acceptable to his Majesty, said Rifai, he would resign with his government— because it was the best arrangement he felt he could achieve.

Rifai had already a foreboding that the agreement would not be acceptable to the King. In a meeting with Hussein two nights earlier, on the 13th, he had sensed that the King's instincts were moving rapidly against reconciliation with the commandos. And now his worst fears were realised: Hussein said the agreement was no good, and when Rifai asked permission to resign, Hussein refused to give an immediate answer and said he would think about it. Rifai heard nothing more until the appointment of his successor was announced on the radio.

Between noon and eleven o'clock that night, the King finally took his decision. He was in the Hummar Palace. With him were a group of advisers, led by Wasfi Tell and Zeid Rifai, and two leading army officers, Brigadier Ma'azen Ajlouni and Brigadier Qa'asem Ma'itah. Hussein's cousin, Zeid bin Shaker had been reinstated in the army in August and was now chief of the operations room at the Military Headquarters. These five men were for strong action against the guerrillas and had been for some time. That same afternoon, Ma'itah's son was killed in a clash between army and commandos in Zerka. The patience of the army commanders was at an end. Before the afternoon was out, they persuaded Hussein that the time for action had come: the agreement with the commandos should be implemented by force which meant by a military government. Abdul Moneim Rifai and Haditha were clearly not up to it, and would refuse to do it anyway: only the army was equal to the task. It would not take long: maybe two days, maybe three. A decisive blow would force the guerrillas out of the towns into the country near the Israeli border, where they had always been intended to operate. But the blow must be determined and thorough.

Some say that Hussein was given an ultimatum that afternoon; that his army leaders gave him no choice but to go along with them. Others say that there was a meeting of minds, that Hussein had long been moving towards this decision himself, and that his advisers and generals gave him the final gentle push.

Whatever it was that finally convinced him on the evening of September the 15th, Hussein's indecision suddenly evaporated. His mind was at last made up. At eleven o'clock, he sent a car to fetch a little-known elderly Brigadier to the palace. His name was Mohamed Daoud.

XX

CIVIL WAR

SEPTEMBER 1970

Late on the night of September the 15th 1970, Hussein received Mohamed Daoud at the Hummar Palace. Daoud had no idea why the King should want to see him; he was an infantry officer and a Palestinian, with many friends among the commandos. For some time now he had been watching the drift towards civil war in Jordan with growing dismay. Like many Palestinians, he deplored the extremism of the Popular Front, and regretted Arafat's failure to exercise more discipline throughout the movement, but he feared the army's indiscipline too, and suspected that the army leaders who could influence Hussein were determined to crush the commando movement regardless of the political consequences.

That night, this tall, fragile-looking, sensitive man was ordered by Hussein to form a military government. In the drawing room at the Hummar, Hussein handed Daoud a piece of paper with the names of his new cabinet written on it and told him that the new government's job would be to implement, once and for all, the measures that Rifai and Arafat had agreed earlier that day, and he reminded Daoud that the two sides had agreed to enforce these measures by eight o'clock the following morning. There was, in other words, just over eight hours left : if the commandos had made no move to evacuate the towns by then—and there was no sign of their doing so—then the army would have to act.

The atmosphere at the Hummar that night was like that of a command post on the eve of battle. Now that the King had made his decision, the uncertainty and frustration of the past few weeks was gone. Plans for military action could now proceed on the assumption that a showdown was inevitable within hours : the agreement between the Rifai government and the commando leadership now appeared irrelevant. Hussein's repudiation of

Rifai and appointment of a military government was bound to be taken as a rejection of the agreement anyway.

Daoud was in an impossible position. He had no choice but to accept the King's order to form a government, though he knew power would be wielded not by his cabinet, but by the King and the group of officers and advisers who surrounded him. Even so, he appears to have clung to the hope that he might still be able to persuade Arafat to implement the agreement of the 15th, particularly as it was now clear that, if he did not, civil war was inevitable. For the next twenty-four hours there was the extraordinary spectacle of Hussein's new Prime Minister struggling desperately to come to terms with the commandos, while Hussein's army leaders quietly moved their men into positions for attack.

Hussein chose Daoud to be Prime Minister during the decisive confrontation because he wanted to present a united front against the commandos. If a Palestinian were to be seen to be in charge it would be less easy for the commandos to argue that they were being suppressed by a Bedouin régime. As a Palestinian infantryman, Daoud would secure the loyalty of the large Palestinian element in the army against their brothers in the commando movement and, as an officer of the King, he would obey his orders and do whatever the King decided was right for the country. But Hussein had misjudged Daoud, whose sympathies with the Palestinians ran deeper than the King had supposed. Far from quietly nodding at the action of the army, which he had no power to control, Daoud tried to restrain it and when he failed, he began to look for an opportunity to show his disapproval by resigning.

At 6 a.m. on September the 16th, Amman radio announced that Hussein had appointed a military government, that Field Marshal Habes Majali had succeeded General Haditha as Chief of Staff, and that the cabinet consisted of seven Generals and Brigadiers, two Colonels and three Majors. Then Hussein addressed the people:

'A situation of uncertainty, chaos and insecurity prevailed in our dear country, and the danger which threatened Jordan has increased. We find it our duty to take a series of measures to restore law and order, and to preserve the life of every citizen, his means of living and his property. . . .'

The commandos took this as a declaration of war. The previous day's agreement still had two hours to run but, as the King and his advisers had expected, the agreement was not forgotten. Arafat summoned an immediate meeting of the Central Committe at his headquarters on Jebel Hussein. All guerrilla forces were ordered to unite under Arafat, and the Popular Front, which had been expelled from the Central Committee after the destruction of the aircraft,* was invited to rejoin. Brigadier Yahya, commander of the Palestine Liberation Army, based mainly in Syria, was appointed Arafat's Chief of Staff. The leadership called for an unlimited general strike to start the following morning, 'until the fascist government is overthrown'.

All through the day, Brigadier Daoud attempted to persuade the commandos to effect the agreement. But he was working in a vacuum. The guerrillas and the army were too busy arranging themselves for battle to heed his feeble, last minute attempts at mediation. The guerrillas regarded him with contempt for accepting the post of Prime Minister, and although he finally succeeded in contacting Arafat by telephone at 8 p.m. on the 16th, and pressed the commando leader to meet him urgently, no meeting resulted.

At five minutes to five on the morning of the 17th, Hussein's army launched a full scale military operation against guerrilla positions in Amman. The King confidently expected it to be complete within 48 hours. Patton tanks of the 60th Armoured Brigade, supported by armoured car units, moved into the city from all sides and concentrated heavy fire on guerrilla strongholds, and in particular on their bases on Jebel Hussein, and in the Wahdat and Al-Husseini refugee camps. It was the first time Jordanian armour had invaded the country's capital, and the effect was devastating: any house from which fire was directed at the advancing armour was obliterated, and the commandos responded with anti-tank and sniper fire. The people of Amman, caught helplessly in the crossfire, sought refuge in their cellars, or tried to escape to parts of the city which they believed would be safe.

Time was a crucial factor in Hussein's strategy. He knew the sympathies of the Arab world were with the guerrillas, but he judged that most Arab governments would withhold their reactions for a time in case they found themselves supporting a lost

* The three aircraft at Dawson's Field were destroyed by PFLP militants, after all the hostages had disembarked, on the 12th.

cause. And he was confident that, for a time, he would have the tacit support of President Nasser. But he knew that the pressure on Arab governments to declare their support for the guerrillas would gather pace with every hour that the fighting continued, and that a prolonged conflict would jeopardise the financial support he received from Libya, Saudi Arabia and Kuwait. The Syrians and the Iraqis, who had 12,000 troops on his territory, had already declared their commitment to the guerrillas, and Hussein had to allow for their active involvement against him if he failed to achieve a swift, decisive victory.

In military terms, assuming the non-involvement of outside powers, the advantage was clearly with Hussein. He had 55,000 men under arms, and at least half were unquestioningly loyal to him. The armour, which was mostly Bedouin, was fanatically devoted to him, and intent on eliminating the Palestinian movement altogether. He had 300 tanks, half of them around Amman, half of them strung out along his northern frontier with one eye on Syria and the other on the Iraqi division based at Mafraq. His air force of 18 Starfighters and 20 Hunters was the weakest link. They were based at Mafraq within range of the Iraqi artillery, and a large number of the Hunter fighter ground-attack aircraft were undergoing modifications. However, he hoped that his air force would not be needed; the battle would be fought not in open country, but in the streets of Amman.

The commandos had some 50,000 men under arms, but of these only about 20,000 were professional fighters. A substantial number of the regular commandos were with the Palestine Liberation Army, which was based in Syria, with a paper strength of 10,000 men: they were believed to possess about 30 old Russian tanks. The commandos controlled most of Amman, and the whole of the northern town of Irbid. They also held large parts of Zerka, Ramtha, Jerash, Ajlun and Salt. Their weakness was their indiscipline, their uncertain chain of command, their vulnerability in open country and their lack of heavy weapons. Their strength was the sympathy they knew they commanded in other Arab countries, which they fervently hoped would be translated into material aid.

For two days, as Hussein's tanks battled their way slowly towards the centre of Amman, against determined opposition from the guerrillas, most of the Arab world restrained itself from commenting. Soon after the fighting began, President Nasser asked Colonel Gaddafi of Libya to meet him urgently and persuaded him to stay his hand until Egypt's Chief of Staff, General Mohamed Sadek, had had a chance to assess the situation. Sadek arrived in Amman on the evening of the 17th and appealed to both sides to stop fighting. But he was careful not to condemn either of them.

Only the Syrians protested. Their President, Dr Atassi, lost no time in declaring his country solidly behind the commandos. Relations between Hussein and the Syrian government were already so bad that the Syrians decided they could lose nothing by aligning themselves from the outset with Hussein's opponents. The real issue for the Syrians was not what to say but what to do. And here there was disagreement within the régime. The militant left-wing leaders, Salah Jedid and Yussef Zuayen, wanted immediate intervention in support of the commandos. These two, supported by President Atassi, saw the trouble in Jordan as an opportunity to eliminate Hussein's right-wing régime, which had long been their favourite *bête-noire*. They set up a kind of unofficial headquarters on the Syrian frontier at Dera'a, and began helping to co-ordinate a major operation to speed men, weapons and ammunition across the border to commando bases in the north of Jordan. But Jedid and Zuayen were opposed by the powerful Minister of Defence, General Hafez Assad, who took the view that open Syrian intervention against Hussein would be unwise, and could provoke Israeli intervention against Syria. Assad was a realist. He calculated that the possible defeat of Hussein's forces by a combined Syrian-Palestinian offensive would only expose Syria to a whole series of political and military dangers. Besides, he had a strong hunch that the Russians, on whose military and economic aid Syria relied almost exclusively, would be strongly opposed to Syrian intervention in Jordan.

But as the appeals of the commandos for outside help grew in urgency and reports of the bloodshed in Amman—most of them grossly exaggerated—swept the Arab world, the pressure from the militants in Syria became irresistible. On the evening of September the 18th—the second day of the fighting in Jordan—the Syrian government contacted the Iraqis with a view to joint military intervention in Jordan.

Hussein knew nothing of all this. He was counting on his army to shatter guerrilla resistance in Amman quickly enough to convince outsiders that intervention would be fruitless and to allow him to move reinforcements from the streets of Amman to secure Jordan's borders. But the army were unable to meet the schedule that Hussein's commanders had set a few days earlier. Guerrilla resistance was desperate, determined and effective. Although Hussein's armour was moving slowly forward, it was clear that there was no prospect of a quick victory within forty-eight or even seventy-two hours. Far from being free to reinforce his borders against external interference, Hussein had to withdraw an armoured infantry regiment from the 40 Brigade area in the north to strengthen his forces in Amman, on the first day of the fighting.

But the pressure on his northern frontier was growing, and Hussein now found himself having to concentrate his attention on two fronts: the battle for Amman, which continued for another week, and the battle for the north, which quickly became the more important of the two and in the end, the decisive one.

The Jordanian 40th Armoured Brigade was hardly in a position to defend the country against Syria. It was deployed mainly west of Irbid, with its guns pointing across the Jordan valley towards Israel, and it was supported in this defensive posture by the Iraqi 12th Armoured Brigade, based on Mafraq: most of the Iraqi tanks were drawn up hull-down in defensive positions along the road between Irbid and Mafraq, also facing westwards. Only one Jordanian squadron of some 15 tanks was based at the crucial frontier town of Ramtha, but it was quite unable to stop the growing influx of Palestinian men and supplies that poured over the border from Syria on the first two days of the fighting.

40 Brigade's commander was a powerfully-built Bedouin called Attallah Ghasib. He was a professional tank commander devoted to Hussein, respected by his men. There was little he and his tank commanders did not know about the qualities and capabilities of their 150 British-made Centurion tanks.

On the evening of the first day of the fighting, Ghasib was injured by an exploding mortar bomb, fired by a group of commandos at his headquarters near Irbid. He was evacuated to a military hospital and operated on that same evening. The following morning he received a personal telephone call from Hussein.

The King told him that Brigadier Muheisen, who had recently taken over command of the whole northern area, had just resigned . Was there anything Ghasib could do to change Muheisen's mind? Hussein knew that Ghasib was recovering from an operation, but it was vital to avoid a failure of command at a time when the northern frontier had to be secured at all costs. Ghasib telephoned Muheisen but was unable to influence him. By 9.30 a.m. on the morning of the 18th, Hussein saw no alternative but to press Ghasib himself to take on the job of Commander-in-Chief in the north. It was a desperate move, as Ghasib now found himself commanding two major units but it ensured firm central control of the army in the north. By the evening of the 18th, Ghasib had moved his command post to the divisional headquarters at Husn. He was just in time.

Late on the night of the 18th, Syrian commandos attacked the Jordanian villages of Et Turra and Shajara and the following morning the Iraqis informed the Jordanians that they were going to withdraw to the east. It was clear to Ghasib that the way was being cleared for a major Syrian incursion, and he had only a handful of tanks at Ramtha to face them. After telephone consultation with Hussein, Zeid bin Shaker, at army headquarters in Amman, told Ghasib to withdraw his main body of tanks— two regiments of them—from the Israeli frontier, and deploy them as quickly as possible to a position north of the Irbid-Mafraq road to meet the expected attack from Syria.

On the evening of September the 19th, the clear night sky over northern Jordan was lit up by green and red flares. These were the signals the Iraqis had agreed their tank commanders would fire as a sign to the Jordanians that they were pulling back to the east. But the Iraqi withdrawal was part of a co-ordinated plan between Iraq and Syria by which, as the Iraqis withdrew, the Syrians would slip across the frontier, firing green and red Very lights as well to confuse the Jordanians. At dawn on Sunday the 20th, Ghasib's tanks were confronted with a major Syrian invasion.

Meanwhile Hussein's diplomatic position had taken a sharp downturn. After two days in Jordan, President Nasser's envoy, General Sadek, had spent a number of hours with Hussein but had failed to obtain his agreement to withdraw his army from the cities. Hussein had replied indignantly that he had no intention of recalling his troops until the commandos agreed to implement the previous agreements and respect his government's authority in Jordan's cities. Sadek had reported to Nasser and Nasser had told him to press on Hussein the urgency of an early end to the fighting. It was clear to Hussein that Nasser's patience would not last much longer. Colonel Gaddafi's did not last *any* longer : he suspended Libya's share of the £40 million that Libya, Kuwait and Saudi Arabia had been paying Hussein since 1967. Hussein had every reason to believe that Kuwait would soon follow suit : the Palestinian influence there was even stronger than in Libya.

At 5 a.m. on the 20th, Hussein was awakened by his chief aide, Zeid Rifai, with the news that the Syrians were at that moment moving across the northern frontier in force. The news drove Hussein close to despair. He and Rifai thought that the war was lost. It seemed impossible that Jordan's military resources could sustain a full-scale attack from Syria particularly as the army were still unable on the fourth day of fighting to spare any units from Amman to reinforce the troops in the north. The Syrians could throw in 880 tanks and more than 200 aircraft : Hussein had 300 tanks—half of them fully occupied in Amman—and only 38 aircraft. To someone of Hussein's mercurial temperament, the situation looked hopeless and, in an onrush of fatalism, he began to prepare himself for the end of his dynasty. He ordered all the women and children to be escorted to Aqaba, which seemed to be the only safe refuge in Jordan at that moment, and he agreed with his military commanders that should the battle in the north be lost—as seemed inevitable— all available troops would be summoned to Amman to make a last stand there.

He then summoned the ambassadors of the four big powers to the Hummar and told them he thought his kingdom faced the greatest threat ever to its existence. He appealed to them to do anything they could with the greatest urgency to preserve the independence of Jordan, and pointed out that the country was now beyond any doubt being invaded by Syria. The author is reliably informed* that Hussein, in his desperation, indicated that

---

* The author was only given this information on the understanding that the source would not be made public. The evidence produced by the source who was at the time in a position of some authority and had no reason to discredit Hussein, is confirmed by two other equally disinterested authorities.

he would welcome *any* intervention, even the intervention of the Israeli air force, that would preserve his Kingdom from the Syrians. This was taken in the West as *cri de coeur*, the natural reaction of anyone as emotional as Hussein to so dire a situation : it was—so the report runs—not even transmitted to the Israelis, who were judged likely to make up their own minds on the merits of intervention, irrespective of the wishes of Hussein. Hussein denies contemptuously that he would ever have appealed for help from Israel, whom he says he has always regarded as Jordan's prime enemy, and a major opponent of the Hashemite régime.

Whether or not Hussein made such an appeal is of little consequence : if he did, he must have known that the Israelis would not allow it to influence their own decision. The episode only underlines—like the rumours of secret meetings between Hussein and Israeli ministers—the essential unimportance of Hussein's relationship, or non-relationship with Israel. Hussein's policies were dictated, just as Israel's were, by the realities of power and the pressure of events in the Middle East. His treatment of the commandos and his hostility to Syria were policies he pursued because he judged they were in his own interest, or because he felt he had no choice—not because he knew or guessed that they would meet with the approval of Israel, America or anyone else. Hussein's experience of power, which he had now enjoyed longer than any other Arab leader, had made him accept the fact that his Arab neighbours were sometimes more of a threat to him than Israel, and that sometimes, if his kingdom was to survive, he must depend on Israel's active or tacit support, as he had in 1958 when only Israel had opened her skies to his supply line. But to infer from this that Hussein and Israel had some furtive alliance to eliminate Israel's enemies in the Arab world is to do an injustice to a man who feels as profoundly as any other Arab the wounds that Israel has inflicted on his country and on Arab pride. And so, if on occasions Hussein's interests apparently coincided with Israel's it is far from an inevitable conclusion—and is only of marginal importance if it is true—that Hussein and the Israeli Prime Minister had mapped out a policy in secret together hidden under a boulder in the Wadi Arava.

That Sunday in September, the Israelis were busily preparing themselves for possible intervention anyway. Their prime concern was not the welfare of King Hussein—many of them were saying at the time that they would welcome his departure from the scene—but the danger of a new Syrian presence on the Jordanian heights overlooking the Israeli kibbutzim in the Beit Shean valley. The Israeli government decided to alert its air force and to mount a massive armoured build-up in the area of Beit Shean in the hope that it would deter the Syrians from penetrating west of Irbid. The operation would also give the Israelis the option of actively intervening on the ground and in the air, if they judged it necessary. The further south the Syrians advanced, the more vulnerable their supply line would become to Israeli air attack : the Syrian armoured thrust depended entirely for its supplies on the road from Damascus to Dera'a, which was within easy striking distance of the Israeli front line.

The reports that reached Hussein all through the Sunday morning and afternoon convinced him that the Syrians meant to overthrow him once and for all. The early morning thrust by the Syrian 88th Armoured Brigade was thrown back by the Jordanians between seven and nine o'clock with heavy Syrian losses, but at noon the Syrians threw in an overwhelming counter-attack. Ghasib estimates that some 217 Syrian tanks of the Syrian 91st Armoured Brigade and the 152nd Independent Tank Regiment, supported by a mechanised infantry brigade (the 67th), three regiments of Syrian commandos and five Palestine Liberation Army regiments, poured over the border. The bulk of the tank force came in well to the east of Ramtha and swept in to the right and behind the Jordanian tanks which were still grouped around Ramtha recovering from the earlier battle.

For six hours the fight went on in the open country around Ramtha. The Jordanians were outnumbered but their Centurion tanks had a 600 yard edge on the range of the Syrians' Russian-built T 55's. The Centurion's 105 millimetre gun is effective against armour at up to 2,400 yards, the T55's up to only 1800. But the pressure on the Jordanians was irresistible, and Ghasib was unable to call on more than one battery of artillery support as his guns were still being transferred from their positions in the Jordan valley. At 5 p.m. one sortie of four Jordanian Hunters from Mafraq flew over the battle, in order to explore the possibility of air attack on the Syrians, but they were fired on by the Iraqis as they returned to land at Mafraq, and Hussein immediately ordered all his aircraft to evacuate Mafraq for the airfield at H5, 75 miles to the east. By the time the transfer was complete it was dark.

At 6 p.m., the Syrians captured the strategic crossroads south of Ramtha, where the Irbid-Mafraq road crosses the Ramtha-Jerash road. Ghasib ordered a retreat to the Husn ridge that runs from Irbid south-east through Husn to join the main road near Nuaimeh. That night the Jordanians entrenched themselves in a strong defensive position along the ridge; by dawn, Ghasib had 110 tanks facing north-east closely supported by the artillery which was also deployed along the ridge. He had had to abandon to the Syrians the whole plain in front of him, from west of Irbid to east of Ramtha.

The survival of Hussein's kingdom and of his army now depended on this thin line of tanks and guns, and on a series of diplomatic exchanges in other capitals. In response to Hussein's pleas, both Britain and America summoned their resident Russian envoys and asked them to press the Kremlin to restrain their Syrian protégés. Nobody was sure, yet, whether the Syrians had Soviet approval for their intervention in Jordan. Some drew encouragement from the fact that the Syrians were denying that they had invaded Jordan, and that there was no sign of any move by the Syrian air force. But would the Syrians maintain their restraint after the success of their first day's campaign? Any further advance by the Syrians would be sure to tempt the powerful Iraqi force in Jordan to take an active role against Hussein as well.

By Monday, September the 21st, Hussein had still not won the battle of Amman, and President Nasser and the ruler of Kuwait had joined the ranks of those Arab leaders whose patience had run out. Kuwait announced that she too was suspending her subsidy to Jordan, and Nasser cabled Hussein that the fighting must stop immediately.

The crisis in Jordan had now given rise to the spectre of a major war in the Middle East: the United States was moving some 20,000 combat troops into the area of the Eastern Mediterranean, and Russia had reinforced her Mediterranean fleet. The Israelis seemed poised to launch themselves on the Syrians. But, throughout Monday, the Syrians were unable to press much further forward, and the prospect of a quick Syrian victory began

to recede. At midday, Hussein's aircraft, Hunter Mark 9's, armed
with anti-tank rockets, began to attack the Syrians with devastating effect. They flew in from H5, in waves of eight aircraft every
half hour or so, and picked off the Syrian tanks one by one in
the plain below the Husn ridge and in the area south and west
of Irbid where they were trying to press forward. Because only
a few of Hussein's aircraft were operational, the pilots were toss-
ing coins in their enthusiasm to decide who should fly the next
sortie.

Hussein had now grimly attuned himself to a fight to the finish,
and he dismissed President Nasser's rebuke and rejected an Egyptian invitation to a summit in Cairo while the threat to his
kingdom persisted. Instead, he sent the unhappy man he had
appointed Prime Minister, Brigadier Daoud, who took the opportunity of announcing his resignation in Cairo a few days later.*

For two days the crucial battle in the north went on without
the Syrians achieving a breakthrough. It was becoming clear that
Damascus did not after all intend to commit all its resources to
the overthrow of Hussein. Assad had refused to commit the air
force in support of the armoured thrust, and the Russians were
now bringing pressure to bear on the Syrian leaders to withdraw
the tanks as well. Hussein's aircraft and artillery had taken such
a toll of the Syrian armour in the plain below the Husn ridge,
that the Syrians were now expending almost as much effort in
retrieving their disabled tanks and armoured vehicles as in pushing forward against the Jordanians. Ghasib intercepted one message from the Syrians to a regimental commander ordering him
to break through to Jerash and join up with an Iraqi regiment
which Ghasib knew was manœuvring in the area, but the Jordanian line across the main road from Ramtha to Jerash held
successfully. By the evening of Tuesday the 22nd, Ghasib felt
strong enough to order a counter-attack by his tanks on the ridge
against the Syrians in the plain : it was timed to begin at 5 a.m.,
the following morning.

But soon after dusk on the Tuesday evening, the Syrians,
assisted by Iraqi tank transporters from Mafraq, began a rapid
withdrawal from North Jordan. By dawn the Jordanians observed
that all the forward Syrian positions had been abandoned and
that the invading force was in full retreat. Ghasib ordered his

* Daoud was a very sick man : he died early in 1972.

tanks and infantry to pursue the Syrians, but it was a cautious pursuit : the Iraqis still threatened the Jordanian right flank, and the Jordanians could not afford to expose themselves to another counter-attack in open country. Besides, the Syrian withdrawal was very efficient : they managed to retrieve all their stricken vehicles—they had been pulling them out steadily on transporters during the past 48 hours—and there was no sign of panic. Even so the Syrians are estimated to have had a total of 62 tanks destroyed in the three day battle and to have lost another 60 trucks and light armoured vehicles. By the end of Wednesday the 23rd, all the Syrian tanks had withdrawn and the external threat to Hussein had disappeared. He could turn his attention to consolidating his position in Amman.

Hussein had spent much of the previous night closeted in the Hummar with a four-man peace mission from Cairo. Its leader was President Numeiry of the Sudan. Hussein was already aware that the military balance was moving in his favour, and he felt able to demand favourable terms for any ceasefire with the guerrillas. He presented Numeiry with a plan that had four main points :

1. The guerrillas should move their bases from the cities. The army would leave too.
2. Guerrilla activity should be restricted to the area of the frontier with Israel.
3. Only the Palestine Liberation Organisation should be recognised as the legitimate representative of the commando movement—a move clearly aimed at the extremist PFLP and PDFLP.
4. The guerrillas should agree strictly to observe Jordanian laws and Jordanian sovereignty.

Hussein succeeded in persuading Numeiry's four-man team to accept these peace terms, and was also able to announce that four guerrilla leaders—one of them a deputy of Arafat's who had fallen into the hands of the army—had approved them too. Together, Hussein and Numeiry broadcast their agreement on the terms, and appealed to both sides to observe a ceasefire.

But the agreement collapsed because the guerrilla leader Yasser Arafat was not a party to it. Numeiry and his team had tried to find him in order to obtain his approval, but Arafat had been moving from place to place, and had only narrowly escaped death a number of times in the fighting. As soon as Arafat heard of the agreement, he announced on the guerrilla radio that he disowned the four men Hussein claimed to have captured, and rejected the terms. The fighting went on. The guerrillas were now claiming that 20,000 people had been killed : Field Marshal Majali retorted that this figure was well over ten times too high : it was more likely to lie between 1,300 and 1,600.

President Numeiry was determined to achieve a ceasefire, and he was back from Cairo the following day, Thursday the 24th, with a new eight-man peace team. They drove over to see Hussein at the Hummar, and he again agreed to a ceasefire, and promised to try to help the team locate Arafat. But this time Arafat was anxious to see them himself, and late that evening he used a commando radio broadcast to invite them to find their way to the house he was occupying on Jebel Webda. With great difficulty, Numeiry made his way to Arafat's headquarters : he complained afterwards that he came under fire from Hussein's troops a number of times, although the King was supposed to have ordered them to stop firing. By dawn, Numeiry had persuaded Arafat to agree to a ceasefire. Arafat made the following announcement on his Damascus based radio :

'Our great people, our brave revolutionaries, to avoid more innocent bloodshed, and so that the citizens may care for their wounded and get the necessities of life, I, in my capacity as supreme commander of the Palestine revolutionary forces, and in response to the appeal by the mission of Arab heads of state, agree to a ceasefire and ask my brothers to observe it provided the other side does the same.'

With the northern frontier sealed against supplies from Syria, and the hope of outside help apparently vanished, Arafat decided that he would be wise to call a halt to the fighting. Hussein's tanks had still failed to penetrate the centre of the city, and there was still strong guerrilla resistance in Irbid, but Arafat judged that the Palestinians, having resisted Hussein's army with some success for more than a week, had established their right to political support from the rest of the Arab world and to a favourable compromise in any new agreement with Hussein. He decided, on Numeiry's advice, that he should fly immediately to Cairo.

Numeiry's aircraft reached Cairo at 8.30 p.m. on Friday evening, the 25th. The triumphant peace team walked down the gang-way under the glare of television lights. A few minutes later, the aircraft taxied away to the military side of the airport, and quietly deposited its last passenger—Yasser Arafat. Within an hour, he was at the Nile Hilton Hotel, where he received the welcome nor-mally reserved for a head of state, and his suite of rooms on the fourth floor was renamed the 'Palestine Suite'. At 10 p.m. Presi-dent Nasser arrived at the Hilton and received Arafat and the peace team in the Hall of the 1001 nights. For four hours, Arafat and the delegation gave Nasser an account of the situation in Jordan that was hardly favourable to Hussein. President Nasser personally cabled Hussein at 2 a.m. on the morning of the 26th and said he now understood the full dimension of what he called the 'horrifying massacre' that had been perpetrated by the King's men in Jordan.

Hussein had been, until then, more concerned with consolidating his position in Amman and around Irbid, and assuring himself that the country was secure from any further foreign interference, than with the gathering political storm that was waiting for him in Cairo. It was only when he read President Nasser's telegram and, shortly afterwards, the agency reports of the Press Confer-ence President Numeiry gave on the Saturday morning, that Hussein felt he should go to Cairo himself.

He left on Sunday morning, piloting his own Caravelle in a wide sweep over Syria, Lebanon and then out to the west of the Nile Delta and into Cairo from the south-west. President Nasser greeted him at the airport, but there were no spectators in the stand, and no press photographers. It was 12.30 when the two men arrived at the Nile Hilton, and an hour later the leaders of the Arab world began to file into the Hall where Arafat had addressed them nearly 40 hours earlier. Arafat entered first, clean-shaven for the first time that many could remember, with a black revolver slung at his right hip. He was followed by King Feisal of Saudi Arabia, El Sabah of Kuwait, Colonel Gaddafi of Libya, General Numeiry of Sudan, Bahi Ladgham of Tunisia, President Franjieh of Lebanon, El Shamy of the Yemen, and President Nasser. Ten chairs were set in a horseshoe shape in the middle of the room. Nasser took the centre chair, and the others sat down.

Then Hussein came in. He was wearing his air force uniform,

with his pilot's wings on the left side of his chest: on his left
hip was a service pistol. Only he and Arafat were armed. He
stood at the door for a moment, smiling rather shyly, as he often
did, and then walked over and took the chair at the end of the
horseshoe opposite Arafat.

The meeting lasted six and a half hours, with a two hour break.
And the agreement that came out of it was considerably less
favourable to Hussein than the agreement he had first laid before
President Numeiry four days earlier. Instead of compelling the
guerrillas to leave the cities and 'restrict their activities to the area
of the frontier with Israel', the Cairo Agreement said they would
merely move to 'appropriate positions for the battle against
Israel'. Nor did the agreement, which had fourteen points, order
the guerrillas to 'respect Jordanian laws and sovereignty', as the
earlier one had. It ended with these words:

'Full support of the Palestinian revolution is ensured to enable
it to carry out its sacred duty: the liberation of its land.'

Somehow, with the coaxing of King Feisal of Saudi Arabia,
Hussein was persuaded to shake hands with Arafat, and the civil
war was officially at an end.

XXI

THE END OF THE RESISTANCE

1971

Hussein had not beaten the Palestinians. His army had demons-
trably failed to crush them; the imprint of the tooth-marks of
Hussein's tanks in the tarmac of the streets of Amman ended
well outside the centre of the city. The Generals had forecast
victory in 48 hours: ten days later, there was still resistance.
Hussein and Arafat were faced with the choice of prolonged civil
war or an honourable truce. The destruction and loss of life had
become an intolerable strain on both sides. The Cairo agreement
appeared to be a recognition by each side that an outright victory
was impossible.

The commandos had won a burst of approval and sympathy
from much of the Arab world for their resistance to Hussein, and
the final safe release of all the airline hostages had soothed the
outraged feelings of the West. But Hussein had faced the greatest
threat of military and political annihilation of his career and survived. Moreover, the conflict had provided him with reassuring
proof of two key elements in the balance of power. The overwhelming majority of his troops had remained loyal to him: a
few hundred—mainly from Palestinian infantry units—are reliably
understood to have deserted, and over the next few months a
brigade of some 5,000 deserters was said by the Palestinians to
have formed in Syria. A handful of senior officers, like Muheisen,
either refused to fight or left to join the commandos, but the
core of his 55,000 strong army never wavered in its devotion to
him despite the precariousness of his position.

Hussein also drew comfort from the fact that the commandos
had been unable to provoke decisive support from any other Arab
state. The Syrians appeared to have been restrained not only by
internal pressures but by the threat of Soviet disapproval and
the fear of Israeli counteraction. And the Iraqis had made only

desultory moves in support of the Syrians, clearly indicating their unwillingness to risk military involvements so far from their home base.* Hussein—and indeed Arafat too—now had their suspicions confirmed that Arab support for the Palestinian resistance went no further than words and economic aid.

But it had been a close-run thing. Hussein had not even been secure in his bunker-like existence at the Hummar. He says he discovered during the fighting that his own driver was a commando, and there was an attempt on his life by one of his cooks who tried to poison his food and was then arrested in possession of a grenade. The commandos' successful penetration of his immediate entourage appeared to be confirmed when the army, soon after the fighting, published what they claimed were captured commando sketch maps showing every detail of the defences of the Hummar down to the positioning of machine-gun posts and minefields around the perimeter.

In this beleaguered fortress, surrounded by a handful of his closest advisers and most trusted generals, Hussein passed the most harrowing ten days of his life. He issued the orders from his study: outside the window a captured Israeli armoured car—a trophy of Karameh—protected the glass from being shattered by the daily salvoes of commando rocket fire. In the evening, for company, he would tune in on a radio wavelength that put him in touch with amateur radio operators all over the world. At the sound of his call-sign 'Juliet Yankee One', people he had never met in Britain and America would wish him well and he would tell them that he was 'putting the house in order', and that soon all would be all right. It was his only real contact with the outside world. Muna and all the children were in London: he had not been able to talk to her since the crisis began, but they were both used to that.

Hussein emerged from the civil war in a conciliatory mood. He was anxious to repair his financial links with Kuwait and Libya, and to reassure the Arab world that he meant to honour his commitments to the commandos under the Cairo agreement. He

* There were rumours soon afterwards that Sherif Nasser and his agents had been busily, and successfully using every inducement on the Iraqis not to intervene against Hussein.

appointed a civilian government under Ahmed Toukan,* and welcomed a new Arab Truce Supervision Committee under Bahi Ladgham, the Tunisian Prime Minister, whose job it was to see that the Cairo agreement was put into effect.

Meanwhile Hussein threw himself energetically into the task he enjoyed most : visiting the troops whose loyalty had once again secured his throne. It was something he did well, moving freely and fearlessly among them, shaking hands, even embracing them, speaking to them as one soldier to others, always thanking them for their courage and steadfastness, promising them they were dear to his heart, and telling them that they were the real guardians of Jordan's destiny and independence. The soldiers received him with wild enthusiasm, shouting his name 'Hussein ! Hussein !', fighting to get a glimpse of him : if they were lucky, they would touch him, shake his hand, even kiss him; he would often lose his beret as the soldiers struggled to get near him. These frenzied scenes, often repeated when Hussein visited Bedouin tribal gatherings, were the very essence of Hussein's hold on his supporters, evidence of the almost mystical bond that he had carefully fostered between himself and the kernels of power on the East Bank over the twenty years of his rule. The fact that he could not so much as drive with any security through the sprawling Palestinian refugee camps where over half the population of his country now lived, only underlined the political importance of these demonstrations of loyalty by the people he knew he could trust.

The polarisation of these opposing forces in Jordan that had come to a climax in the civil war, did not ease off in the aftermath of the fighting. The number of dead, variously estimated at between 1,500 and 20,000, had cut too deep a wound : the bitterness and mistrust which had obstructed implementation of the numerous agreements before the civil war, were only aggravated by the bloodshed. It soon became clear that the only way the Cairo agreement would be effected was by the exercise of force. The Palestinians, lacking firm leadership, picked isolated fights with the army, and Hussein's commanders lost no time in

---

* One man who made a bid for the premiership, using a close adviser of Hussein's as his intermediary soon after Daoud's resignation, was Ali Abu Nuwar, now securely restored to the King's favour—with his own office in the Basman Palace. Hussein admired Ali's gall, but told him that for the moment he would have to be content to take up the post of ambassador in Paris.

extending their influence, by force if necessary, in areas where they considered the guerrillas posed a threat. Bahi Ladgham and his team tried desperately to maintain a balance between the two sides, but their task was impossible. Hussein, sensing that the decisive showdown with the commandos was yet to come, urgently appealed to the British and Americans for more weapons and ammunition, and was gratified two weeks later when the first aircraft in a major airlift of American military supplies touched down, with a nice irony, on the airstrip at Dawson's Field where the guerrillas had staged their spectacular coup a month earlier.

Meanwhile attention was diverted from Jordan by the death of President Nasser in Cairo. Hussein flew straight back to Cairo with other Arab leaders and attended the funeral. For a time Arab differences were forgotten in the mourning for the father figure of Arab nationalism, whose heart had succumbed to the strain of the past few weeks of crisis. It was a curious bereavement for Hussein. He had never quite known whether to regard Nasser as a friend or an enemy. In the 1950s he had been sure that Nasser was plotting his downfall, but as the two of them matured through the 1960s, Hussein felt he was coming to be accepted by Nasser, as their interests increasingly coincided. He valued Nasser's support in the search for a settlement with Israel, and firmly believed that Nasser supported his drive against the commandos, even if he was unable to say so publicly. Hussein was quite unable to establish the same rapport with Nasser's successor, Anwar Sadat.

Throughout October 1970 Egypt's preoccupation with her own internal problems after the death of Nasser, and political disturbances in Iraq and Syria relieved the pressure on Hussein as he worked with his advisers to map out a new strategy after the civil war. By the end of the month, he was ready. Toukan's stop gap government was sacked and Hussein appointed the uncompromising Wasfi Tell Prime Minister. Zeid Rifai, the other adviser who had sat close by Hussein through the turmoil of 1970, was despatched to London as ambassador. Britain's enthusiasm for Hussein appeared to be cooling, and Hussein wanted all the British support he could get in the months ahead : he relied exclusively on Britain to supply ammunition for his Centurion tanks, which had expended a large proportion of their stocks against the Syrians in September.

In the ensuing nine months Hussein and his army commanders totally eliminated the commando presence in Jordan. It was a masterly exercise in unremitting military pressure : one by one, guerrilla positions were isolated, attacked and absorbed into the army's sphere of control. Constant harrassment and provocation of the army and police by extremist groups, struggling to assert their continued militancy provided the army with useful pretexts for pursuing their slow advance. But it would be wrong to portray this as a coolly predetermined campaign. If the opportunities provided by the incidents delighted those elements in the army which were working for the elimination of the commando movement in Jordan, Wasfi Tell himself was constantly trying to restrain the army and persuade the commandos to accept Hussein's authority. The final demise of the commandos was brought about as much by their own constant provocation of the army as by any deliberate policy on the part of the government.

However the army commanders made no secret of their determination to restore Hussein's rule throughout Jordan, and treated with contempt the protests of other Arab states, who loudly and frequently condemned the Jordanian government but did nothing to aid the commandos. Strengthened by promises of American military and financial aid, and confident after the experience of September 1970, that there would be no external intervention, the Jordanian leaders were able to pick off the weakened and divided guerrilla forces as opportunities presented themselves. Diplomacy, which Tell regarded as of secondary importance anyway, was quietly relegated to the background; although efforts were made to revive the Kuwaiti subsidy, Palestinian pressures in Kuwait and the uncompromising hostility of the Libyan government made it inevitable that as long as the campaign lasted, Jordan would have to write off the £25 million a year she had formerly relied on from these two countries. Only Saudi sensitivities remained unaffected, and King Feisal continued to pay his annual contribution of some £15 million.

The campaign against the guerrillas had two stages. From November 1970 to April 1971, the army's objective was to drive them from the towns : Amman, Irbid, Jerash and Ajloun. Then, between May and July, the remnants of the guerrilla army, camped in the woods and villages between Jerash and Ajloun and southwards across the Wadi Zarka, were systematically annihilated and no other Arab country lifted a finger to help them, though many of them expressed their horror. The guerrillas who escaped death or imprisonment fled to Syria, Lebanon and even Israel. By August 1971, military activity by the Palestinian resistance movement in Jordan was at an end.

Crucial to the success of the government's campaign was the weak and indecisive leadership of Arafat and the split between the Fateh and Habbash's Popular Front, which lasted right through the decisive first stage, allowing the Jordan government to use the PFLP's constant provocation and rejection of agreements between government and commandos as an excuse to move against the whole commando movement. Arafat and Hussein signed an agreement in Amman in October 1970 confirming the Cairo agreement: Habbash refused to have anything to do with it. Another agreement was signed in January 1971: again Habbash rejected it, and was even condemned by the Fateh leadership. Habbash repeatedly demanded the overthrow of Hussein's government: Arafat, throughout the first stage, attempted to come to an accommodation with the government, but failed to persuade his followers to adopt a stance that would have demolished the government's case against them. It is perhaps remarkable that Arafat continued to work for an understanding with a government that appeared to be committing itself more and more to a clean sweep of the commando movement, but his military position was weak and most of his financial supporters had always made it clear that their contributions to the Palestine Liberation Organisation were for the pursuit of the campaign against Israel—not against Hussein.

Fighting broke out between the army and the commandos almost daily up to the end of March 1971. On the 26th of March, Wasfi Tell announced that he had ordered the army to 're-establish security' in Irbid after 'repeated attacks against police posts' there. Two days later the fighting spread to Amman. The government accused the commandos of attacking police posts and the oil refinery at Zerka 'in league with the Israelis'. The commandos retorted that it was the King who was in league with the Israelis, and fought back at what they thought was a final move to push them out of the cities. Egypt, Syria and Iraq said they would not let the Palestinian resistance movement die, and President Sadat said the Arab nations would hold to severe account those responsible for crushing the commandos. Colonel Gaddafi of Libya urged the Jordan army to overthrow Hussein. An Arab summit was called to discuss the fighting in Jordan. But Hussein said he had no intention of attending it, and on the 6th of April he gave the commandos two days to move all their weapons out of Amman.

'The land where weapons should be wielded and resistance should be planted is the occupied territory, so that every citizen here may live in peace and security.'

Six months earlier, the commandos would have taken this as a challenge to a showdown with the government : but by now they were exhausted and demoralised by Hussein's war of attrition. For the next few days truckloads of them took to the roads northwards out of Amman. Within a week, all armed guerrillas had evacuated the city. They settled, apparently by agreement with the government, in the woodland area between Ajloun and Jerash—about five thousand of them in the cold, clear, mountain air of the early spring. Some of them found houses for shelter in and around the villages of Sakib, Dibbin, Burma, and Sumiya, some dug themselves bunkers in the earth, others pitched tents. Some talked vaguely of the new phase in their struggle for the liberation of their homeland over the Jordan; others concentrated their attention on organising some kind of defence against the Jordan army which quickly moved up and encircled them. All of them sensed that the days of their survival in Jordan were numbered.

On the 13th of April, Bahi Ladgham finally resigned and returned, exhausted, to Cairo. King Hussein was, he said, now 'liquidating little by little' the Palestine resistance he had failed to crush the previous September. He accused Hussein of a 'patent determination' to extinguish the commandos, and said that the Arab truce team had never really been welcomed in Amman, where Hussein had considered it was meddling in Jordanian affairs.

Hussein shrugged off this and other attacks with contempt. 'The situation in Jordan is now very healthy indeed,' he told *The Times* on April the 17th. 'Now the silent majority in Jordan can speak with complete freedom.' He had not been so confident

for years. On the 2nd of June, he ordered Wasfi Tell to take
'bold and tough action against the handful of professional
criminals and conspirators who would use the commando movement to disguise their treasonable plots. I want no hesitation,
tolerance or compromise in handling them.' The day before the
King's broadcast, a government spokesman had announced that
a 65-year-old farmer had been killed by guerrilla mortar fire near
Jerash. By now the number of besieged commandos had dwindled
to about 3,000. There were frequent clashes between them and
the army : the army claimed the commandos were attacking local
farmers and disrupting the life of the villagers in the area.

For another six weeks the army held back. Then, in five days
from the 13th to the 17th of July, came the final reckoning.
Armoured columns moved into the mountain redoubts and
crushed all remaining commando resistance with overwhelming
force. The guerrillas, running for their lives into Syria and even
across the Jordan into Israel, talked of massacres and killings in
cold blood. Wasfi Tell reported 2,300 commandos captured out
of a total force of 2,500. The army suffered 120 casualties—
dead and wounded. Hussein announced that the fighting was
now finally ended, and that he had had no choice but to act
against the commandos 'because they were a nuisance to many
people and to the armed forces'. The guerrilla forces, who had
been officially welcomed to Jordan in 1964, were now officially
extinct. In a last desperate attempt at unity, in the middle of
the battle with the Jordanian army, the guerrillas announced
that the Popular Front had joined the executive committee of the
PLO. But it was too late : by the 18th of July, it was all over.
Most of the captured guerrillas were packed off across the border
into Syria two days later : half a dozen were hanged for proven
murders of civilians, the remainder were held prisoner and, except
for a few, released over the next few months.

Twelve days after the final collapse of the commandos in the
Ajloun Woods, Colonel Gaddafi of Libya called an Arab summit
conference in Libya to discuss Hussein's total victory over the
resistance. The leaders of Egypt, Syria, and Yemen joined Gaddafi
together with Yasser Arafat : Kuwait, Lebanon, Iraq, Saudi
Arabia and Tunisia made no appearance. Hussein sent a message
to Gaddafi; thanking him for the invitation, 'which did not reach
me', and noting that the conference would discuss the affairs of

Jordan in the absence of its leader. Hussein said he wished to remind all the delegations present at the conference that Jordan had fought valiantly in the 1967 war, and that of all Arab countries it had the longest front line with Israel.

The four Arab leaders at the conference condemned Hussein and threatened to impose sanctions against Jordan: Syria and Iraq had closed their frontiers to Jordan soon after the fighting ended. All this had little effect on Hussein, who noted with gratification that the Syrians themselves were acting vigorously to control the commandos in their country, and were even confiscating commando arms shipments arriving at Syrian ports and allowing Jordanian trucks through Syrian territory to collect arms shipments for the Jordanian army from the port of Latakia.

But Hussein's victory had made him over-confident. In his exuberance, he allowed his army to press their attacks on the retreating commandos across the Syrian border—at first, apparently, with the tacit approval of Syria. But in the middle of August his army went too far: they shelled a Syrian village near Dera'a and the Syrians retaliated. Tension on the border rapidly mounted and shots were exchanged between the Syrian and Jordanian armies. Syria closed her air space to Jordanian aircraft, and Amman was again cut off from direct air access to Beirut. People began to talk of an outbreak of war between Syria and Jordan, and it was only after a visit to Damascus by President Sadat of Egypt, who was strongly opposed to this, that the situation became calmer.

The Egyptians now attempted to achieve a reconciliation between Hussein and the commandos. A conference was arranged in Jedda, with the help and encouragement of the Saudi Arabian government, and after much hesitation in the guerrilla camp, delegations were finally despatched by Arafat and Hussein. But at the end of September, the talks collapsed. The commandos had nothing to bargain with except the provisions of the Cairo agreement a year earlier, which the Jordanian government had long forgotten. Hussein would not consider the re-establishment of Palestinian armed groups in Jordan,* unless they came under his army's express control.

* A small group of some 500 Palestinians said to be from the Palestine Liberation Army, were re-established in Jordan in a tented camp at Khaw, near Zerka, in Autumn 1971. But they were kept firmly under the control of the army.

As 1971 drew to a close Hussein appeared to have restored his unquestioned control over the whole of Jordan. But his economic situation was serious. The buoyancy that had begun to take hold of the economy in 1969, despite the loss of the West Bank to Israel, began to recede in 1970, and collapsed with the withdrawal of the Libyan and Kuwaiti subsidies at the end of the year. Gross National Product for 1970 was 13 per cent down on 1969 (reduced from 231 million Jordanian dinars to JD 204 million). Taxes were increased but looked like providing only a fraction of the revenue needed to balance the budget for 1971. A 30 million dollar grant from the United States after the civil war of September 1970 made up for the loss of the Libyan subsidy, but there was still a gap of some £15 million to be made up. Military aid had been generously provided by the Americans and the British had, after much persuasion, finally agreed to provide 3,000 of the 12,000 rounds of tank ammunition that the Jordan government had been requesting to make up their losses in the tank battles in the same month. Britain had also agreed to increase her budgetary aid from £1½ to £2 million. But Jordan's economy, further stifled by the closing of the Syrian and Iraqi frontiers at the end of the summer of 1971, was in its most precarious state ever.

The political state of the country, by the spring of 1972, was never so uncomplicated. Military rule was total and uncompromising; the militant Palestinians had been extinguished as a political force. But the wounds Hussein and his men had inflicted on the commando movement and its supporters throughout the Arab world ran deep, and the thirst for vengeance found desperate expression in the murder of Wasfi Tell in Cairo in November 1971, and the attempted murder of Zeid Rifai in London a month later.

Tell was gunned down by a Palestinian group calling themselves the Black Hand of September as he returned to his hotel after a session of defence talks with other Arab leaders. Hussein, who had begged Tell not to risk the journey to Egypt, had lost his best administrator, and he nearly lost his best friend when a gunman discharged an entire magazine of automatic fire into the rear window of Zeid Rifai's Daimler as it rounded a corner near his embassy in London: Rifai dived to the floor of the car with a bullet wound in his hand and shouted to his driver to accelerate. The car stalled, but the gunman failed to follow up his attack, and Rifai survived.

These bullets did nothing to upset the restored calm in Jordan : they had been aimed at the wrong man. Hussein had long lived with the threat of assassination, and he now knew that as long as the bullets missed him, the régime would survive. With political opposition effectively eliminated in Jordan, and the commandos crushed, the danger of a political coup or revolution had vanished, and the army had proved itself well able to frighten off any external intervention. The country was ruled more decisively than ever before by Hussein and a small group of close advisers who were dedicated to preserving Jordan as an independent Hashemite kingdom.

Hussein felt strong enough to explore more thoroughly the prospect of a working relationship with Israel, whose presence on the West Bank was fast becoming established as a permanent reality, although it still stopped short of formal annexation. He was disturbed at the possibility of Egypt's President Sadat negotiating a separate peace with Israel that could reduce Jordan's bargaining power and her chances of winning back the West Bank in a general settlement. It is clear that, at the beginning of 1972, contacts were resumed between Jordan and Israel (see footnote on p. 202) and the first visible result of these negotiations was the easing of travel restrictions across the Jordan.

But it went deeper than that. Hussein gave an interview to the Israeli evening paper *Maariv* on January the 28th 1972 in which he said it would have been preferable to try for a global settlement of the Arab-Israeli dispute, but that he did not rule out the 'right of any party to search for a solution to his own problem'. Six weeks later he presented the world with his plan for a 'United Arab Kingdom'—a federation of the two banks of the Jordan that would allow the Palestinians a large measure of autonomy under the Jordanian flag. Hussein was reasserting his claim to the West Bank in language that he hoped would appeal to moderate Palestinians; and—a few days later—he tried to re-assure the Israelis by adding that he ruled out a military solution to his dispute with them.

But the Israelis rejected his plan mainly, they said, because it was Hussein's business to negotiate the return of his territory before he presumed to regulate its future. Reaction among Palestinians on the West Bank was mixed: some welcomed the prospect of a Palestinian identity within Jordan, others spurned the attentions of the man they felt had neglected them in the past. The commandos and most other Arab states denounced the plan as a Western plot.*

The suspicion that Hussein's plan was in some way linked to a secret deal with Israel seemed to be discounted by the apparently genuine indignation and scorn of the Israeli rejection, and the fact that it appeared to be unrelated to any discussion of the terms for peace with Israel. Yet for all its apparent unreality, there were features of the plan that appealed to the Israelis: it was clear, for example, that Hussein was no more ready than they were to contemplate a separate Palestinian state between Jordan and Israel. The speculation began again: was Hussein publishing his ideas because his secret talks with Israel had broken down? Or was this the prelude to disclosure that a deal was already agreed? Or was the whole episode evidence that no talks had taken place at all?

The author believes it very likely that Hussein *has* held secret discussions with Israeli leaders, not because there is any concrete evidence or any convincing leak from the Israeli side, but because it is unthinkable that Hussein would not want to examine for himself any opening for a settlement with Israel that would benefit Jordan. His only fear would be that the Arabs would reject any agreement he made with Israel as a betrayal of the Arab cause rather than accept it as a means of regaining lost territory. It is too early—at the time of writing—to guess at the progress of these discussions, if indeed they *are* going on; but it is likely that, in the short term, the hard stand of the Israelis on their demand for the retention of the whole of Jerusalem and for other substantial changes in their old frontiers with Jordan will make it unnecessary for Hussein to face the awesome task of presenting an agreed settlement to the Arab public. But if he or his successors can one day persuade the Israelis that they can have security without substantial annexations of Jordanian territory, then Jordanians and Palestinians alike may yet applaud their Hashemite

---

* Egypt broke off relations with Hussein. The feeling was mutual: Hussein bitterly resented President Sadat's courts releasing Tell's assassins on February the 29th.

rulers for winning back as much as any reasonable man could expect.

But reason comes hard to the Arabs, who blame Hussein as much as Israel for their present helplessness in defeat, and if Hussein has a vision of a land that will one day be reunited, peaceful and free of political turmoil, it is a dream that will probably not be fulfilled in his lifetime.

CONCLUSION

THE GREAT SURVIVOR

For twenty years Jordan's existence as an independent state has depended solely on the continuing survival of its king. It is questionable whether a Jordanian republic would have been willing or able to maintain its sovereign independence. It is certain that the fall of the monarchy in the 1950's or early 1960's would have heightened the danger of Israeli intervention and the possible involvement of the Great Powers. Of course, a number of Jordanians, particularly the more extreme of the Palestinians, would have welcomed Jordan's absorption into a larger Arab state and the tension with Israel that would inevitably have followed. But Hussein's leadership, if it has been intolerant of any opposition, has fostered the development of a Jordanian nationhood and begun establishing the social and economic framework for a lasting independent state. Jordan's nationhood and even its conservative system are accepted—and even, with reservations, positively desired—by a substantial proportion of its population. And, although the country's political framework contrasts sharply with that of its neighbours, it is more stable and no less democratic than, for example, the régimes in Syria and Iraq.

Hussein's importance is that he represents a different style of Arab leadership—one that has proved itself an alternative to Nasserism and the 'pan-Arabism' of the Baathis. His strength is that he has occasionally tried to lead rather than follow the emotions of Arab public opinion—particularly in regard to Israel. His weakness is that he has taken too long to decide whether to throw his resources unequivocally behind the demands of the other Arabs, or to follow through the logic of his policy and come to an arrangement with Israel. On the one hand, the lesson of his grandfather's murder, his tendency to flights of military fancy and Islamic prowess, and the unremitting popular pressure of a showdown with Israel have sometimes urged him to the side of Arab

nationalism : it was these factors, egged on by his own rash judgement that led to the disaster of 1967. Conversely, his own
recognition of the reality of Israel's unassailable position, his links
with the West and his ideological conflict with 'Arab Socialism'
have as often inclined him the other way: and here again he became
the victim of his own impulsiveness and nearly overreached himself on a number of occasions. The contradictions of his policies
have earned him the contempt of other Arabs and the exaspera-
tion of the Israelis and his friends in the West who demanded
a consistency of him that was neither in his nature nor within
his power.

Hussein's central problem in 1972 remained essentially what
it was when he succeeded his father in 1952—the management
of a country split by the conflicting demands of the Palestinians
and the East Jordanians. His own tribal roots and the pressures
of his power base on the East Bank made him an East Jordanian
first, and the bloody clash with the commandos became unavoidable. But would any other leader—of any other political
affiliation—have maintained the balance? It is very doubtful.
Certainly, his violent subjection of the Palestinians was the product not of the ruthless mind of a miltary dictator but of an
agonising process of decision-making.

It is the author's conviction that, in spite of all his short-
comings, Hussein's perception of the realities of the Arabs' predicament and his courage in frequently giving voice to what
other Arab leaders may privately approve but publicly condemn,
far outweigh any more selfish reason for his personal survival :
and if he has, for his own purposes, inflated the mission of the
Hashemites to ridiculous proportions, his rule has nevertheless
made a positive start to the formidable challenge of making the
best of Jordan's highly vulnerable economic and political situation.

We are left with Hussein himself—a gentle, sensitive man
with a deep sincerity and personal charm that even his bitterest
enemies admire. His family life is more English than Arab, his
friends men of action rather than intellectuals. He still regards
life as an adventure and likes to be thought of more as the Brave
Young King at the head of his army than the sophisticated statesman. His views are unashamedly conservative, and he shows no
sign of relaxing the patriarchal authority of the crown over all

matters of importance. He believes naïvely, passionately in his family's divine right—and duty—to rule, even if it is assailed from all sides. He has grown powerfully into the task he inherited when he was little more than a boy, but, beneath the surface, he is still troubled by the complexes and uncertainties of his childhood. He enjoys life, but is somehow too modest in his tastes and too inhibited to be described as a playboy. He derives great pleasure from laughing loud and long with his friends in private over his continuous feud with his Arab neighbours. He revels in living dangerously.

To many of his people, and most of his neighbours, his whole make-up is alien and out-of-date, impervious to the demands of a fast maturing population. But whether or not people regard Hussein's leadership as desirable, it is a fact. After twenty years as King of the most turbulent country in the Middle East, Hussein has demonstrated that what decides events is not the shouting of slogans and the search for acclaim but the exercise of power.

BIBLIOGRAPHY

Politics and the Military in Jordan. P. J. Vatikiotis. Cass 1967.

Jordan: State of Tension. Benjamin Shwadran. ME Affairs Council. New York 1959.

King Hussein: Uneasy lies the Head. Heinemann 1962.

Bedouin Command. Peter Young. Kimber 1956.

The Arab Revolt. Michael Ionides. 1958.

Hussein of Jordan: My War with Israel. Vance and Lauer. Peter Owen 1968.

Soldier with the Arabs. Glubb. Hodder and Stoughton 1957.

The Sandstorm. Kinche and Bawly. Secker and Warburg 1968.

The Arab Cold War 1958–67. Kerr. Chatham House 1967.

Jordan: A Political Study. Abidi. Asia Publishing House 1965.

No End of a Lesson. Antony Nutting. Constable 1967.

The Road to War 1967. Laqueur. Weidenfeld and Nicholson. 1968.

Memoirs of King Abdullah of Transjordan. Jonathan Cape 1950.

Leila's Hijack War. Snow and Phillips. Pan 1970.

The Middle East in Revolution. Lord Trevelyan. Macmillan 1970

Suez the Twice Fought War. Love. Longman 1969

The Struggle for Syria. Seale. OUP 1965.

The War Business. Thayer. Weidenfeld and Nicholson 1969.

Republican Iraq. Khadduri. OUP 1969

Full Circle. Lord Avon. Houghton Mifflin 1960.

A Crackle of Thorns. Kirkbride. London 1956

INDEX

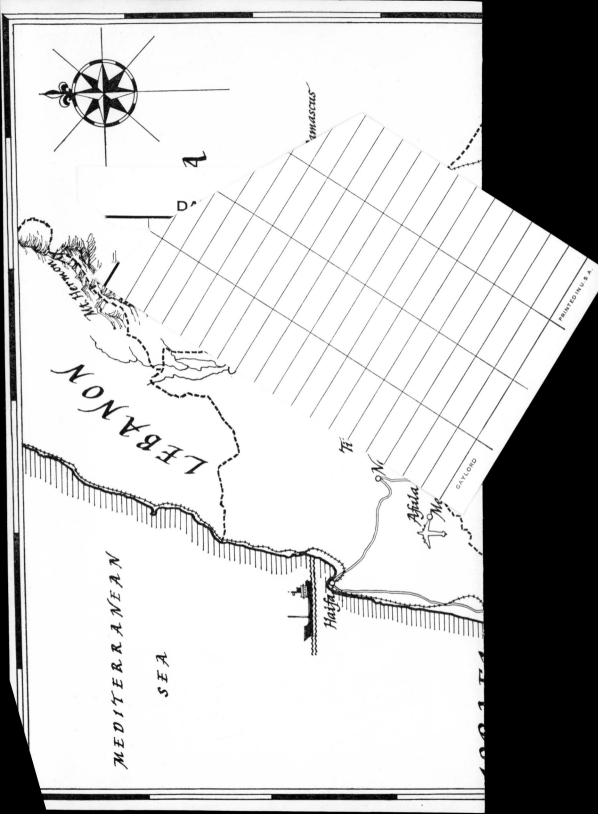